Praise for *Adventureman*:

'I laughed. I cried. I absolutely loved reading about Jamie's journey – just incredible. It's not just his 5,000-mile Canadian run, but also, more profoundly, the fact that he was sick as a kid and yet still achieved and experienced so many amazing things that makes this book so damn good. What struck me deeply is his humanity and unfailing ability to never give up... It was also great to read about all the people who helped Jamie across our vast country – I couldn't be prouder to be Canadian. This book is unputdownable – a true must-read for anyone looking to find the superhero within themselves.'
Clara Hughes, OC OM MSC

'Jamie McDonald proves that the ordinary can be extraordinary. *Adventureman* is an uplifting story of grit and stick-to-it-iveness that both superheroes and everyday heroes will find fascinating.'
Dean Karnazes

'Jamie is extremely tough. What he has put his body through both physically and mentally takes a tremendous amount of determination. Not many people could even attempt these challenges. Whether you're 3 years old or 93 years old, we all dream of and long for adventure, but the way Jamie's managed to combine it with fundraising and helping the world is inspirational. His book is a must-read for all!'
Sir Ranulph Fiennes, OBE

'Having run many marathons, the last thing I'd do is run across Canada. Jamie, you are proof that grit and determination are what you need to succeed.'
Paula Radcliffe, MBE

To Jace &
Halle &
Trevor, Bryce,

ANYONE CAN BE A SUPERHERO

It's
true

Kashlyn,
LiBa!

DVENTUREMAN
THE ASTONISHING TRUE STORY

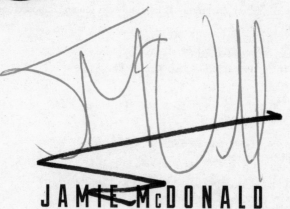

JAMIE McDONALD

summersdale

ADVENTUREMAN

Copyright © Jamie McDonald 2017

Inside front cover photos © Jamie McDonald
Inside back cover photos © UAV (www.danforth.ca), Gloucestershire Live,
Shonna Morgan and Jamie McDonald

All rights reserved.

Jamie McDonald has asserted his right to be identified as the author of this
work in accordance with sections 77 and 78 of the Copyright, Designs and
Patents Act 1988.

Summersdale Publishers Ltd
46 West Street
Chichester
West Sussex
PO19 1RP
UK

www.summersdale.com

Printed and bound by CPI Group (UK) Ltd, Croydon, CR0 4YY

ISBN: 978-1-84953-969-2

Substantial discounts on bulk quantities of Summersdale books are
available to corporations, professional associations and other organisations.
For details contact general enquiries: telephone: +44 (0) 1243 771107, fax:
+44 (0) 1243 786300 or email: enquiries@summersdale.com.

CONTENTS

*Dedicated to all the sick children and their
families around the world*

*100 per cent of all royalties from the sales of this book will
be donated to Superhero Foundation – a charity that empowers real-life
superheroes to change and save lives.*

ONE WRONG TURN

I finally collapsed on the edge of a snow-dusted road in Newfoundland that had looked identical for the last 5 miles. My chariot – whom I'd christened Caesar because he needed to be strong at all times – toppled with me and spilled out all my equipment onto the icy grass: my tent, tins of fish and spare clothes. My gut ached from hunger, my ears and fingers were numb with the cold, and my legs – that had caused me so much distress in my early years – felt like they'd been plunged into an incinerator. I was only a month into my year-long challenge, but maybe it was time to admit defeat.

I screamed like a terrified schoolgirl. I couldn't help it. Trying to take my mind off the pain in my legs, I checked my map. I checked it again. Then I screamed once more so loudly that I didn't hear a Land Rover approaching. It stopped beside me and the driver, a woman in her sixties, wound down a steam-covered window. She wore little circular glasses and her grey hair in a bun. 'I heard a scream out here,' she said. 'Are you hurt, son?'

'I've gone the wrong way,' I sobbed.

'But are you hurt?'

'I don't care about that!' I yelled, bashing my fists against the ground. 'I've gone east instead of west. East not west! It's the wrong way... I've gone the wrong way.' I pointed to the sign that read: BIRCHY NARROWS. 'I've seen that sign once already today. Do you know what that means?'

She peered at me with, understandably, no idea what I was talking about. 'No.'

'It means now I've got 186 marathons left – 186!'

'Look, son, I live in a cabin about a mile away and when I heard the scream I figured somebody must be hurt.'

'I told you, I'm not hurt.' I picked up my phone and tried to work out from Google Maps why I'd run in completely the wrong direction.

'You headed anywhere particular?'

'A restaurant. I've been eating fish and butter for days. I'll eat anything else they have, even dog food.'

'Why don't you drive there?'

'Because I'm running.'

'Why are you running? It's real cold and everything is real far.'

My spirits lifted as soon as I told her – and reminded myself – exactly why I was putting myself through this torture. I was making my way across Canada on foot to raise money for children's hospitals in Canada and the UK. I'd been pretty ill as a kid, I told her, and it was only through the help I got from children's hospitals that I was able, in adulthood, to charge around her country doing a marathon a day and sleeping rough in freezing temperatures.

'Oh my,' said the woman. 'Well, I hope you make it, son. Can I give you a ride to the restaurant? I think I know the place you mean.'

'No thanks,' I said, easing back onto my feet. My legs were still painful but they had enough life in them to run the 10 miles I needed to reach my destination. I hobbled over to my chariot and started putting my possessions inside him. I summoned all my mental strength, seized Caesar's handlebar and sprinted back up the road.

I looked over my shoulder and said to the woman, 'Goodbye, ma'am. Just another 5,000 miles to go!' She went mute, as her eyes expanded to fill her glasses.

PART 1

I'LL NEVER WALK AGAIN

It's not something I want to remember, but I always will. When I was six years old, I went with my mum to see a doctor at Great Ormond Street Hospital who told us, in a deadpan tone, 'Jamie has a syrinx on the spinal cord – a cyst filled with fluid. It's a condition called syringomyelia, and if it progresses, it will damage the nerves of the spinal cord. And where the syrinx is located, it will affect Jamie's legs.' My mum went pale and her features seemed to age 30 years in a matter of seconds. I don't remember being shocked or upset myself – I wasn't sure if I understood the full meaning of what we'd just been told. In fact, I was more shocked by my mum's reaction than the doctor's bad news. My mum feared I'd be in a wheelchair for the rest of my life, or even worse, that I might die.

I was immunodeficient from six weeks old until the age of four, meaning that I picked up all kinds of coughs and colds, and I also suffered epileptic fits during sleep. Worst of all, though, sometimes I just couldn't move my legs. The first time it happened, I woke up in the night feeling as though I had concrete blocks weighing down on them – I just couldn't move them. I was so scared, I wailed until Mum and Dad told me that everything was going to be all right. Sometimes though, I'd be in remission and have bouts where I'd feel well.

My uncertain future prompted my parents to make the most of the present. They scrimped and saved and took me to Disney World in Florida, which was such a sweet and loving gesture. 'It's the holiday of a lifetime,' my mum said – and she was right. My first-ever crush was on Minnie Mouse, but when I met her in real life she struck me as a bit too bulky for me at the time.

When we got back to our hometown of Gloucester, my mum asked me one summer's day if I'd like to play tennis. I put my hands over my face and shook my head. I felt sick, my legs were aching and I just didn't want to put myself through the humiliation.

'Come on, J,' Mum insisted. 'Bet you can't beat me!' She passed me an old racket held together with Sellotape and took me into the garden where she tied a piece of string between our two fences. We weren't very well off in those days. She gave me a ball that had turned from fluorescent orange to white from age. 'Just throw the ball up in the air,' she said, 'and hit it with the racket, hard as you can.'

I did as she told me. WHACK! The moment I struck that ball I forgot about everything else in my life, especially the pain in my legs. 'Yeah!' I shouted in glee. 'Yeah!'

My mum didn't look too happy. 'J, you're supposed to hit the ball *over* the string not *under*!'

I didn't care. Just to have hit the thing was proof that I could have an active life after all. We played for the next two hours and even managed to get some good rallies going. I guess, despite my illness, I had a bit of a natural flair for the sport – and I was hooked. I just loved to move, whether it was throwing a ball for a dog or charging around the garden.

My older brother Lee was a bit of a daredevil. One afternoon he said to me, 'Don't tell Mum and Dad, but shall we climb over the garden fence and play around the railway line?' I knew even then that the railway line was not exactly a safe place for kids. As if that wasn't hazardous enough, Lee suggested we might find some adders in the long grass.

'Don't like adders!' I said. 'Please let's not go there.'

'Oh stop being such a baby!'

Not wanting to be left out of what 'normal' kids get to do, I reluctantly followed him over the fence. Lee had 'armed' himself with a hedge trimmer. As soon as we were on the other side, the small, raisin-like head of an adder popped out of the grass. Its horrible beady eyes stared me out as it got ready to strike. Terrified, I turned to try to climb back over the fence, but pains started shooting through my calves and my knees began to shake. I gasped, tears forming in my eyes. I couldn't lift my legs at all. Lee raised the hedge trimmer over his head like Conan the Barbarian and swung it at the snake. I don't think he hit it, but at least the snake left us alone.

'I shouldn't have come here,' I wept. I rubbed my calves to ease the pain, but it didn't work. I knew there was a long way to go before I'd conquer my illness and be fully fit like every other kid I knew.

However, the more tennis I played, the less trouble I had with my leg pains and other symptoms of the illness. And I played a lot of tennis. I graduated from knocking balls over the string in the garden with my family members to my uncle Kev, along with my cousins Kiera and Karley, helping me to join a proper club and playing matches against other boys in the Gloucester area. My parents bought me a brand new Slazenger racket, decent Adidas shoes and sweatbands (an all-important tennis fashion accessory in the nineties).

When I was ten, we went back to see the doctor and this time it was his turn to look shocked, albeit in a good way. 'This is a bloody miracle!' he exclaimed as he showed us the graphic of my MRI scan on his computer. 'No guarantees of course, but it looks to me that the syrinx has not progressed on your spinal cord.' He looked me in the eye. 'Jamie, have you been feeling well lately?'

'Yeah,' I beamed.

'No fits or anything like that?'

'No.'

'Well, there's no evidence I know of which proves that exercise can help with a condition like this...' He looked back at the screen, still quite dazed. 'But I suppose you ought to just keep on doing what you're doing, as it seems to be working.'

I turned to my mum. 'Can you take me to the tennis club now?'

One day, a man called Keiran Montagu interrupted me as I was about to serve. He had broad shoulders and curtain-like brown hair. 'You could go all the way to Wimbledon one day,' he said.

'Don't take the mickey!' I laughed. But he wasn't. Keiran took me on free of charge because he believed in me and he knew that my family didn't have the money for private lessons. Up until that point, thanks to my love of movement, tennis had been the centre of my life, but from the moment I met Keiran, it also seemed like a viable career. Unfortunately, I stopped taking secondary school seriously. When I wasn't daydreaming about thrashing Henman in the Wimbledon final, I was making life difficult for my teachers.

One particularly boring morning, I threw a wet piece of paper in a teacher's face. I'm not proud of having done that, of course, but it was the sort of thing that less academically inclined pupils liked to do. The teacher peeled the paper off his cheek and sent me straight to see Mr Montagu, the head teacher. He also happened to be Keiran's dad.

I knocked on his door and I heard an exasperated voice say, 'Come in.' I was often sent to see him so I think he knew it was me.

'Look, Jamie,' he sighed. 'You know I'm going to have to give you three detentions, don't you?'

I tucked my chin in and said, 'Yes, Larry.'

'You can't call me that inside this school. Do you understand?'

'Yes, sir.'

'How's the tennis going, anyway? Really well, I hear.'

I left his office feeling great – even with three detentions under my belt. Larry always had a way of making you feel like there was a purpose in life, even when you'd annoyed him.

My mum was the caring, nurturing type who wanted to help everyone. My cousin Nathan came to stay with us while he was trying to kick his heroin habit. Friends and neighbours would often say to my mum, 'Are you sure it's wise to have someone who's addicted to drugs in the house, given that Jamie is so young?' My mum didn't care what anyone else thought. She was going to do her best for her nephew and that was that.

It wasn't easy for her. Every time she tried to help Nathan get clean, he'd relapse and it would break her heart. Nathan would pull stunts like borrowing my bike for the day and then claiming it had been stolen, when in fact he'd sold it to fund his addiction. I lost three bikes that way.

At the age of 15, I felt very connected to Nathan. He was a good, generous-hearted person who had a weakness. I remember him asking me where my life was going. He may have been high at the time, but it was a fair question. 'You can talk to me about anything,' he added, sweetly.

I opened up to him. 'I'm not sure if tennis is really for me.'

'No way! But you're so good at it.'

'I don't think I'm good enough to live up to Keiran's expectation that I go professional. I feel indebted to him because he's supported me.'

Nathan put his arm round me. 'J, you gotta do what you want. It's your life.'

This little exchange seemed to do Nathan some good too. He quit the heroin and got himself a job.

Almost a year later, though, Nathan appeared in court, charged with beating someone up in a McDonald's restaurant for shouting, 'I support Bin Laden.' I asked, and so did my mum, to go with him to court and support him, but Nathan didn't want any of the family to be there. Later that day, the police knocked on our door. It was an ominous sound. 'We're really sorry to inform you that Nathan has passed away.' He'd overdosed in the court toilets just moments before his hearing was due to begin. As his body had been clean for nearly a year, that fix had been too much of a shock to his system. This broke my heart, but I had been incredibly lucky to have someone like Nathan in my life through those years as a positive role model.

With Nathan's advice ringing in my ears, I decided to quit my dream of being a pro tennis player. Nobody trained harder than I did, but I just didn't have the talent – that extra element – you need to get to the top. I thought it better to admit this at the time rather than get even more disappointed later. Still, it wasn't easy to accept.

It didn't help that I was at that age when beer and girls were most alluring. Nevertheless, with adult freedom comes adult responsibility. My dad, who'd been a hard-working bricklayer all his life, said to me, firmly but respectfully, 'You need to start paying your way, son.' So I got a job at Asda, stacking fruit and vegetables. I couldn't be the obedient drone, though. If a customer was ever rude to me, I'd take the hidden water pistol out of my pocket and shoot them with it. Somehow I didn't get sacked for that, but management strongly advised me to leave. I then worked as a lifeguard for a year before qualifying as a tennis instructor.

However, the conventional life wasn't quite doing it for me. I needed adventure. By the age of 18, I'd saved up enough money to go travelling. I bought a round-the-world ticket and planned for a year's worth of bumming about. It turned into three years during which I visited the US, Fiji, Cook Islands, Australia, New Zealand and Thailand.

On the whole, it went smoothly, apart from one incident in Australia when I blacked out after drinking a box of cheap wine (which contained fish eggs, for some reason) and awoke to a girl screaming, 'Why am I wet? Jamie!'

I remembered that I was on the top bunk of a bed and that an Irish girl – whom I quite fancied – was on the bottom one. I then realised that my pants were wet. I wanted to die there and then when it dawned on me that I had urinated over this poor girl while we were both comatose.

To atone for my bad behaviour I went out and bought her a bouquet of flowers, chocolates and a teddy. I wrote a note: 'I'm so sorry. All I can do now is shower you with gifts.' Unsurprisingly, the romance that I was hoping would blossom between us simply didn't.

I was 20 when I got back to the UK. I was broke, exhausted and tired of partying. I was also clueless about the direction in which I wanted my life to go. At that age I'm sure nobody really knows what they want to do. Was I going to travel again or settle down in Gloucester? I was constantly swaying between these two paths – there were good reasons for following either.

Most of the people around me were settling down, having kids, buying houses or trying to save up for a fancier car. I met up with Keiran again, who now had his own tennis academy at St Peter's High School. His passion for teaching and inspiring the children made total sense to me, given how he had helped my development. He asked me if I wanted to work for him at the academy. I said yes – here was a job I'd enjoy doing and an opportunity to help Keiran's dream along just as he had helped mine.

So here I was working at my old school, with all the teachers that had kicked me out of their lessons. More practical assistance was to come from Keiran's dad: 'Why don't you come back to school and take your GCSEs again?' he said to me when I bumped into him. 'I know it didn't go too well back then, but you're a mature lad now and you'll fly through them – I know it.'

'I'm not too sure, Larry. I'm 23 years old and schoolwork never really was my bag. You know that.' I was petrified I'd fail my GCSEs all over again and my greatest fear – that everyone would think I'm stupid – would come to pass. I told him I'd think about it and I did for a while, before finally deciding that he was right. I nervously sat in class with teenagers six or seven years younger than me to study science, maths and English. The latter scared me the most – I couldn't write a thing and was certain I had some form of dyslexia, but wasn't comfortable telling anyone. Most of the students thought I was a teacher's assistant, but in reality I was at the back of the class doing the same work they were.

I knew that what I lacked in natural academic talent I could make up for with hard work. I was no stranger to graft, having managed to conquer a serious illness through hard work. Some of my classmates were even calling me 'sir' by the end, even though by then they'd figured out that I wasn't an assistant but a student just like them. It was endearing, anyway. On results day, I got As in science and maths, and a B in English. All I kept saying to myself was: 'I can't believe it – all I did this time round was try.'

The next step in my quest for normality was saving up to buy a house. While I was saying to my mum that I just wanted what everybody else my age seemed to aspire to, my dad came in from work, flopped down on the sofa and said, 'Did you know that I've been a bricklayer for nearly 25 years?'

'Course we do, Donald,' said my mum, a bit puzzled.

'And I really don't like doing it no more.'

Mum and I looked at each other and simultaneously said, 'Well, don't do it no more!'

Dad lay back on the sofa and made a kind of relieved sighing noise.

He quit bricklaying, accepted a serious pay cut down to minimum wage, and started working with people with mental health and learning difficulties. Many of them had violent tendencies and after his first day, Dad burst through the door sporting a black eye.

'What the hell happened?' I asked.

'I got punched by one of the people we were trying to help. I'm sure he didn't mean it.' Then, weirdly I thought, Dad started grinning. 'Anyway, that was the best bloody eight hours of my life.'

Dad's example made me pause and wonder what life was all about. I had an adventurous spirit, even then, and felt I had to nurture that side of me too.

I continued to save for a house. Every day I woke up and said to myself, 'I want a house; I need a house. It's the only way I'm going to progress in life and be happy.' In the meantime, my mum started talking again about fostering children, something she'd been keen on since Nathan had lived with us. She made the necessary enquiries and soon got a call from the fostering agency. When she got off the phone, she told us that we'd have a new member in our family, a 14-year-old boy called Aziz. He had fled from Afghanistan during the war and had no idea whether his family were alive or not. My mum's major concern was that some of her more conservative friends and relatives had expressed dismay that she was taking in a young Muslim. She asked my Dad and me what we thought. We couldn't make the decision for her, but we knew it was a big one to make. 'Just do what feels right and we'll support you,'

Dad said. We knew she'd be a great foster mother, as she lives and breathes family. She's the sort of person who feels guilty if a guest leaves her house without a full stomach.

She thought about it for a day and then decided to take Aziz in. He was a quiet, humble boy with little self-confidence. Whatever our other relatives thought, Dad and I were clear in our own thoughts: Aziz was another human being and, regardless of his skin colour, he needed our help. In the event, some people stopped visiting after we'd taken on Aziz. It wasn't easy to see Mum getting upset about it. At the time, I struggled to understand these people who couldn't accept others from different walks of life. Despite the initial stress, my mum knew she was doing the right thing.

Around this time I heard some news about a local guy my age called Graham, whom I'd met once. He'd struck me as pleasant enough, but I recalled nothing remarkable about him. What I found out, though, was that he was cycling around the world all by himself. *That* was remarkable. Once again, I asked myself if there was a little more to life than slaving away to buy a house. By then, I'd coached enough tennis hours to save up more than £20,000. This was it: the moment I'd waited for, for nearly three years. I found a house that I liked and had an offer accepted, but when I started going through the legal process, I felt knots in my gut and thumps in my heart. This was such a commitment, a decision I couldn't back out of and would mean being locked into my job and Gloucester forever – or at least for a long, long time. I realised that I was buying a house only because everyone else around me was doing the same. It was like the 'thing to do'. But it wasn't the thing I really, fundamentally, wanted to do.

I sent my apologies to the estate agent.

Then I went into deep thought, asking big questions about who I was and what sort of a life I desired. 'What the hell do you want?' I said out loud to myself, hoping people wouldn't overhear and think I'd lost my mind. 'My parents seem to have found it.'

I recalled the time I spent in Gloucester Children's Hospital and had this intense urge to go and visit it again. I got in touch with the Pied Piper Appeal, the charity supporting the hospital, and met its lovely head, Wendy Fabian. I asked if we could look round the hospital, but never mentioned I'd been a patient there. I was wowed when I met all the kids that the Pied Piper was assisting. 'I should be giving back like this,' I said to myself afterwards.

As hard as it was, I called Keiran to tell him that I wanted to quit. Coaching just wasn't my calling. Thankfully, he understood, although he wasn't happy about it as he feared for my safety.

I called up Wendy once more. 'I never mentioned it before,' I said, 'but I spent a lot of my childhood in Gloucester Children's Hospital. The way you're supporting kids and their families is incredible. I'd like to help and I have an idea I'd like to run past you.'

'Go on,' said Wendy.

'I'm going to cycle 14,000 miles to raise funds for the hospital.'

'You what?' she gasped.

Later that day, I told Mum and Dad about my adventure. They went pale and frowned at each other.

'You've both found your pathways,' I said. 'This is mine. I know it's ridiculous, but I just have to do it.'

'J, I can think of better ways to help the world than this,' sighed Mum.

'What route will you cycle?' asked Dad.

I put my arm around Aziz. 'How's Afghanistan this time of year, little brother?'

PART 2

NEVER PEDAL BACK, ALWAYS PEDAL FORWARD

I was cycling merrily through Bangkok, every face smiling, every hand waving at me, when my front tyre burst with a horrible farting noise. Served me right for buying the bike advertised in the newspaper for £50. I lost control and skidded a few feet, almost colliding with a Buddhist monk in an orange gown who hadn't seen me coming because he was tapping away on his iPhone. When I came to a halt, I realised that I had no clue how to fix the tyre. I didn't have a spare one and didn't know where in Bangkok I could get one. 'How am I supposed to complete 14,000 miles across 25 countries now?' I hissed, as I reluctantly got off the bike. The anger turned to stomach-spinning anxiety, as I remembered my duty here: raise funds for Gloucester Children's Hospital, which had helped me to get over my syringomyelia.

The flat tyre could cause a massive, potentially trip-ruining delay. Luckily, I managed to walk my bike to a hotel where the amiable receptionist was able to hook me up with a mechanic. He couldn't understand a word I was saying, so never found out about my childhood illness, the help I'd got to overcome it or the reason why I was fundraising for the charity – but he fixed the tyre for free anyway. This act of kindness would be the first of many over my adventures.

In Vietnam, I started videoing myself with my camera, making silly comments and then posting them on social media so friends and supporters at home could follow my movements. At lunchtime, absolutely starving, I dropped into a restaurant and ordered a $2 bowl of *pho* (noodle soup). The waitress took my $10 note and didn't give me any change. I ended up arguing with five waitresses. 'I am not a cycling cash machine,' I said. 'Give me my change now!' It was more about the principle than the money – I didn't want to be the cliched dumb tourist. But in this instance, as I was getting nowhere, I helped myself to a packet of cookies from their restaurant by way of compensation.

Cycling was such a lovely way to travel. You have the speed and the ease of moving around, while you also get to see attractive places and meet interesting people.

To this day, Laos is possibly the most beautiful country I've ever visited. I could barely believe that the turquoise waterfalls at Luang Prabang were real. I don't think I've seen anything that stunning even in travel agent brochures. I shouted, 'Who's the man?' as I swung off a rope and into the crystalline pools at the bottom of the falls.

Sailors talk about getting their 'sea legs', whereby they get used to the trials of sea travel. China was where I got my 'cycling legs', if you like. After three months of intensive pedalling, my fitness came on quickly. That's what I love about cycling: you get noticeably, physically stronger each day you do it.

But in other ways China crushed my confidence. The alpine terrain was tough and I struggled to ascend some of the bigger mountains. Nobody understood a word I said and everybody stared at my flip-flops – hardly the correct shoes for this kind of travelling. When you're pushing yourself physically, you need good food but every time I ate in China, I had no clue what was going in my mouth. Put it this way: it's not like the Chinese food you get at home.

I bumped into a local man named Xei and, mercifully, he spoke a little English. 'I take you for speciality meal, for our city. We are very proud.'

Yes, I thought, *finally a decent meal*.

Whatever it was, though, it didn't do much for me. 'What exactly is this, Xei?' I asked after a few mouthfuls.

'I'm not sure what English word is. Wait, I translate on phone. Ah yes, look.' I looked at his phone screen. I was eating pig's ears. I thought, *I won't be getting a decent meal in 3,000 miles then*.

I zoomed out of the city of Xining, my legs feeling frail, my mind whisking me back home to my creature comforts. I traversed more mountains and a stretch of desert, head down all day every day, surviving on only five hours of sleep per night.

Realising that I had only ten days before my Chinese visa expired, I picked up my pace and covered 900 miles in that time. Before I knew it, I was 245 miles away from the visa office in Urumqi, which shut the next day at 4 p.m. The wind blowing in my face the whole time didn't exactly help my progress. My legs went so numb that they felt like artificial attachments bolted on to me.

There was no choice but to pedal right through the night. I found a small store that was selling Coke. Bingo! That should sustain me for a while.

At 3 a.m., I fell asleep at the handlebars and crashed on the highway, grazing my elbow. I leaped back up, more awake than a newborn baby. At midday, I sensed I was close to Urumqi, but there were so many people, cars, bikes and motorbikes about that I got lost amongst them. I stopped and asked every person I could for directions. At last I found the office – it was 3.30 p.m.

I jumped off my bike, sprinted to the shutter and found this sign: SORRY, ON WEDNESDAY AFTERNOONS THE VISA OFFICE CLOSES EARLY.

'No!' I bellowed at the sky. 'I won't survive a Chinese prison.'

I went back to the visa office first thing the next morning, fully prepared to beg. The officer said, 'No problem, sir. You can overrun your visa date by two weeks. We'll extend your visa in one hour.'

'Are you kidding me?' I replied.

'No problem,' she said.

'No problem? No problem?' This woman had no idea about the problems I'd had to overcome just to get here on time.

I was fairly proud of myself too, though. I wondered if I'd broken a world record, what with cycling for 34 hours straight. I typed this into Google: 'What's the longest bike ride without stopping?'

This is what came up: 'World Record for Non-stop Static Cycling: 224 hours, 24 minutes, 24 seconds set by Patrizio Sciroli in Italy, 2011.'

Bang went my pathetic effort.

With renewed confidence, I smashed through Kazakhstan, the mountains of Kyrgyzstan and up to Tajikistan, which is a country I'd never heard of before. By that point, I was beginning to run low on food so I was relieved when I spotted some silhouettes of people in the distance. Getting closer, I realised they were border guards. I couldn't speak the lingo so I put my hand to my mouth and shouted, 'Food? Food?' They looked blankly back at me.

I had to choose whether to cycle back two days in order to avoid Tajikistan and get hold of some much-needed grub or take the risk of cycling on an empty stomach for three days. The map was showing 300 miles of sheer emptiness.

However – did I forget to mention it? – there was another rule on this journey: never go back, always go forward. So off I went with my last few ABC biscuits.

By day two my stomach was growling like a wild animal for sustenance. It was a catch-22: I'd pedal harder in the hope of finding some food, but the harder I pushed myself, the more calories I burnt. This was not a healthy approach.

Then, thankfully, I spotted a house in the midst of the barren mountains. I gathered all my remaining strength to get there.

I knocked on the door and an old woman opened it. She took one look at my face and offered me bread and yogurt. I stuffed my face to the point where I felt like the lower half of my body was full of concrete – I hadn't realised how much my stomach had shrunk.

I noticed that all this kindly woman and her husband had was bread and yogurt. They owned no furniture. They remain the poorest family I've ever met anywhere in the world and, to this day, I can't figure out how they could survive. That being said, they constantly smiled at me and each other. What they lacked in material things they made up for with happiness. They even let me stay on their floor.

Before leaving the house the following morning, I didn't ask for anything because the couple had nothing. But the husband gave me water and the wife handed me a loaf of bread. I thanked them but handed it back. They insisted I take it. The woman's nurturing expression, her ragged clothes and the way she gently handed me the provisions touched my soul.

My throat clamped up as I cycled off and, within minutes, tears were torrenting down my cheeks. Unbelievable kindness. But what made me feel guilty was a memory of my mum serving me Brussels sprouts during a childhood dinner and how I shouted, 'Get that off my plate!' All she was doing was trying to keep me healthy and strong, just like the poor woman I'd just stayed with.

———

Arriving at a hotel on the Afghan border at 4 a.m., I thought I could hear fireworks. After digesting the noises for a few minutes, I realised it was way worse. It was real gunfire and explosions. My heart fluttered.

Another guest, a Dutch guy, said to me, 'I've just heard that one of the generals was killed last night by an Afghan. A war is going off, man.' I went into the garden with my camera, thinking *I must capture what I can*. As I started self-filming, I heard shots being fired nearby. I was so foolish that I hadn't realised there was a powerful red light on my camera which resembled a sniper's laser sight. As a result, shots were fired at me and pinged off the wall just beside where I was standing. If I'd been killed that night, it would have been entirely my fault.

As the sun came up, Rob, an Englishman who was on holiday with his wife, gathered us all around the veranda. 'Listen everyone, rebels are out there and the army won't stop until it's killed them all. We have no idea how long this is going to take. We're stuck—' He was cut off by a loud bang about 10 feet from where we were standing. We all ran indoors.

We grouped together again a few hours later. 'How is everyone doing for food?' I asked. Some people had several days' worth, while others had next to nothing. 'Right then,' I said. 'Let's share it out, but we'll need to ration it. We should stay put in our rooms and ride this out as safely as we can.'

Throughout the day, it sounded like heavy machinery was arriving outside. We guessed it must be tanks. Everyone was fearful of either being blown up by the army or kidnapped by the rebels.

That evening I checked on all five rooms to see if everyone was all right. I walked into one and found a French-Canadian called Max and his wife eating a vast stack of biscuits, bread, cheese and chocolate. Max looked up at me, frowning guiltily. 'Erm, Jamie, do you want some food?'

I wanted to tell him that he was scum of the earth for not sharing his food, but it wasn't worth getting into an argument, so instead I replied, 'I'm OK, thank you.'

We ran out of food the next day. Someone pointed to pear and berry trees in the hotel grounds. Understandably, no one wanted to go out into the open space for fear of being targeted. Fuelled up on adrenaline, I said, 'I'll go.' I took tiny steps out to the pear tree and grabbed what I could as quickly as possible.

'Jamie!' Max called behind me. 'Don't forget the berry tree.' The berry tree was even further into 'no-man's-land'.

'Why don't you go, Max?' I snapped back.

During the rest of the day, Max managed to irritate everyone else, which amped up the anxiety level of the whole group. He kept making tactless comments like, 'Why don't the army just hurry up and kill them all so I can get out of here?'

The battle outside raged for 30 hours before a Tajik man turned up at the hotel with blood all over him. 'No shooting for two hours, but after it gets even worse. Everyone must leave now.'

I cycled out with two of the other guests, Julie and Adam. We went into a state of shock when we saw the houses with shell holes in them, the smouldering wrecks of tanks and fresh blood streaked across the pavement. I counted two or three dead bodies too.

As we were about to leave the town, a Western-looking woman and her little girl stopped us, their eyes wide with fear.

'Where are you from?' I asked.

'Germany. We were on holiday here, but then… Well, we just don't know what's going on now.'

Adam picked up the girl and put her on his bike. 'We'll stay with you until we make it to a safe area,' I said to the mother.

Further along, we bumped into Max and his wife. They waved down an eight-seater vehicle and jumped in it. Feeling my blood rising, I cycled over to them and threw open the door.

'Get out Max, get out now! There's a mother and child here – they go first.'

'I have a plane to catch,' he protested.

That annoyed me even more. 'Get out now!' I yelled. Everyone, including the mother, was telling me to calm down. Max managed a nervous smile, slammed the door and the car pulled away.

'I knew he was going to do that,' I spat.

Car after car passed us by while we made our way through the war zone. Then one stopped. Two Tajik men got out and offered the mother and daughter safe passage. Julie, Adam and I decided to race out of there. After a mile, we bumped into Max on the side of the road. For whatever reason, their lift hadn't taken them out of town and they were stranded. I pulled out my camera to film Max and screamed at him, 'You are a disgusting human being!' I just couldn't help it.

Later on I found out that over 600 people had died in those 30 hours of combat. Thankfully, everyone I met was OK: the

German woman and her kid made it out of there, but Max missed his flight.

As I crossed into Uzbekistan, I felt like I'd seen and had enough of suffering. I focused on the finish. I raced through the near-vacant deserts of Turkmenistan in 50°C heat, breaking off to find shade under a tree whenever one appeared. Before entering Iran, I posted on Facebook and Twitter to let my followers know that I was close to crossing the border. The responses were panicky.

One read: 'Jamie, do you know what's going on there at the minute? They recently attacked and burnt down the British Embassy.' I'd seen enough violence already and didn't want more.

I crossed the border into Iran and whenever I made eye contact with someone, I would worry that I was cycling into jeopardy once again. My first few hundred metres of Iranian turf went smoothly, until I reached a gate where I had to stop to speak to the guards.

'Where you from?' one asked.

My head spun. I knew I shouldn't say I was British, given recent events. *Say, 'I'm from Italy'*, I thought. *I have dark hair, dark eyebrows – they'll believe that. Come on Jamie, you can pull this off*. Then for a reason I'll never understand, I blurted out, 'I'm from England.'

The guy eyeballed me. 'Me, you – we are not brothers.'

'No, we're not,' I shrugged.

'Wait here,' the Iranian said, showing me his palm. He walked off. I didn't know what to think apart from, *I shouldn't be here*.

My knees started to shake as I agonised over whether to run away from this situation. The man came back a few moments later and handed me a cup of tea. 'Welcome to our country.'

I cycled off, pleased that my intuition had been right – I'd trusted the man just as I'd trusted so many other people over the last seven months, in all of the other countries.

I found Iran to be one of the most hospitable places so far. One guy stopped me as I was cycling to ask if I'd like an apple. I nodded. 'Follow me,' he said. He started jogging and I followed him on my bike. After 3 miles we came to an apple tree.

Whilst I made my way easily across Iran, I couldn't get a niggling thought out of my head: how *did* that man break the world record for cycling ten days non-stop? If somebody has done that, it must be possible.

Iraq was an equally pleasant surprise. OK, so a lot of people were carrying guns, but the level of hospitality was even better than in Iran, or anywhere else I've been before or since. I queued in a supermarket to buy some bananas, and the cashier wouldn't take my money.

'Please take it,' I insisted, a bit embarrassed.

'You're a guest in our country,' he said. 'Please accept our gesture.'

As I walked out of the supermarket, the cashier's friend, Omid, invited me to stay at his tiny shack for the night. I accepted. That night he laid a blanket and some food out on the floor. I sat down with Omid, his wife and children to eat bread, yogurt and chicken. Noticing that no one was going for the meat, I offered to share it.

Omid shook his head. 'You're our guest. You need it more than we do to keep your strength up,' he said. 'You know, Jamie, I spent quite a bit of time in England a few years back, in Birmingham.'

'How was it?' I smiled.

'Your country is amazing, full of opportunity and the people were great.'

I felt pretty proud to be British at that point, chinwagging away with my new Brummie/Iraqi best pal. We then spoke about current affairs in the UK. He said he was disappointed about the way his country was perceived by Britons. I told him I was disappointed too and that my first impression of Iraq was that of a special place. I could see that this filled him with joy.

To be honest, I thought I'd be dead by the time I'd neared Afghanistan and passed through Iran and Iraq. But my positive experiences in these countries completely changed my view of the world. Like so many other Westerners, I'd been brainwashed into thinking that anywhere outside the West was scary, hazardous and depressing. The truth I learned was that bad things happen all across the world. Back home, watching the news, all I'd heard about the Middle East was connected to war, murder and terrorism. Yet, the vast majority of the people I met in these countries were charming and friendly. Obviously, some bad things had happened to me on this trip, but those incidents were few and far between; along the way, people were just... people: incredibly kind.

I was on a high when I crossed into Turkey. 'Turkey! Turkey! Turkey!' I would chant whenever I saw a Turkish person. They could have thought I was a nutter but instead, they were always very kind in response and cheered back at me.

After a day of hard pedalling, I made it into the city of Batman – yes, there's actually a city named Batman. Even more astonishing was the fact that my cousin Kev, also on a bike, was waiting for me on the outskirts of the city. We cycled towards each other in what felt like slow-motion and embraced. It was like a scene from a romantic film. Then Kev brought me down to earth by mocking me for how skinny I'd got. We went to a bar for a well-deserved beer. 'So why did you fly out to meet me, you mad bastard?' I asked him.

'Just wanted to support you. I did worry about what other people would think of me coming all the way out here. But you know what? I don't care what other people think; I just care about what you think.'

'Kev, I've done this trip solo for 12,000 miles. The last 2,000 miles will go faster now I've got my best mate beside me, supporting me, wanting to have the adventure of his life.' I slapped him on the back. 'Kev, let's do this.'

'Oh, I've got a surprise for you.' Kev pulled out Batman and Robin outfits from his bag.

'What's all that about?' I asked.

Kev giggled. 'Back home I managed to get an interview with ITV West Country at the Gloucester Children's Hospital. I was wearing a Robin outfit the whole time.'

'I don't get it, Kev.'

'I told them I was meeting you in the city of Batman and I'd be bringing with me Batman and Robin outfits for me and you to wear while we cycled back home.'

'You said what? You have to be kidding me.'

'I'm not kidding. The story reached hundreds of thousands, so we have to do it now or we'll disappoint a lot of people.'

We laughed like a pair of naughty toddlers as we put on our outfits. At 6'2", Kev is much taller than I am and his Robin costume was as tight as a duck's bum. By contrast, my Batman costume was drooping off me because I had lost so much weight. We resembled a bad comedy duo, like Del Boy and Rodney from *Only Fools and Horses*. We cycled around for the day, taking videos and pictures of Batman signs until a car that looked like the Batmobile showed up. It was the anti-terrorist police.

They leaped out, shotguns in hand, and asked us for our passports. They detained us for five hours, but the only words they said that we understood were: 'You are terrorists?' Eventually, they realised that we were just a couple of British idiots having a bit of fun and they let us go.

All over Turkey people embraced us, although they didn't know who Robin was. They would always point their finger at Kev and say, 'Hey Superman!'

Unfortunately for Kev, the superhero suit didn't give him enough power to allow him to cycle all the way home. He was trying to keep up with someone who had nearly 12,000 miles in the bank and his knees just couldn't take it. He began hitchhiking ahead of me.

I met up with him in the next town. He was shaking and all the colour had gone from his face. 'A big Turkish trucker picked me up and let me put my bike in the back. While I was riding next to him, he kept saying "sex" and then laughing his head off. I laughed nervously along with him. It was like he only knew one word: "sex". Then he started pointing at his you-know-what. Without any warning, he leaned over and grabbed my dick! I went completely nuts, waving my arms and shouting. So I grabbed my cape and covered myself.

'He then started phoning his friends and speaking Turkish. I thought he was lining them up to rape me. Luckily, when we got to a busy town, I opened the door and talked him into getting my bike out.'

Kev hadn't had the nicest of times... Didn't stop me laughing at him, though. After he had recovered from his ordeal, Kev sat with me in an internet cafe while I submitted an application to attempt the longest marathon static cycling record. I knew this had to be my next challenge after the epic bike ride.

Just as we set off, I got an email that read:

Thank you for your application. The current record (current as at the date of this email) is 224 hr 24 min and 24 sec and was achieved by Patrizio Sciroli (Italy) in Teramo, Italy, from 6 to 15 May 2011.

Please see the attached guidelines.

We wish you the best of luck in your record attempt and we look forward to hearing from you!

Turkey was nearly over and I had Europe left to do before the record attempt. My training needed to start right away. I pedalled like a man possessed for hours upon hours, whizzing through the countries. I'd only need to blink and I was in a new one: Bulgaria, tick. Serbia, done. Hungary, another one bites the dust… and so on.

From time to time I would only give myself a couple of hours' sleep to see what it would be like to be sleep-deprived. Every time I did that, though, I risked falling off the bike from fatigue, as well as putting myself in a disgusting mood – I like my sleep.

I whooshed through Austria, Germany, Belgium, Netherlands, France and then, finally, England.

PART 3

RECORD SMASHER

'Ten, nine, eight...'

My head was about to pop off my shoulders from anticipation.

'Three, two, one...'

I stamped on the pedals and my feet went faster than a spin dryer. 'Don't drop beneath 12 mph,' I kept saying to myself. 'That's the rule.'

My dad rushed over. 'Calm down, J, this isn't a race, remember?' I was glad for his support because my mum's first reaction to the news that I was going to attempt the world static cycling record had been quite different: 'What's wrong with you, Jamie? You're going to get yourself killed.'

I glanced around the marquee and came to terms with the fact that this would be all I'd be seeing for the next ten days. There was a big digital clock in one corner, counting the seconds. 'Get rid of that!' I shouted after an hour. 'I don't want to watch paint dry.' In the other corner was my 'table of health': elete (for salts and minerals), vitamin C, fish oils, some fruit and loads of Chamois cream (lube to stop the skin chafing).

There were also hundreds of Snickers bars on the table. They definitely weren't in the food plan that my dietician Jamie Richards – a tall, lanky Londoner with an infectious passion for life – had devised. His wise words from when we first met rang in my ears as I pedalled: '"Paleo" is better known as the "caveman diet". In essence, it's meat and veg. No carbohydrates at all – no pasta, no rice, not even potatoes.' I'd stuck slavishly to that regime in the build-up to the big day.

It was when the marquee started to get busy that I needed to pee. I asked my Dad to pass me a bottle. 'Don't look, everyone,' I said. Even though they all turned around, I was still too nervous to go. I went red as a glow stick. A serious case of stage fright.

'False alarm, everyone!' I was concerned that, if I couldn't pee in front of people and cycle at the same time, I'd have to get off the bike and go to the toilet – but that would eat into my sleeping time. Again, I could hear Jamie's words in my head: 'The theory behind the paleo diet is that carbohydrates have starch and in starch there's sugar. Sleep deprivation will be brutal enough, but if you have to battle a sugar crash, you might not wake up again. How would you feel about cycling for 24 hours and then taking a two-hour break? That way you could fit in one sleep cycle and then have a spare 30 minutes to visit the toilet.'

A few hours later I asked for the bottle again. The smaller crowd meant I was chilled enough to pee. It felt as good as cycling without stabilisers for the first time.

At 5.30 a.m., I'd been cycling for 20 and a half hours and decided to sleep. The bed was situated in the same marquee, about 6 feet away. As I lay down, I put on my eye mask and earmuffs but I wasn't tired. With each minute that passed – and each minute I wasn't sleeping – I could feel the pressure building. After a quarter of an hour like this, I knew there was no way I was going to sleep.

I jerked upright, walked back to the bike and hopped on. As the sun rose, my mind lit up too and I was ready for another day. People were gradually popping in to see how I was getting on. However I felt, I'd always tell them, 'Good, thank you, all good.'

After the thirtieth hour, my head began to nod with fatigue. Ed Archer, a short, well-built South African physiologist friend, advised that I should keep going until I reached the next night. Ed speaks very slowly and wisely, so I thought I'd listen. By hour 41, it was dark again and I went for a second attempt at rest. As soon as I was unconscious, I was woken by a big, cold lump of fresh air striking my body. I heard my dad's voice: 'Come on J! We need to do this quickly – every minute counts.' He ripped me out of bed – I was wearing nothing but a pair of pants – and dragged me by the arm over to the bike. I was delirious and my head was splitting, but nothing could come out of my mouth to tell him to stop.

While pedalling again, I asked Kev how long I'd slept for.

'Don't worry, J, you got an hour and a half. How do you feel?'

'Not good, Kev. Why was I so cold? That was traumatic. I can't go through that again.'

'I think your dad went a little too quickly. He's worried about saving minutes.'

I told him that saving my life was more important than saving minutes. 'Wake me up slower next time.'

Ann Wooldridge, who holds the UMCA (Ultra Marathon Cycling Association) ladies 50+ transcontinental record, had a plan to let me know how I was progressing. Each morning, after my sleep break, she would attach a yellow flower to my handlebars. It seemed a bit pointless to me at that stage, but would grow in significance throughout the attempt.

I was into day three with 63 hours of pedalling behind me. One visitor kept glancing up and down at me and then whispering into his mate's ear. What was I, a circus freak? I knew he was saying that there was no way this guy could keep this up for another week.

The fatigue got bad. Every ten seconds my head would drop. The skin on my cheeks felt as if it was drooping like that on a bulldog's face. The doubting whispers continued all around the marquee. I didn't know if they were real or just a figment of my paranoia. *Either way, I'll show you*, I thought. *As long as I'm alive, nothing will stop me.*

As day turned to night on day four, I got a hellacious craving for fatty food. All I could think about was fat dripping off roast lamb and rivers of cheese flowing into my mouth. I also longed for sleep.

Ann came back. 'Jamie, you look amazing,' she said in her quiet, unassuming way. I smirked at her. I knew she was lying through her teeth. 'If you think what you've been through over the last four days is tough,' she added, 'it's only going to get harder from here, so prepare yourself.'

I looked straight through her. 'Righto, Ann.'

At 2 a.m. my legs carried on pedalling but the rest of my body started to shut down. I was struggling not to topple off the bike. Ann moved closer to me. 'This is how it's going to work: you're going to fight through these worst hours – 2 a.m. to 4 a.m. – and then we're going to let you sleep. When you wake up, you'll enjoy the sunrise over the beautiful water of the docks. How does that sound?'

'Great, Ann, flipping great.' My head was now slouched between my shoulder blades.

'Jamie, look at me, will you?' I lifted my head up slowly. 'Now listen: look to the left. Not with your head, just with your eyes.' I did as she said. 'Good. Now look to the right.' I did that too. 'Good. Now down below. And up.' After five minutes of this I felt much more alert. The eye movements had somehow stimulated my exhausted brain.

I repeated these exercises with Ann for the next two hours. They likely saved the record attempt because, without them, I don't know what would have kept me awake. Before going to bed, I asked Ann if that was what she'd be doing with me for the next few nights.

'Yes,' she said sternly.

As I fell asleep, I thought, *I hope I don't end up punching her in the face*.

I must have only blinked when Kev said, 'J, it's that time again,' in a really quiet voice. Then music started playing.

It was 'Lovely Day' by Bill Withers – one of my favourite tracks, and the song that Kev and I played over and over again when we woke up in Turkey, before another gruelling cycle. I couldn't help but grin even as I awoke from my third one-and-a-half-hour sleep in the space of just four days and nights.

I was given a Christmas hat to celebrate the moment I reached the 100-hour mark. Everyone cheered, and euphoria surged through my veins and head. My bum was stinging horribly, but I was too gleeful to be bothered by it. I went into hysterical laughter, cracked jokes and pedalled like a crazy man. 'I've never felt so good in all my life!' I roared. 'I'm going to smash the record, whaooooo!'

Ed approached me cautiously. 'Jamie, what you're experiencing is very natural when you're sleep-deprived. It's not going to last forever so just calm down.'

I wanted Ed to clear off – he was killing my buzz.

Father Christmas walked through the door. 'Hey, Jamie,' he said in a feminine voice. 'Are you all right, Jamie? It's Liz Gooding here, one of the volunteers.'

'Father Christmas isn't so manly after all,' I laughed.

A few minutes later, my head dropped like a ton of bricks. Unconsciousness was seeping in and I had to fight it. Ed placed a pillow on the handlebars. I put my head against it and somehow managed to keep pedalling. I turned to Keith

Gooding, the volunteer who was keeping an eye on my monitor. 'Have I dropped below 12 mph?' I muttered.

'Not yet.'

Phil Vickery, ex-captain of the England rugby team, appeared later on. The surprise nearly made me fall off my bike. He's a huge, stocky man with a dulcet voice. 'You, my son, are walking the walk.'

Once Phil left, people kept saying every five minutes, 'How are you, Jamie?' Eventually, I snapped at one woman who asked me that. 'How do you think I feel? Honestly? I'll tell you how I feel: like a piece of shit!'

I'd never spoken to anyone like that before and instantly felt bad. I apologised.

Jamie came up with a solution to the problem. The team created posters and put them up everywhere in the marquee, including on the door. On them was an illustration of a big yellow face with a tongue hanging out and they read:

THANK YOU FOR THE SUPPORT, BUT PLEASE DON'T ASK HOW I AM. I'VE BEEN CYCLING A LOT. TRY TO DISTRACT ME INSTEAD, AS THE TIME WILL GO MUCH QUICKER.

To make things less dull for me, the team put a map of the United States up on the wall to inform me how far I would have cycled across that country, had I set off from New York instead of being stuck here on a static bike. I'd done almost 2,000 miles and was, as it were, halfway across America. Suddenly, it felt like I was actually going somewhere, although I never actually moved more than a few feet throughout the record attempt.

On the evening of day six, distractions from the agony came in the form of Ed's kids running around the marquee and hassling spectators with donation buckets. I looked on, realising that everyone was feeling good: the kids were having fun and the people walking past could take pride in giving. In turn, I was chuffed about all the good things the money would be spent on.

My friend Dan Snowdon and his band came in to play some live reggae. People cracked open beers, sang along and danced. A party was happening right next to me, but I couldn't go to it. Instead, I was stuck pedalling myself stupid. I didn't mind – I was feeding off their energy.

Once everyone had cleared out, though, I couldn't keep my eyes open or my body from falling off. Ann popped in to do some more exercises. 'Now, Jamie, look up—'

'Ann!' I hissed. 'Just fuck off. I've had e-fucking-nough.'

Ann took a little step back and snickered. It wound me up even more. 'What's so fucking funny?'

She snickered some more.

A few minutes later, once silence returned, I realised that I was the most awake I'd been since I'd begun this challenge. Ann was deliberately winding me up and it was working. Once I figured out her ploy, I calmed down. 'Sorry, Ann.'

By day eight, hour 150, people in the marquee had a different air about them. The whispering had stopped. They really believed I could break the record. Unfortunately, though, the pain in my bum worsened. I could think of nothing else. If people engaged with me, I could only think of my bum rather than focusing on what they were saying. When someone handed me food, I'd think of my bum while I scoffed it.

Soon it felt as if someone were using an industrial sander on my behind and then sprinkling salt on it. The tears were spraying out of my eyes but I kept on keeping on. Trying to maintain a straight face, Ed informed me that he was worried my bum had got infected. Two nurses came in with lots of medical gear. They took a photo of my bottom and grimaced at it for a while. When they showed it to me, I nearly vomited. All I could see was white pus oozing out of a puddle of blood. 'Why did you show me that?' I demanded.

'Quite honestly,' one of the nurses said, 'we've never had to deal with anything like this before. We're really sorry, but there's nothing we can do. For this to heal, you have to get off that bike.'

Clearly, that wasn't an option. I thanked them and said I'd keep pedalling. At that moment, a kid in a Spiderman costume walked in with a £5 donation. It was a reminder of what all the pain, blood and pus were for.

I can't say I wasn't worried. If the infection worsened, there was a good chance I'd get sick, and that would then end all hopes of smashing the record.

An hour later, Jamie came bursting through the entrance, waving a small tube in the air. 'Manuka honey! It's an antibiotic, one of the strongest you can get.'

Not convinced, I slapped the honey on.

Steve Jones, who sorted the bike out, also tried to come up with a solution and arrived with five different saddles. 'This could help. Which one do you want?'

'Whichever one that's going to help my arse.'

The saddle relieved some pressure for about an hour.

At 2 a.m. the next morning, Ann started to drive me insane again. She spoke to me as my eyes were shutting down. 'What are you seeing, Jamie?'

'A helicopter... It's flying about in the air.'

Ann's voice perked up. 'Oh nice, what's it doing?'

'It wants to land.'

'Jamie!' she screamed. 'Your helicopter must not land. Whatever you do, it must not land. Do you hear me? Open your eyes right now!'

I was already half asleep. 'Sorry, Ann, it has to land.'

'No! Jamie!'

I then felt a stinging sensation on my face and my eyes slowly opened. 'Did you just slap me?' I squeaked.

Ann was towering over me. 'Well done, you're awake!'

At 6 a.m. I stumbled off the bike, barely able to walk. The volunteers carried me to bed. My head slammed against the pillow.

I was back on the bike, at the rear of a slow-moving truck with a team of grinning people around me. The sun was blazing down on us. I could see pink flowers in turquoise fields rolling past in slow motion. It was the definition of bliss and tranquillity. Had I ascended to another world?

I heard Kev's voice. 'Jamie, are you OK?'

My head was foggier than if someone had dosed me up on tranquillisers. 'Wha-what happened?'

'After you went to bed you never quite woke up. We managed to carry you to the bike and you somehow got pedalling, but you weren't all there. We were ready to call an ambulance.'

I looked down and my legs were still going round. They didn't feel like they were under my control.

'Should I call that ambulance, Jamie?' asked Kev. 'Talk to me.'

'I can't tell you exactly where I've been, but it was a happy place.'

'Bloody hell, you had us all worried. Well, at least you're alive, even if you're not making much sense. Not too long now and you'll be a new world record holder.'

The Gloucester rugby players Charlie Sharples, Freddie Burns, Jim Hamilton, Tom Savage, Jimmy Cowan and others came to support me and give £500 to the hospital. The donations were really starting to fly in now, both online and via people coming in and putting notes in the buckets.

As I clocked 175 hours of non-stop cycling, my mum started hovering around me, trying to perk me up with her positivity. 'J, I know you're in pain,' she said.

I thought to myself, *Mum, you haven't got a flipping clue*.

'You know,' she said, 'the experience is nearly all over now, and you'll never have to go through this again. So you may as well enjoy it.'

My mum had never ever said anything like this before. Maybe she was coming round to this adventure stuff.

As the day slipped into night, the marquee looked radically different. I wasn't quite sure how or why, but I just knew it had changed. I shouted over to Kev. 'How come we're in a new room? I didn't think I was allowed to switch rooms?'

Kev opened his palms to me in bewilderment. 'You haven't gone anywhere in nine days. Don't lose the plot now, not when you're this close!'

Later, hundreds of people gathered in the marquee. Crews from the BBC and ITV crowded round me, their cameras rammed in my face. I heard a countdown from ten and then... Bang! The place erupted. 'Jamie,' said a journalist. 'You've just broken the world record, but you're still going. Why?'

'I'm starting to believe that there's no limit to any human being,' I said. 'The only limits we have are us.'

'But aren't you tired?'

'How could I be tired when I've got all these people around me that I love? I'm absolutely buzzing!'

That collective energy kept me soaring for a further 20 hours. I didn't want to just break the record, I wanted to smash it. I told myself that the longer I went on, the more money would come in for the hospital. My original target was £5,000 and now it had reached £20,000. I just kept pedalling.

The tall and fuzzy-haired figure of Jody Gooding, an ex-Great Britain volleyball player, appeared by my side; he'd been following my progress online. He has this infectious energy that fills you with confidence, so I thought it vital to listen to him. 'You've got to keep going, you know. You should go for another week.'

Light-headed, I gazed at him and said, 'Yeeeahhh!' You could have told me my dad was Elton John and I would still have said, 'Yeaahhh.'

'Let's keep it going,' agreed Kev.

'I think it's over now; there's nothing more to prove,' said Phil Vickery.

'I think you've all gone mad,' argued Jody. 'Jamie should keep at it.' He then looked over at me. 'What do you think, Jamie?' It seemed to take a decade for my brain to absorb Jody's words.

Before I could open my mouth, Ed stepped in. 'Jamie's achieved something none of us could have dreamed of. He's done it. Not only has he done it, he's smashed it. Everyone here is extremely tired, not least Jamie. More than that, we have no bloody idea what this is doing to Jamie's health. Right now he's somewhere no man has been. I say let's stop, get him healthy and let him prep for the next one.'

Had I really heard Ed say 'the next one'?

I stepped off the bike at 268 hours, 32 minutes and 44 seconds. More than 11 days. At the time of writing, this remains the world record.

I stumbled off the bike, out of the marquee and into a waiting car. As we left, someone shouted that there was a party happening there in six hours.

I turned in slow motion to try to look at the person. My eyes couldn't focus.

'Well, are you in? The party is for you!'

'Goodnight,' I muttered.

Back home, I lay down and set my alarm for four hours later. I wasn't going to miss the party. *My* party.

Indeed, I made it: I drank a few beers and swayed the night away to Michael Jackson's 'Thriller'. I didn't even need to dress up as a zombie – I was a zombie.

Afterwards, I went back home and slept for 17 hours straight. On the second night I slept for another 14 hours but it took another week for me to feel anything approaching normal again.

Once I'd rested up, I visited Gloucester Children's Hospital. Wendy took me into a dingy little room. 'How would you feel if we spent the money you raised on a new playschool right here?'

The lump in my throat was so big I couldn't answer her. As a sick kid, I'd never had much education. I could never have guessed I'd get the opportunity to help provide one for other sick kids. Finally, I was able to say to Wendy, 'That would be incredible.'

I then received a Facebook message from Dave O'Reegan:

Dear Jamie, I just wanted to send you a little message to let you know that your project has inspired me and is the greatest and most inspirational thing I've seen in a long time. My friend showed me your posts on your page, all your videos on YouTube and they are amazing. Also, seeing you actually getting on a bicycle and cycling has pushed me to finally take my own project on. I'm now going to cycle around the world for charity. I know, I'm terrified but

you've shown me that if you can do it, I can do it. Anyway, I don't want to waste any more of your time. Thank you once more for the inspiration, love Dave.

I went on Google and typed 'define: inspiration', as I didn't really know what it meant. This is what flashed up: 'The process of being mentally stimulated to do or feel something, especially to do something creative.' Underneath was another meaning: 'A sudden brilliant or timely idea.'

I will always remember Dave's message as a milestone because it was the first time I ever inspired anyone with my adventures. But I'd been inspired too. I remembered the story of average Graham who'd cycled around the world and how that persuaded me to give up on the suburban life I was aiming for and live my dream. I wondered who Dave was now going to inspire with his own trip. I was in the middle of an enormous chain reaction and it was wonderful.

I went for a meal at Peppers Cafe in Gloucester with all the people who had helped me to achieve the world record. Jody, Jamie R, Ed and my dad were there.

Jody was waving his arms about. 'Jamie, Jamie, you could be one of the next great adventurers. If you carry on, in ten years' time you could raise millions. Instead of funding a school playroom you could raise enough to build a hospital.'

'All right, Mr Positive,' I chuckled, 'did you overdose on your meds this morning?' All I was thinking about was which coffee to choose. He went on like that all day.

Sometimes people would stop me in the streets of Gloucester and ask what my next big adventure was going to be. I kept thinking, *What do they mean, what's next? Haven't I done enough already?*

The next morning I went to my parents' house and the dreaded question popped up again. 'What are you going to do with yourself now, J?' asked my brother Lee.

'Don't know,' I sighed. 'I've got a working visa for Canada so I'd like to travel around there a bit.'

'"Travel around?"' scoffed my dad. 'That sounds a bit too...' he struggled for the right word. 'Too *easy* for you, son.'

That evening, I kept thinking about the new school playroom in the hospital that was being built and I also kept going over Dave O'Reegan's kind words. Was I really going to just bum about in Canada after achieving all this?

I went to the toilet and had a eureka moment. It was indeed 'a sudden brilliant or timely idea'. I ran back into the living room and shouted, 'Mum, Dad, Lee, I'm going to run across Canada!'

Mum looked horrified. 'Not again. Please don't put me through this again.'

My dad started yelling, 'Yes, son, that's exactly what you should be doing!' The vein on the side of his head was pulsating.

'Let's see if anyone else has been mad enough to do this before,' said Lee, opening up a laptop. All together, as a family, we typed 'run across Canada' into Google and came across a short YouTube documentary about a man called Terry Fox. A keen athlete from childhood, Terry had his knee amputated after contracting osteosarcoma, a form of cancer. He was fitted with an artificial leg and in 1980, against every sensible person's advice, he decided to run across Canada to raise money for cancer research. Terry got halfway, to a place called Thunder Bay, before he was forced to give up because his cancer had spread to his lungs. He died nine months later, but not before he'd raised 24 million Canadian dollars and saved thousands of lives. In the years since his death, the organisation has gone on to raise over 600 million dollars.

After the film, we stared at each other, speechless. None of us could believe how incredible Terry Fox's story was. Suddenly, that word – 'inspiration' – took on real meaning. It was a human driving force, I was sure of it. If Terry could attempt to circumnavigate the second largest country in the world with one leg and cancer, I could give it a crack too.

PART 4

BIGGER THAN THE ROCKIES

'It always seems impossible until it's done.'

Nelson Mandela

NEWFOUNDLAND

The moment I dipped my hand in the Atlantic Ocean at St John's in Newfoundland, on 9 March 2013, that was it. All the fear transformed into blissful hysteria. As I got running, I screamed over and over again: 'I'm running 5,000 miles across Canada!'

That's nearly 200 marathons in less than a year, almost a marathon every day.

People waved at me as I ran along George Street – was it because it has the most bars per square foot of any street in North America? It might also have had something to do with the fact I was still yelling, 'I'm running across Canada!' at the top of my voice.

I'd prepared myself for camping every night and in all weather conditions. But I really had no idea what I'd be faced with. I hadn't bothered researching – might have put me off. All I knew was that I'd be catching the end of the winter at the start of the run on the east coast and hoped to make it to the other side before the bad weather hit on the west coast.

Running out of town, my first Canadian sign popped up: TRANS-CANADA HIGHWAY. On the plane over, a nice Canadian told me that this highway starts on one coast and ends at the other.

'Happy days,' I said. 'Shouldn't be too difficult to get lost then.'

The miles disappeared quickly thanks to adrenaline – the best fuel known to man. NTV News showed up in a fancy car on the side of the highway. A reporter named Nancy jumped out, camera on her shoulder. I got some words out between the panting.

'Brilliant,' she said. 'This will go out at 6 p.m. and reach more than 100,000 viewers.' I didn't know who contacted them, but I was glad to get the media coverage – and I was only on day one.

At the end of that first day, I was ready to set up camp. There wasn't any grass in sight, only snow – mountains of it that were as tall as me. I spied a house in the distance with a small patch of greenery beside it. I brewed up the courage to knock on the door, something I'd never do in England, but for some reason, being a foreigner and feeling vulnerable, I thought it worth a try.

A middle-aged guy with glasses poked his head out.

'Hi there. I know this might sound a bit odd, but my name is Jamie McDonald and I'm running across Canada.' He looked suspicious. 'Anyhow, do you mind if I camp on your lawn? I won't do any harm. Promise.'

'Yes you can,' he said, a little uncertainly, and shut the door.

Since I'd stopped running, my body temperature dropped. My breathing was heavy, as my heart worked like a miner to pump blood around my system to counteract the freezing temperature. At −15°C, it was the coldest I'd ever encountered. Before the run I'd had my body fat tested. It was at 5 per cent. 'Ultra lean,' the testers had said. Why did I flipping pick Canada?

Shaking, I assembled the tent and curled up in my sleeping bag, still buzzing from my first day of running. Could I really do this for nearly a year?

That night I dreamed of being back in Gloucester, talking with a guy I met in the pub who'd been in the army and knew what it was like to lug heavy equipment about the place.

'How are you going to carry all your stuff across the country?' he asked.

'With a backpack, stupid.'

He laughed his head off. 'Have you ever run with a backpack? You're in for a treat.'

By the next morning, I'd got his joke. My backpack weighed in at 30 kg – half my own body weight. I was now, in a sense, obese. Or at least, I was carrying with me as much weight as an obese person would be.

After a few miles, my calves felt like Pinocchio's wooden legs, but with actual pain. I reached an enormous highway where a few cars whizzed by me at 120 mph. Anxiety crept into my head. 'What if I need water?' I asked myself. 'I can't stop cars at that speed.'

A mile later, a house popped up on the side of the road. A woman answered the door and in a thick Irish accent said, ''Ello dere, wha' can I do for you?'

'I'm running across Canada. Any chance of a glass of water?'

'Of course! I'm Bonnie, by the way. Are you hungry, too?'

'Jamie. And yes, I'm starving.'

The door swung open. 'Lucky for you we got a Jiggs dinner on.'

'I have no idea what that is,' I said, catching my breath. 'But I love most food.'

It turned out to be my favourite home-cooked meal: a roast dinner. 'Why didn't you say it was a roast dinner?' I asked.

We were joined by Bonnie's niece, Ginamay, and her dad Scott, and we spent the whole meal chatting away. I found it extremely weird that, in 2013, I was sitting down in Canada with people who sounded like they were fresh off the boat from Ireland.

'Ah, we all sound like this, us Newfies,' said Bonnie. 'You must know tho' that we're only a boat ride away from the Irish folk.'

After the fantastic dinner, the conversation moved to why I was running. The moment I said that I was fundraising for children's hospitals, Bonnie looked sombrely at Ginamay, who was wearing a bobble hat. 'Go on, darling, remove it.' Ginamay slowly slid her bobble hat off.

'A shaved head?' I blurted out. 'Why?'

'My friend Shantell has cancer. She's lost her hair and the use of her legs. I wanted to show her that she's not alone. To show my support, I donated my hair to make wigs.'

Running on from that house, I couldn't help but be amazed by a 12-year-old girl who was prepared to be as bald as Bruce Willis. I always thought a girl's hair is her prized possession.

Her commitment was the motor that propelled me through the next day.

At a crossroads I saw a sign that read: DILDO. I thought I was going blind – or mad. I ran closer again and DILDO just got bigger until eventually it *was* what I thought it was: Canada had a town named Dildo. I hauled out my camera to take a selfie. 'Oh no you didn't, Canada,' I smirked. 'Oh no, you didn't.'

By dusk I'd only managed another half-marathon. That was my fourth day managing only 13 miles. I couldn't see how I was going to be able to hit a full marathon of 26 miles. I'd never really attempted anything on this scale before, and certainly hadn't trained to run the breadth of a vast country like Canada. Finding water took a lot of time out of the day. I'd keep my eye out for lakes and use my trusty pump purifier. The problem was that sometimes the ice was inches thick and I'd have to smash through it with a rock.

I checked into a motel for the night. It wasn't kind on my budget, but it was so cold outside. In the morning, I opened my door and saw a total white-out. Snow started flying in my face. How was I supposed to get anywhere in these conditions?

I put on a ski mask, balaclava and gloves – in fact, every item of clothing I owned – and ended up looking like a ninja. I went to reception and asked the owner for advice. 'The Trailside Motel and Restaurant is 15 miles up the road,' he said, 'but what are you doing, man, are you crazy? People won't even drive out in this, let alone run in it. It's –20°C. Just stay here.'

I anxiously waved goodbye and ran into the wind, which shoved me back and cut like a stiletto into the gaps between my gloves and sleeves. I trudged on. With every step, my foot sank a little so then I'd have to make a big effort to get it out of the hole I'd made and repeat the process. After 20 minutes of this, I was warm and actually finding being out in a snowstorm quite exhilarating.

My Achilles tendon and quad muscles deteriorated fast. My pace slowed down and then my temperature dropped. My chin ended up buried in my chest. There weren't any vehicles around. I just had to keep moving forward.

The motel hoved into view. I explained to the lady in reception that I'd just run from the last motel. 'Can I camp somewhere near?'

'Don't be silly,' she said in her Irish brogue. 'If you camp out in this, you'll be dead by morning. How about I talk with the owner and see if I can get you a room?'

'You're a literal lifesaver,' I said.

The next morning the storm had vanished. The roads were clear and I had only 14 miles to the smallish town of Clarenville, population 6,000. Halfway there, I heard a crack in my foot. I stopped and moved it around but felt nothing. I ploughed on and, with each mile, my foot grew more painful. With 2 miles left, I was limping. A week in and I realised that my dream of running the breadth of Canada might already be over.

A car pulled up. 'Hey, are you that runner guy?' asked the driver, a skinny guy in a baseball cap.

'I might be,' was my tentative reply.

'I'm Keith and I've just signed up to Twitter. You were the first person who popped up.' What a fluke! He was probably my first Canadian follower on social media. 'You want to come and stay at our house?'

I was in a bad mental state, which I didn't want to tell him about. Then again, a motel would be lonely and expensive so I accepted his offer. He asked me to hop in. As much as I wanted to get off my possibly broken foot, I said, 'I'll run, thank you.' I had one rule on this journey: I'd always run to where I'd sleep.

Keith's place was warm and cosy. I met his lovely wife, Lynn, and found out that they were both keen runners. They called their doctor friend who took one look at my foot and told me that there was a high possibility I had a bone fracture, but needed a scan to be sure. 'The worst case scenario,' he said, 'is that you'll need a couple of months off running.' No way could I do that. My visa would run out and the winter in the Rockies would be savage.

I decided to take a couple of weeks off instead. I'd do the strengthening exercises that Ed had taught me, taking care not to aggravate the foot. I started to doubt my ability to run across Canada, so why not cycle it instead? I knew I could do that. But no, I'd promised myself and everyone else that I'd run.

I ended up staying for those two weeks off with Lynn and Keith, who spent most days chatting with me and keeping super positive, telling me that I'd love it out west in the gorgeous Rocky Mountains. Their lovely friends came round to cheer me up and give me hope.

They also invited me to their ski chalet to take my mind off things. Lynn noticed that one of the skiers sliding down had a trailer behind him with a baby in it. 'See that trailer? It has wheels like a stroller.'

I didn't get it. 'What's a stroller, Lynn?'

'It's a buggy type of thing where the baby goes and the mother can push it along.'

'I get it. That's what we call a pram in England.' Of course! What an excellent idea – a much easier way for me to carry all my stuff while running, so Keith and I ordered one online.

After two weeks, I went to see the doctor about the results of the bone scan. He told me there was a big white spot on my foot where it was inflamed. However, he'd been wrong in his first diagnosis. There was no fracture but I did have tendon damage.

I punched the air as I left. As long as the bone wasn't damaged, I could run. I was sure of that.

Before heading off, I gave my old friend and head teacher Larry Montagu a call. I'd heard just a few weeks before that he was suffering from cancer. He didn't sound well and couldn't talk much, so I thought I'd share a true story with him.

A 70-year-old man with cancer was given weeks to live by his doctor. He'd always had the ambition to skydive, so he did it. He loved it so much that he did another 20 jumps after that. He was so into skydiving that he decided to get a qualification which would allow him to help other people to jump. Weeks went by and then months. When he visited the doctor again, he was astonished to find that his cancer was fading. That 70-year-old man is now in his eighties.

The next day I saw on social media that Larry had passed away. I shrivelled up on my bed and sobbed. Composing myself, I remembered what a great role model he'd been to me and many others. He'd given me the confidence to take the small steps in life, which led on to bigger and greater things. He was another hero, and now he was gone.

I dubbed my new trailer 'the chariot' – I was expecting it to fight a kind of battle – and set off again. As I was making good time in Terra Nova National Park, a ranger pulled over. He was wearing one of those classically Canadian fur hats. 'Hey, what you doing out here?' I told him all about my trip. 'You must be crazy,' he gasped. 'Camping out, too? Do you have any protection with you?'

'I think I have a can of beans that could do some damage.'

He smiled and then straightened his face. 'You got pepper spray? The bears are sleeping right now, but in the next month they'll be out and they'll be hungry.'

I looked down at my emaciated body. 'They won't get a good feed off of me,' I quipped and then ran on.

'Be safe,' he shouted.

I could feel a niggle on the inside of my knee. I set up camp in the woods and hoped that the pain would be gone by the following day. Morning came and the pain was worse. I'd only been back on the road for a few days after a three-week break – and I was injured again.

I kept reminding myself what Ed Archer had said before I left home: 'If you get a small injury, just stop, rest up, heal and know that you can make up the time later on.'

I spent a few days in that wood and eventually built up enough courage to get going. I could only manage 10 miles that day. I made new calculations, bearing in mind having had so much time off so early on – as a result, I had 190 marathons left to go, and just 230 days to complete them.

I managed another 10 miles before I stopped for the night. I was about to drop off when I heard some tapping noises above and around the tent. As it was pitch-dark, I rummaged for the torch but I was frightened it might be a bear, so I didn't turn the light on. I didn't move.

The tapping grew louder and more frequent. Could it be rats? My food was out there – what if they ate it? My heart was going like a bass drum. I lay there for hours until eventually I calmed down and went to sleep.

Unzipping my tent at dawn, I wasn't sure what I'd find. The place was covered in snow. Was that what I'd heard in the night: snowfall tapping against the tent's walls? I was annoyed with myself for letting my imagination run wild and for getting frantic about snow. There was going to be plenty more of that in this part of the world and I needed to man up!

The next town in my sights was Gander, in the northeast of Newfoundland island. I got a Facebook message about it:

Hey Jamie, I'd imagine your body is fairly sore now so I've called the Radiance Salon and Spa for a complimentary spa. I thought it might help.

The miles flew by with the thought of a bit of pampering at the end. Halfway through the run, the sun disappeared and the temperature plummeted. Hailstones pelted down. I put on my puffy jacket, and wrapped my hoodie around my head and face to stop the stinging.

Bursting into the spa, I was greeted by three lovely women. 'Come here, you poor thing, and take your coat off. You shouldn't be out in that nasty weather.'

Unbelievably, the sun came out the following day, melting the snow and signalling spring. The streams around me started to rustle, and the colours of the trees grew bold and vibrant. I even slapped some sun cream on my nose. I love the smell of it. For a moment it was like I was on holiday – except I had about 186 marathons left, that's all.

A few days went by and I saw nothing. Then, quite late into the night, somebody stopped to assure me that there'd be a restaurant 5 miles up the road. My legs were too tired to make it so I resolved to go there for breakfast the following day.

I woke up looking forward to sausages at the restaurant. Once it felt like I'd run 5 miles, I stopped to check Google. It seemed that I'd somehow run further away from the restaurant. So I ran on and noticed I'd gone even further. That's when I realised I'd gone the wrong way, melted down with anger and managed to frighten a poor, unassuming motorist.

I finally got to the restaurant and shared my story with ten punters. When I got to the part about the driver thinking that somebody was hurt, everyone roared with laughter. I went blank. It didn't seem funny to me then. After my meal, I watched my reaction on a small camera that the BBC had given me to capture footage for a short documentary due to be made when I got home.

Seeing myself writhing on the ground, more upset about taking a wrong turning than all the physical pain I was in, I had to laugh. I looked angrier than the Incredible Hulk himself. This legging it across a country business is as draining emotionally as it is physically.

I took my wallet out to pay for breakfast, but the waitresses said, 'Don't be stupid.' Before leaving, the people who'd enjoyed my story gave me donations for SickKids, one of the main Canadian kids' hospitals I was raising money for. As if that wasn't enough, the waiting staff handed me food to take with me.

I ran off with a full belly and more than $100 for SickKids. What generosity!

Near Badger, a settlement on the Exploits River, was an isolated road that cut across the province. Taking it would save me more than two marathons. Firstly, though, I needed to set up camp. I went over to a shack and asked the woman who answered the door if I could sleep in her garden.

She glared at me as if I were wearing a suit of slugs. 'No you can't!'

As I turned away, she asked who I was, what I was doing and why I was doing it. I told her.

'Wait there,' she said. She slammed the door on me, which was confusing. Five minutes later she opened it again. 'I've just Googled you and... You're real.'

As I was constructing my tent on her lawn, the lady came over to me. 'I'm Daisy. Stop that, please.' She explained that she had phoned the motel over the road and booked a room for me: 'A key is waiting for you – it's all paid for. But first why don't you come to mine?'

At her house, Daisy introduced me to her sister Sylvia and her husband Ron. We drank tea, ate biscuits and chatted the evening away. Daisy phoned a ranger to ask whether I could take the shortcut I had been considering. She put her phone on loudspeaker so I could hear him. 'No, man,' he said. 'There's no way you can get through that road cos it's full of snow, knee-deep or worse.' I decided it would be wise to listen to him.

Daisy had shown such kindness; I entered her house a complete stranger and by the end of the evening I was a friend.

The following morning posed an almighty climb, perhaps the steepest of the whole journey. My legs were so frail that all I could do was lean forward as far as I could and start with baby steps on my tiptoes. It was worth it – as soon as I conquered the summit, I was looking down on the beautiful city of Corner Brook. Ornate buildings and trees full of crimson leaves overlooked a sparkling blue lake that shimmered as deep as the ocean.

Ron, whom I'd met the previous night, popped up out of nowhere and said, 'You know that me and Sylvia live in Corner Brook?' So I ran behind his car as he led me to the nearest bike shop. Inside, a family greeted me. 'You're Jamie McDonald, aren't you?' I was introduced to a little girl called Brygette. Much of her early life had been spent in hospitals. We had that in common.

'She was in constant pain,' said her mum, 'with vomiting, fevers and such. Her outlook wasn't great until doctors found out what was wrong with her after sequencing her DNA. She's the second kid in the world to have been diagnosed. Doctors at the hospital in Toronto gave her a stem cell transplant and she's been symptom-free ever since.'

I was glad to be reminded about the material difference that fundraising makes. Unless you get out and meet kids like Brygette, it can all seem a bit abstract, just numbers on a fundraising web page. I gave Brygette a hug; she gave me a SickKids jersey. It made sense to be wearing the logo of one of the charities I was helping.

I stayed with Ron and Sylvia that night and it just so happened that Dwight Ball, the leader of the Liberal Party of

Newfoundland and Labrador, came to dinner. He loved what I was doing and got on the phone to spread the word. 'I'd love for you to reach out to a school to speak to the kids.' I nodded vigorously, even though I hadn't done any public speaking before and the very thought terrified me. But this journey was all about saying 'yes'.

Sylvia woke me the following day with some extraordinary news. 'I've just called CBC News and they're going to cover your story.'

'You can't do that, Sylvia,' I yawned.

'Sure I damn can.' I knew local papers across the province had mentioned me – but this one was big.

I tried to get up and couldn't move my neck. I realised that I'd been pushing Caesar – my new name for my chariot – for more than 20 days, and my shoulders and trap muscles were stiff as hardboard. If I looked left, or right, my entire body had to move with my head. I must have looked like the Terminator.

I got back on the road, but after a few miles my legs were getting sore again. I did some yoga moves on the side of the highway, which earned me some odd looks from macho truckers driving by.

I bumped into two cyclists who were cycling across Canada on a tandem bike each. 'Hey, you must be Jamie?'

'Yes, how do you know that?'

'You're famous, man. Every town we've been through, everyone's like: "Make sure you catch up with Jamie – he's a crazy British guy running east to west. Send him our love."'

'Thanks, that really warms my heart.' I asked them about their adventure.

'We have a tandem each cos we want people to ride with us.'

I couldn't help but think, *But what about if you pick up a nut job?* Instead, I said, 'What an amazing idea: friend-collecting.' They cycled off and I was a tad jealous of their speed.

By the end of the day, I was worried that I was in physical decline. Just turning my head or wiggling my toes was agonising.

Seven miles into the next leg of my journey, another guy in a baseball cap pulled up to invite me for breakfast. I accepted because I was quite sick of butter and tinned fish. I ran nearly a mile off route, but it was worth it. When I entered his wooden cabin, I was greeted by his wife JoAnn and their 13-year-old son, Liam, who has learning difficulties. Liam started writing a letter, which he read to me once he was finished with it. 'Trust what you know,' he said. 'Keep going forward. Never give up. Are you going to take off your shoes and quit or are you going to tighten your laces and go for the big prize?'

Liam had received so much assistance himself and here he was offering someone else beautiful words of support. It was a sweet gesture and made me feel churlish for having even considered taking off my shoes and quitting.

Back on the road, I hit one of the windiest places on the planet, the Wreckhouse. Before my trip I'd found some quotes about it online. 'That place blows over trucks for fun. The wind is trapped and turns into hurricane force – constantly.'

Indeed, the wind was howling so loudly I couldn't hear a thing. I went head-on into it, yelling 'I feel so alive!'

I couldn't go fast but I did eventually get to the town of Port aux Basques, the ferry port to the next province. People were cheering and giving me $5 and $10 donations for SickKids. Dwight, the politician I'd met at Ron and Sylvia's, texted me to ask if I'd speak at a local school. 'Of course, I'm all ready to do it in the morning,' I replied. He then directed me to the Hotel Port aux Basques, where the receptionist asked me to sit down to a meal already paid for. I couldn't, because I stank like a beast. Once I'd showered, though, I demolished a humongous rack of ribs. The best part about it was that it was hot. I'd been eating cold, boring food for nearly a week. When you're doing mad challenges like this, the simplest things become so meaningful.

As I was tucking into some cheesecake, I cheekily asked the waitress what time she got off work.

'I have to leave here and go to another job,' she said quickly.

I was loving Canada so much, I was already on the hunt for a lady, and perhaps a visa too!

Well rested, I made it to the school assembly at 9 a.m. The hall had over 500 seats and basketball hoops everywhere. It was so Canadian! A teacher gave me a microphone and I accepted it with a shaking hand.

I rigged up my laptop to a big screen and showed a video of people hurling themselves down Cooper's Hill in Gloucester, chasing a giant wheel of Double Gloucester cheese. The kids bawled with laughter. 'That's where I'm from,' I said. 'We run after a dairy snack and sometimes break our arms and legs doing it.' I got more guffaws for that. This was my first time doing public speaking and I loved it. I even got a standing ovation while the head teacher gave me a $300 cheque for SickKids.

When it was time for me to leave, three of the kids ran 2 miles with me to the ferry terminal. 'I wonder if I could run across Canada too?' asked one of them.

On the ferry three stewardesses handed me my boarding card along with more donations. I just couldn't believe that my expenses were being paid for *and* people were giving to the cause too.

What a time I'd had in Newfoundland!

NOVA SCOTIA

I was surprised to find a weighing machine on the ferry. I was worried that I'd lost a lot of weight, so when I hopped on the machine and looked at the display, I thought it must be broken. I was heavier than ever before: 66 kg. I'd run over 800 miles and somehow gained more than 10 per cent in weight. It just showed that the Newfie women like to feed their men, especially with great cheesecake! It was time to slow down in the food department.

I Skyped Jamie Richards, my trusty diet guru. 'Everyone thinks you need lots of calories to run tons of miles,' he said. 'In fact, all you need to be doing is eating meat, fats and veg when you can get it. Cut out the sugar and turn into a mean, lean running machine.'

The next day it was raining hard, as I sprinted onto narrow Seal Island Bridge. Then I saw a foreboding sign: YOU ARE NOW AT THE BASE OF KELLY'S MOUNTAIN. YOU WILL CLIMB 1.4 MILES FOR THE NEXT 4 MILES. My legs burned as the lactic acid built up in them. It was Caesar that was holding me back.

Once I reached the other side, I received a text from Sylvia with a number for CBC Nova Scotia. I called it and explained what I was doing.

'Yeah, yeah,' snorted the man on the other end. 'We get lots of runners and cyclists call in. I'm sorry but we can't run a story on this.'

'What, you get lots of people running alone across the whole of Canada?'

'Look, man, we get lots of these requests.'

After the media buzz in Newfoundland, this was weird. It also sank in that not one single car had beeped since I'd come to Nova Scotia. People didn't know who I was or what I was doing. I had to start all over again – moving to another province was like moving to another country.

I knocked on a door. A guy called Zac made me a cup of tea and we chatted for an hour. I was hoping he'd let me snuggle up on his sofa, but he kicked me out into his shed. It was a roof over my head, after all.

I complained via Skype to Rich Leigh, a PR expert back home who was generously giving his time to support my trip. 'Jamie, I know I said that the media back in the UK would be covering and they're not, but they soon will be. It takes time. As for

Canada, I've no doubt things will pick up again there, too. Keep focused on your current followers on social media – they're your true supporters. You already have thousands following you on Facebook, and Twitter is going strong, too. Carry on with the YouTube videos. Make an impact there and the media will come to you, rather than the other way round.'

Once I was on the move again, a cyclist appeared and rode along beside me for a few hours. His name was Marcus and he was doing a five-day trip, away from his wife.

'How has it been, going it alone?' I asked.

'I sing to myself.'

'What does your wife think of this?'

'Honestly? She thinks it's a bit odd.' She sounded like a wise lady.

Once I finally reached the lakeside village of Baddeck, I saw a house that was bright pink. I jogged over and gave the door a knock. A huge face appeared in the window, nose pressed against the glass. He began to scream at me. I panicked, turned and ran off. I didn't think I looked that scary.

I ran to the next home, a mile up the road, and was welcomed in for a cup of tea with Ron and Debbie, a middle-aged couple.

'Who lives in the pink house down the road?' I asked.

'Ah, he's very weird,' said Debbie. 'No one talks to him and you were lucky not to be invited in.' I guess this was the risk of knocking on random people's doors – one could be the most wanted serial killer in North America. Ron and Debbie seemed sweet enough, though, and they let me sleep in their garden.

A couple of miles into the following day's run and I needed to go for a 'number two', so I left Caesar at the top of the road and went down into a forested ditch. As I was squatting, I heard a car pull up and then kids' voices. They got nearer. I thought *Why, oh, why did I leave Caesar in plain view?* Now I was going to be caught in my worst-ever moment. Then the kids appeared at the top of the ditch. I made eye contact with one and he groaned 'yuck' at me. 'Sorry,' I said. I leaped up and ran onto the road, where I saw them all pile into their car and speed off. I grabbed my temples with shame and as soon as I did that, I realised I hadn't washed my hands.

Some miles later an SUV stopped beside me. The driver passed me a rather large Canadian flag. 'Thank you for all you're doing here in Canada, you're making us proud.' I stuck the flag in Caesar and it flowed beautifully as I ran on. I felt half-Canadian, or wished that I was.

Halfway through the run that day, the heavens opened just when I needed to do my yoga. I went into a garden centre and the manager let me do it there. As I was doing my moves, another employee kept skulking around me, making me feel self-conscious.

'Am I weirding you out?' I asked at last.

'I'm from New Jersey,' she said. 'You have to do a lot more than that to weird me out.'

Back on the road, I could begin to feel that my body was hardening to the mileage but soon it was time to set up my tent – this time at the back of a petrol station, next to a stream.

I was woken up by a phone call from Chuck, a presenter on local radio station 1015 The Hawk. We talked about my trip so far and he said he'd try to air it. Perhaps this would get the media ball rolling in this province.

The following day, I walked into a cafe adjoining the petrol station and ordered breakfast. When it came to the bill, the waiters and waitresses brought me $100 for SickKids. 'Don't worry about your meal, it's all covered,' the manager said.

'How did you know it was me?'

'Well, there's not too many other British folk round here – certainly not charging about with a baby stroller – and we heard your voice on the radio. We think it's amazing what you're doing. Keep it up!'

I ran off, pleased that this was the first donation received in Nova Scotia.

I developed a strategy for this part of the journey: I'd face the traffic and wheel Caesar on the smooth tarmac with my right hand, while I ran slightly to the left of him on the soft broken-up stone or dirt track. It felt a lot easier on my joints and ligaments, especially with another 170 marathons to go.

I was nearing Antigonish, a town about 100 miles northeast of Halifax, the capital of Nova Scotia. Outside the town hall I was greeted by two lovely ladies and a cop, Shaun, who leaned close to me conspiratorially and said, 'Hey man, I brought you some spray paint.'

I couldn't help but think: *Didn't he have something more useful to give a runner than spray paint?*

Then it all became clear. 'I brought this for you so every night before you go to bed on the side of the road, you can spray an arrow in the direction you're supposed to be running. We wouldn't want you running 5 miles in the wrong direction again, would we?'

We all laughed at that because we were all well aware of my YouTube meme by now.

'I'm going to write "feed me" on the side of my tent,' I told him. 'That way I'll never starve on this trip.' Shaun went into the back office, grabbed a Budweiser and said, 'I just confiscated this off some kid last night. It's all yours but don't tell anyone. Anyway, follow me.'

He opened the door to a motel room. 'You can handle this for the night can't you, kid? Here's your key and your coupon for your free hot breakfast in the morning.'

I had a feeling I might not see much for a few days so I did a little bit of a supermarket sweep in Antigonish. Sick of sardines, I chose a tin of Turkey Flakes. That had to be an improvement.

Setting up camp the next night at the busy highway, I thought I'd stay true to my word about the spray paint. I played the *Oliver!* musical soundtrack on my phone and got in the mood for spraying. In a massively luminous orange colour I wrote 'FEED ME' on my tent. The truckers loved it and gave me plenty of horn honks. Sadly, no one stopped so I got stuck into my sardines and thought I'd save the turkey for a special occasion.

In the morning my tent looked like it had been vandalised, so bright was the orange paint in the sunlight. Running up to a bridge, I noticed I could take a detour; it would mean adding an extra 6 miles over 55 miles, but I thought those extra miles would be well spent, as the highway was so mind-numbingly dull.

There were no cars or people on the road, just the odd house from time to time. My belly started to rumble and I thought I'd treat myself to the turkey. It was all mashed into one consolidated lump and as I spooned it in, I grimaced and almost retched. I knew exactly what it was: spam. I remembered it from my childhood – it's not fit for your pets to eat.

An old boy pulled his sports car over to where I was sitting and eating. 'You're not planning on staying here for long, are you?'

'Well, I'm not too sure yet. Why?'

He frowned. 'Only a few hours ago a huge bear was standing *exactly* where you are right now. I'm not sure you'd like to meet him, especially with that in your hand.'

'Honestly, if there's one thing I'm sure about, it's that the bear will not be attracted to spam.'

He knew more about bears than I did, though, so I took his advice and jogged on.

As I headed back onto the dreaded highway, another car appeared and a guy called Mike jumped out. He gave me a massive warm hug and asked if he could run with me for a while. I agreed. As we got going, he told me he used to be a keen runner. I couldn't help but notice that he was a bit chubby.

'I kinda lost my way this last year,' he said. 'See, Jamie, I read about you online and watched your YouTube videos and learned that you were doing all this for sick kids. It will be, next week, exactly a year ago since I lost my daughter. She was born premature and was taken up to the Halifax hospital, but sadly she only lived for a week. Your quest reminded me of all the things the hospital did for my daughter. Anyway, I just had to join you. It's amazing what you're doing, buddy.'

From then on, he put his arm around me as we ran together.

Mike said his goodbyes as we neared the city of Amherst, on the edge of the picturesque Tantramar salt marshes. A little later, a car ground to a halt on the other side of the road. The window rushed down and a fist popped out. 'What the hell are you doing?' a gruff voice shouted. 'The flag is dragging along the floor.'

I turned to Caesar and saw that the man was indeed right. I put my hands up, shrugged innocently and said, 'I'm so sorry.' I tugged the flag into an upright position.

That wasn't good enough for this guy. 'How dare you disgrace the Canadian flag like that?' He continued to rant and I allowed him to get it off his chest.

When he was done, I said, 'I had no idea it was dragging – I couldn't see it behind me. Again, I'm really sorry.' I spoke those words in the calmest way I could, but it only fuelled his fury.

'You're a total disgrace to Canada!'

The moment I heard those words, I flipped. I pointed my finger at the guy and shouted in an irascible teacher's tone. 'How dare you!' Without checking if there were any cars going by, I stomped over the road to him. 'I'm running across Canada at the minute, trying to help some of your fellow Canadians. How dare you!' When I got within a few feet of the car, I noticed that there were children in the back seat. I was speechless. 'Jerk,' said the man and wheel-span off.

I ranted to myself about this incident all the way to Mike's sister's house where I stayed the night. In the morning, her kids – Mia, Lauren, Bailee and Tanner – wanted to run with me to the border with New Brunswick. A mile in, I turned to them and asked what it was like to be off school and running with a crazy Brit. They pumped their arms up and screamed for joy, over and over again. I could barely hear a thing. 'Stop the racket,' I pleaded, in danger of acting like a grumpy old man.

It was beautiful how, in the space of just 5 miles, their minds had opened up to what I was doing. OK, so they were missing out on education for a day, but I secretly hoped that they'd learn more from pushing themselves mentally and physically, while helping to do some good.

When we reached the border, it seemed like I'd made my way through an entire province in the second largest country in the world in the blink of an eye. I was a little step closer to my goal: two out of nine provinces completed. Or, put another way, 165 marathons out of 200 to go.

NEW BRUNSWICK

The temperature rose as the days – and the country road – rolled by. I managed to force out half-marathons in 30°C heat, sweating like crazy. Even way into the evening, there'd be no shade around, so I'd put up my tent and leave the door open. Rather than cool me down, the heat went up another ten degrees. Every morning my little blow-up mat would be drenched in salty sweat.

I ran out of water after a couple of days in this environment. I grew dizzy, unable to focus on anything. On one particularly bad morning, once I was all packed up, I woozily ran off, pleading with whatever higher forces there might be for water. My mouth got drier with every step, as each intake of breath sucked more saliva out of my mouth. I was almost hyperventilating. The road seemed never-ending: no cars, no people, no buildings – just bush.

At last I spotted a house. I ran down the driveway and saw a topless man pottering about. I tried to speak, but my lips were sealed shut. 'Can I... please have... some water... please?' I eventually squeezed out. He rushed off and returned with a glass of H_2O. 'I bet you people in England think of Canada as ice and cold. Well, we literally have everything.'

'I was definitely a member of that naive group,' I said, downing the glass in one.

I could have stopped there for a bit but there's a perverse side to me that makes me want to push myself harder when the challenge gets tougher. So I cracked on in this, the hottest day of the year, and completed a full marathon.

That night in my tent the mosquitoes attacked me. Foolishly, I had no spray to keep them at bay.

In the morning, I told the insects off for all the bites they'd given me overnight and packed the tent away. As I was approaching a corner shop, a guy called Darren Hansen asked me how I was funding the trip. I told him that I'd spent the deposit I had saved up for a house. He handed me $100. 'Here, this is for you and I'll be making a donation to the hospital online.'

It was the first time somebody wanted to give *me* money, for my journey. It was a generous gesture. I thanked Darren and he walked off. In the shop I went to buy myself some tinned fish with the $100 bill, but something didn't feel right in my gut. Instead I used $20 of my own cash. I really appreciated Darren's gift, but it deserved to go into the donation pot. The kids in hospital would make much better use of it.

That night I scored a camper van in a 70-year-old woman's backyard. Next day, I went to Scotiabank and deposited just over $2,500 in cash, which I'd collected along the way. When I told the cashiers about my adventure, they all clubbed their own money together, adding nearly another $100. Before making the deposit, I wanted to go outside and take a picture of all the cash, so I ran out of the bank, waving the bundle of notes about. When I shared a post on Facebook with the image, I got quite a few private messages telling me that I was opening myself up to getting robbed.

I then went into a health food store. A hippy called Ralf came up to me with a basket. 'Knock yourself out, dude. This is on us.' I'd always wanted to walk into a supermarket and shop till I dropped. Firstly, I went for my trusty canned fish, knowing that I could take that everywhere. Next up I chose fruit, cold meats and then my one and only: nuts. One bag of cashews. Oh, I better have some almonds, too. OK, let's get some Brazil nuts as well. I walked over to the counter, sheepish about how much stuff I had in the basket. Ralf took one look inside it and said, 'That's not enough. Come with me.' He then added mango slices, a first-aid kit and a tub of expensive Manuka honey. I left with a week's worth of supplies.

Darren showed up again, asking me if I wanted to speak at his local Rotary Club, Moncton West & Riverview. I talked for ten minutes, telling silly stories about my adventures and my childhood, to raise awareness of the kids' hospitals. My audience, who were all businessmen wearing suits and ties, put cash in a giant pot. Darren counted it up and handed it to me. 'There's $500. That enough?'

'Not bad for ten minutes' work,' I grinned.

Jogging down Route 104, I noticed how smelly I was. This might have had something to do with not having showered for the last two weeks. Luckily, no one else was around to judge me for it. I stopped in at a little cottage and was welcomed by a granny called Joy. 'Do you need a shower?' she said instantly.

'What you trying to say?' I frowned.

'Oh sorry, I didn't mean—'

'No worries, Joy,' I laughed. 'I was only messing. I know I smell like bear droppings. It's even starting to irritate me!'

There's nothing better than being filthy for a long time and then feeling that hot water pour over your face.

A short distance on, once back on the road, I heard a loud and rapid ringing noise. I glanced around to see what it was and saw my first woodpecker. He was perched on a pole and headbutting metal. He must have been the dumbest woodpecker in the world.

Near Grand Falls, famous for its river that spills down over a 20-metre drop, I knocked on a door and a woman called Jane answered. In a distinct Manchester accent, she invited me in to meet her husband Terry, also a Mancunian. 'What's your biggest obstacle?' he asked me.

'To be honest, it's this bloody tent. It's just way too hot to sleep in for this time of year.'

'Hang on, mate.' Terry went upstairs and came back with a netted pop-up tent and a waterproof army sheet. 'I served in Afghanistan and brought this lot back with me. It'll be a lot cooler and hardier than the crap you're using at the moment. It's yours.'

After thanking them profusely and saying my goodbyes, I set off again and ran through Grand Falls. I saw a shortcut on Google maps, but the downside was how bushy the terrain was. It was a drag pushing Caesar through the weeds and sticks, and I could feel the force holding him back. The foliage got thicker and thicker, but it was still worth doing that to shave a few miles off my route.

At Edmundston, a town on the frontier with Quebec, I called into the Lotus Bleu Cafe. The French-Canadian owner, Louise, had long, dark hair and blue eyes. 'What are you up to?' she asked in a sexy French accent. Not for the first – or last – time on this trip, I justified my mad mission. 'Whatever you want is on the house,' she purred.

'You really don't have to do that.'

'And you don't have to run across Canada.'

Getting back to my journey, it wasn't Louise's delicious food or her beauty that fuelled me; it was the big-heartedness of her gesture.

Charles, a local reporter, joined me on his mountain bike and led me to the 100-mile Trans Canada Trail. Just before the sun went down, I saw a sign: WELCOME TO QUEBEC. I fist-bumped Charles. Three provinces down, only six to go.

QUEBEC

I camped on the border and decided it was time to share my progress with the world so I posted on Facebook:

BONJOUR! I'm about to enter Quebec, where everyone speaks French. Any advice?

I got comments in reply such as 'run faster than the wind' and 'don't stop' from other Canadians. I guessed they were joking, but at the same time, I was aware of a major division between

Quebec and the rest of Canada. It's political, and politics isn't something I know much about.

I thought about this for a while before I went to sleep and I couldn't understand where all this animosity came from. The following morning I found a nearby diner for breakfast. While I was munching, the waitress asked if I would sign my name on a napkin. 'But why?' I asked.

'You're famous, Jamie. That group over there have been talking about you all morning.'

'Don't be silly. Once I've signed that, it'll be worth even less than it was before.' But she wouldn't be put off; she waved her friend over and handed me the napkin. I couldn't believe it. I felt like a good-deed rock star. Although I couldn't have a long conversation with her because I only know a few French words and she didn't speak a lot of English, I did get a selfie of us hugging each other.

With a full belly, off I plodded on to the Trans Canada Trail, trying to remember my schooldays French. 'Bonjourrrrr,' I said to myself, practising. 'Bonjourrrr Miserrrrr', 'Jabit Glawsterrrrr.' I had hoped I'd remember more, but that was it for now.

After running a half-marathon on the delightful trail, I noticed a sign with the image of a swimmer. It was still 30°C so I set up my new army tent, lobbed my clothes in and made my way down to the Madawaska River to cool off. As soon as my toes touched the water, it felt like I'd dipped them in a bucket of ice. I gingerly made my way in, my teeth chattering as the water rose to my waist. I held my breath and dived in. My head froze like a lolly. I swam to the surface and got the hell out of there. If I'd stayed in, I'd have got hypothermia. I did feel fresher, but I decided that was the last time I'd be swimming in Canada. Back in my Afghanistan tent, I played a game: how many mosquitoes could I flick through the netting and kill with one blow?

The next morning I found a small white cafe near the lake. I was the only customer and the chef didn't speak a word of English. I checked out the menu and all I could see were different variations of *poutine*, which I knew was the traditional meal of the province. I'm a gambling man so, without being sure exactly what it was, I pointed to one of the *poutines*. Ten minutes later chips, cheese and gravy arrived. I couldn't help but mumble, 'What... This is the traditional meal?'

It was the food I normally ate at 3 a.m. after a Friday night on the beer. The only difference was that now I was staring at it sober, and it was laid on a fancy plate, with napkins, a knife and a fork. I'd never used cutlery for this meal before. But the first mouthful was amazing. It was the best kind of filler after burning so many calories.

Back on the road, I came across a Dutch family who'd converted a truck into a very cool mobile home. They were touring Canada for an entire year. JJ, the 35-year-old dad, said, 'Everyone in the Netherlands is working all their life for the golden pension, but then they die. As a family, we don't have much money. We're renting our house out back home to cover the mortgage.'

He showed me around the gigantic truck, which even had a car in the back so that when they visited a city they could use that to drive around. 'During the trip,' said JJ, 'we are schooling our children ourselves.' I admired the fact that this family were going against the grain and pursuing a life just how they wanted to live it. Even having children wasn't holding them back. On the side of the truck was the slogan: LATER IS NOW. I liked that.

I love people who make me think differently about life. I began writing a short blog about them on Facebook, in the hope that others would think differently about life as well. This was the first time I really wrote a more in depth piece, even though it wasn't my forte. The grammar and spelling weren't perfect, but I just had this powerful urge to communicate with people on social media about this remarkable family. I took two hours to compose a short paragraph and read it back to myself more than 20 times. I hit the 'post' button and went to sleep.

In the morning, I checked the Facebook post's performance: it had 330 likes and had reached more than 6,000 people. If it inspired one person to make a life-changing decision then it would have been worth writing it. Dan Trueman commented:

Your journey is bringing you into contact with so many people, both mobile and settled, and you are touching their lives as they touch yours. Just following your adventure this way touches all our lives every time you share with us.

Glen Louwrens wasn't so kind:

As long as Jamie isn't helping to teach the kids grammar (it's 'their' not 'there' house). Ignoramus. Sorry, Jamie. Pot calling the kettle black.

I closed my eyes and sighed. That ecstatic feeling was gone. I Googled 'ignoramus' and found that it meant 'an ignorant or stupid person'. I was suddenly back at school, feeling glum because I couldn't write.

There was only one thing to do: get out of the tent and work my legs. As the steps accumulated and the pain amplified, I kept asking myself why I was so thick and why I was put on this planet with no brains. I screamed like a madman in answer and then ran harder, pushing Caesar harder, taking it out on him... Harder and harder, just keep going harder.

After 15 miles, I still hadn't run off my frustration. I rang Rich on Skype. 'I've been called stupid for writing on Facebook,' I moaned. 'I don't know what to do. I'm so hurt I never want to write again.'

'I saw it, Jamie. I know it must have hurt, but it's only one person out of thousands of people who don't care whether you can spell. Look, if it's really bothering you that much, why not post about it? It might help to shut future critics up.' I was terrified at the thought of sharing one of my darkest fears, but he had a point. 'Why don't you write it out from the heart,' he continued, 'and then send it on to me to proofread?'

'OK, let's do it.'

Here's what I wrote:

After a few people have mentioned my spelling during this adventure, I just thought I'd say that sometimes I will, as we all do, make mistakes with my spelling and grammar. Three years ago – as a twenty-three year old – I went back to school to retake all the subjects I'd failed at sixteen, including English. I sat at the back of the class and I'm sure some of the kids thought I was a teaching assistant! I'm proud that I made that decision to go back and, to any adults that struggle, I'd recommend finishing any education you missed or weren't able to complete at the time. If I'm honest, I was the class clown at school 24/7 and I flunked almost everything. It's not something I'm proud of, but it was a time that I wouldn't change. It shaped my personality through learning the hard way. I do have mild dyslexia and I'm certain to make errors now and in the future, but I will try my best to get it right. I'm not perfect, but actions speak far louder than – sometimes misspelt – words and I'm trying my hardest to make a difference.

That post was almost as big as the last one, with 300 likes, another 6,000 readers and over 100 comments. Corla Benzie wrote, 'As an Aussie Sheila would say, "Good on ya mate, you're a rippa."' Hilary Wakeham remarked: 'I already considered you to be inspirational and a fabulous role model to young people but you have just managed to impress me even further with your strength and determination!'

My insecurities about dyslexia and feeling stupid gradually disappeared as I read people's comments. Then I had to laugh when I saw what Kev had posted: 'I fink ur gr8'. Thanks to the speed and ease of social media, the support that came in was everything I needed to keep on writing and sharing – and keep on running.

———————

Caesar's wheels sank into the ground as we hit loose gravel. That must be the most irritating terrain to run on. I kept grinding through it, though, taking breaks every 100 yards. Another obstacle was being attacked in the face by flies. You had to run fast to escape those buggers.

A Mercedes pulled up on a quiet country road. A man with wild staring eyes jumped out and began screaming in French at me. I had no idea what he was saying, so I just kept nodding, pretending to understand his every word. He wouldn't let me utter a reply but instead kept pointing to his number plate, which read THE BOSS. After ten minutes of this nonsense, I was exhausted. The sun was close to setting and I needed a bed for the night. I just had to get away from this nutty French-Canadian.

Further up the road, a man in a hockey shirt was waiting on the pavement with a shopping bag. 'Err...' he said in the strongest French accent I'd heard so far, 'My name is Steve and this is for you.' The bag was full of food and water bottles. Before I could thank him, the crazy man with THE BOSS number plate pulled up again. Steve explained that the man wanted me to run another 3 miles up the road in order to stay at his house. I think Steve sensed that the man freaked me out, so he invited me to camp in his garden instead.

Steve kindly put down insulation on the grass under my tent, and he also had a power cable to charge my phone and laptop.

With 50 marathons down, and another 150 to go, I decided to put a small plan on Facebook of where I would be heading for the next week, listing the roads that I'd be taking.

The following morning the first thing I saw when I opened my eyes was Steve poking his head into my tent, carrying a huge plate of eggs and fruit. 'Who needs a hotel when you have Steve, hey?' I said, tucking into the grub.

'We can call this Steve's Hotel, *non*?'

No sooner had I hit the road again than a friendly old couple from Newfoundland appeared in their truck. They gave me a sweet hug which they said had come all the way from Newfoundland. Then they handed me a package and said, 'This is from our daughter, Anne Solo. She's a bonkers fan.' I loved reading Anne's comments on my blog. 'I'll surprise myself with it later,' I commented. They were doing a road trip of their own and were already over 1,000 miles into it. It was so cool of them to take a detour to meet me.

I ran on, propelled by the anticipation of opening my present. I found a small veranda by a stream and cracked it open. There was more fish (yummy – or not!), sun cream, lip balm, nuts, and a dark blue superhero cape. On the back of the cape it read: www.jamiemcdonald.org 4 Sick Kids. This was so special and it took me right back to the days I spent cycling in Turkey. My eyes moistened with nostalgia. I put it on and ran like a bullet train. I was a superhero now.

With the placid Saint Lawrence River beside me, I really started to soak up the natural splendour of Quebec. Not so splendid was the fact that the donations had dried up in this province. I wasn't sure why people weren't so approachable round here. Considering my kind of personality, not being able to socialise was depressing me a tad. No one had stopped to ask what I was up to in days. I'd not even had a toot from a car. All I had was Caesar for company and I wasn't going to get much of a conversation out of him.

At 10 a.m., out of nowhere, two women and a man ran up to me. One of the ladies, Marie-France, told me, 'We put a sign in our garden 6 miles back saying WELCOME JAMIE, COME INSIDE. You missed it.'

'Anyway,' said the guy. 'We bring breakfast to you. Welcome to Quebec. It's happy hour.' Marie-France produced a bottle of ice-cold beer. I necked it. You can take the boy out of Gloucester, etc. – you know the rest. I giggled for ten minutes straight, as if I'd just had my first-ever beer, and then I ran on, quite tipsy.

I entered the city of Quebec. I had a powerful urge to party here. Maybe it was the taste of beer on my tongue or the sight of so many people after such a long time on my own. I crossed the river by ferry and checked into the Auberge internationale de Québec, a youth hostel, craving to meet backpackers who could speak English. More pressing than finding company was my need to get a wash – I hadn't showered in 12 days. I jumped in the shower and as soon as I got out, I completely flaked out in bed. My brain was saying: 'Party! Girls!' but my body was shouting, 'Get to bed, you idiot!'

My alarm went off at 5 a.m. I woke up a bit miserable that I hadn't got what I wanted out of Quebec City. That said, I had the pressure of time bearing down on me. I couldn't spend the rest of my life trying to get across this vast nation. Plus, my visa was running out. As I limbered up for the next gruelling leg of my odyssey, I felt jealous of all of the other backpackers still lying in bed, probably hungover, with not a care in the world – and here I was, with the world on my shoulders, locked into a full-time job of running 40 bloody hours a week.

Knowing that I'd be fairly isolated for days and possibly weeks, I decided that it was time to put my headphones in. I'd have different music for different moods. In the morning, I'd be hurting for the first few miles so I'd play tunes like Al Green's 'Let's Stay Together'. This was my comfort music. I think it's because it reminded me of being a kid and sitting in my mum's car as she sang the same song. Any music from my childhood was good for my soul.

As dusk came, I'd often need a pick-me-up. 'Firestarter' by The Prodigy would be exactly the ticket. I'd get these huge surges of endorphins as I smashed another marathon. I knew I simply couldn't have done it without music.

I was more than a quarter of my way through Canada and so far the total raised was $3,380 in Canadian donations (with the aim of getting to $30,000) and £2,269.80 in UK donations, with the hope we'd get to £60,000. This was good progress, but not great. It was time to think of a new strategy to increase the support. En route to Montreal, I thought I'd take the whole superhero gimmick one step further. I asked people on Facebook to vote for one of four superhero outfits which I'd wear for the next two weeks, until I hit Montreal. In order to choose, they had to donate. Not a big ask.

The first choice was Super Mario because he is awesome and I've wanted to be him since I was four. Second up was the Flash, as I'd have to be running in flashes to finish in time. Third was Batman, as a tribute to my Turkey trip, and fourth was Supergirl, for all of those evil people out there who wanted to humiliate me. I was certain the votes would go to Supergirl. I gave the people who were following me on social media three days to decide.

A cyclist stopped by the roadside to tell me that I ought to be carrying the flag of Quebec instead of a Canadian flag. I didn't really grasp the politics, but it did make me wonder whether having the wrong flag explained the often frosty reception I was getting. A few miles down the road I saw a pub festooned with Quebecois flags. I tiptoed over and stole one, imagining that nobody would miss it.

Trois-Rivières, an old and enormous city, seemed to be all suburbs. My phone, camera and laptop were all out of battery and I needed electricity. I tried a couple of doors, but wasn't welcomed inside. Then I saw it: an outside power socket beside an apartment block. The neighbourhood was run-down and there were a lot of homeless people about. Cars with tinted windows sped by, pumping out gangsta rap. I was petrified as I put up my tent. I plugged my gadgets in, climbed inside and placed my survival knife within reach in case anyone disturbed me in the night.

In the morning, a woman from the apartment block spotted me. I thought she was going to hassle me for stealing her power. Instead, she walked over with a chair in her hand and placed it on the ground. While I sat there, a woman in her nightgown came out onto a balcony high up on the block and shouted, '*Café? Café?*'

'Yes, please,' I shouted back. She looked blankly back at me so I nodded my head rapidly in a yo-yo motion. Once the lady had brought my coffee over, the other one who'd brought out the chair handed me an apple. I couldn't believe that I'd gone from a night of terror to a surprise open-air breakfast. The chair, coffee and apple were comparatively small gestures, but those are the ones that count.

I packed up and headed out of Trois-Rivières. I came across a young woman with a shaven head, wearing a wetsuit. She introduced herself as Chantelle and asked why I was running. She turned out to be a freelance journalist and wanted to write about my adventure. I wasn't going to turn this opportunity down – it was my first bit of coverage in Quebec.

'I admire what you're doing,' she said. 'I've just recovered from breast cancer. Now I'm working at my own pace, doing what I love: windsurfing. My shaved head is my way of saying "I'm alive".' I understood. I ran off, thinking how wonderful it was that even a terrible illness can inspire someone to start living the way they truly wanted to live.

Voting was over. I got out my phone, scared to think what I'd have to wear for the next fortnight. In fourth place was Batman and in third Super Mario; Supergirl was second, but only just. The winner was the Flash. I was relieved I wouldn't have to wear a skirt and high heels for two weeks.

One of my Facebook followers sent me a message:

On this date, 28th June, but back in 1981, Terry Fox died of cancer in New Westminster, BC, one month before his 23rd birthday. 'Even if I don't finish,' he said famously, 'we need others to continue. It's got to keep going without me.'

The streets of Montreal were crammed with cars, buses and people. When I finally found the Oya Costumes shop, they were uber-excited to provide me with the Flash outfit. The girls behind the desk couldn't stop giggling. I didn't have the courage to try on the suit there and then – I wanted to take it away and build up the balls to wear it later. I left, feeling genuinely anxious about what the public would think of me.

I ran along the river until I saw a portable toilet. Bingo! It was like every superhero film I'd ever watched – you have to get changed in a loo. As there were lots of people around, I thought I'd give them a shock. I burst out of the toilet door in my mask, cape and bold red onesie with a flash sign on the chest. I lost count of the number of schoolkids who were pointing and laughing at me.

I'd been so preoccupied with using the toilet as a place where I could get changed that I forgot to take a pee. A mile on, I was desperate. I looked down at my onesie and realised that there was no pee hole. Taking the whole costume off just for a slash was out of the question, so I grabbed my pocket knife and cut an opening, just in time. The only problem then was that I was left with a huge hole in my crotch so I wore a pair of boxer shorts on top.

A bit of a crowd had gathered as I left Montreal, and the toots and waves spurred me on nicely. I passed a large dance class going on in the street and thought that I'd have to show off my Flash moves. I joined them, tapping my feet and rocking my head from side to side – I'll call it 'Flash-styling'.

My new superhero powers, however, had limitations. It went dark and I still hadn't hit 26 miles. I carried on, disappointed that I wasn't going as fast as the Flash. By the time I'd completed my marathon it was 10 p.m. and I found myself at a bus stop. I was so exhausted I didn't feel like setting up the tent. I figured that the bus stop was all the shelter I needed anyway. I curled up in a little ball inside my sleeping bag on top of my thin blow-up mattress and drifted off.

I snapped awake to the sound of a Scottish accent. 'Are you shitting me? Is that the Flash?' My chest was protruding from the sleeping bag and I still had the mask on. I rubbed my eyes and saw an evidently drunk – and well-built – guy about my age leaning over me. His breath reeked of beer. 'Flash man, how are you doing?' he asked and then called over his shoulder, 'Hey, Trina, come here – come and meet Flash!' He reached for my mask and I slapped his hand away.

'Hey, Flash, no need to be a villain! I just want a go on your mask.'

'If you go for me again,' I snarled. 'I'm going to jump up and kick your arse!'

He tootled off, a bit embarrassed. This was a stroke of good luck on my part – if we had fought, he would have kicked *my* arse for sure. I went back to sleep and in the morning I wasn't sure whether I'd dreamed the encounter or not.

It was a drizzly day and I chugged on through it, getting myself drenched within a mile. Once I completed my half-marathon, I stopped at a Starbucks coffee shop where I ordered a cup of tea to warm me up. The staff wouldn't let me take off my soaking wet costume. I even had to keep my sodden shoes and socks on. I lay back in my seat, put my mask back on and nodded off. When my eyes opened, a family were peering at me. 'You OK? What the hell are you doing?' After I'd told them, they calmed down and calculated that if I ran exactly another 13 miles – another half-marathon – I'd be at their house. A coincidence or was it meant to be?

A bed and friends at the end of the day were the perfect incentives to get going again. The rain stopped and I made good progress. Two miles from the house, Denis, the father of the family, popped up on a unicycle, with his nine-year-old kid jogging behind him, and accompanied me on his single wheel while his son took Caesar's reins.

At dinner Denis poured me a big glass of red and asked me to give a small speech. It threw me off guard a little, but I just tried to speak from the heart. 'Within minutes of meeting you, I knew you're a really special family. You've made me feel so welcome, and the fact that you invited me back after meeting me for just five minutes in a cafe means the absolute world to me. You put my faith in humanity through the roof, so thank you.' We clinked glasses and I showed them some of my YouTube videos.

For my final marathon in Quebec I was joined by Steve and Christine, two Facebook followers who'd tracked me down. They were both fitness fanatics so the pace was fast. We chatted away for the whole time and it all went so quickly. Magically, I didn't feel any pain in my legs or feet. Steve and Christine, you were a wonderful distraction for the journey to the Ontario border.

ONTARIO

My next destination was Ottawa, the capital of Canada and a taste of home. Lesley Peters, a lady originally from my hometown, had been following me via Twitter and invited me to celebrate Canada Day. 'I'll also make you a proper roast dinner,' she'd promised, 'with gravy and all the trimmings.' Her home on the outskirts of Ottawa was a bit off-route, but I couldn't resist – I was homesick, after all.

I hit over 30 miles that day, my longest run so far. It felt that way, too. Unfortunately, I knew there would be times when I would have to cover more than 26 miles (that is, more than a marathon) a day if I was going to make it to Vancouver before my visa ran out and before the winter struck. I set up camp and was determined to reach Ottawa by the following evening so I set the alarm for 4 a.m., knowing that I'd need to cover over 30 miles once again.

With my first few steps the next morning I was painfully reminded of the fact I'd run nearly 31 miles the day before. That said, the birds were singing so beautifully that it would have been churlish to be miserable. My experience told me that I needed to keep running to loosen up the muscles. As soon as the ache in my legs eased off, my nipples began to sting. When I peeled off my Flash suit, I saw that they were red raw. I slapped on some duct tape.

Lesley met me on the way to Ottawa and we hugged.

'I can't believe this is you,' she said in a rich Gloucester accent. Lesley had never run before, but wanted to accompany me for more than 5 miles to her house. 'What have I got myself in for?' she said, as we went along. After another mile I could hear cheering and the sound of pots and pans clanging. Then we saw them: on the roadside more than 50 people were dressed in red. They came running up to me, holding bundles of cash that they stuffed into every corner of Caesar. He was loving it.

'You're in Ontario now!' shouted Lesley. She was breathing heavily and covered in sweat.

'Are you struggling?' I asked.

'Yes I am,' she panted. She grabbed hold of her breasts, explaining, 'You don't need to carry these around!' Then the *Chariots of Fire* theme tune was playing at full blast. I ran into Lesley's driveway, and gave a skip to the right and then a skip to the left. What a welcome into Ontario!

Lesley took me straight to my bedroom and on the side table were nuts, coconut oil, a shaver and a pot of money containing nearly $200 for SickKids. There was also a note that read: 'Hi Jamie, I've donated my allowance to you. Hope it helps. Toby.'

'Is that your son?' I asked Lesley.

'Yes, he's 14 years old. I told him this month's allowance has to go to your charities.'

'Come on, Lesley, so you forced him?'

'I gently persuaded him. He really does get it, though. He also sold his Xbox game and put the cash in the pot. Believe me, from him, that's huge. He's never given a present in his life.'

We went off to CTV, a television network, for an interview. I think it helped that people could now speak the same language as me. They cut in a lot of my YouTube videos and the presenter, Terry Marcotte, told millions of viewers, 'You gotta see this guy, he's flipping hilarious.' Although I was made out to be a bit of a joker, they still canvassed the public for donations to the hospitals.

Back at Lesley's house, she served me, as promised, roast beef with Yorkshire puddings. Instinctively knowing how much music means to me, she put 'My Girl' by The Temptations on the stereo. We sang the night away.

Lesley and her family had a holiday planned and they generously let me house-sit for them. I spent many days editing my videos, one of the hardest mental challenges I'd ever undertaken. As you've probably guessed by now, I'm not one for sitting down for too long. A support crew would have come in handy.

By the time the family returned, I'd shared most of the videos on YouTube and they'd gone down a storm. The donations were rolling in. The Peters family came out to hug me goodbye. Lesley shed a tear like a good mum should and said, 'Be careful.'

Before I left, her husband Giles, who built live trackers for the army, fitted a tracker onto me so that my social media followers could see where I was at any time.

It was an eerie misty morning that day, when I reached an important crossroads – a literal and a figurative one. If I went right, I'd be on the shortest possible route across Canada. On the other hand, I could turn left and go to visit the SickKids Hospital in Toronto, but that would mean an extra 13 marathons, as well as running the risk of overstaying my visa. This was the decision that would change everything. I had my lazy brain pulling me one way and my heart pulling me the other. I kept repeating these words in my head: 'I'm only running Canada once.'

After an hour of indecision, I leaped up and took a left. I was heading to SickKids – it just felt right.

An hour later, something else felt far from right. The inside of my knee suddenly twinged and I could hardly walk, let alone run. Was this it? The end? I hobbled on and my wish for a house was answered.

An old man with missing teeth answered the door.

'Any chance I can camp in your garden?' I winced.

'Of course you can. You might prefer a bed in our house, however.' Without waiting for my reply, he flung open the door. 'Help yourself to anything. Our house is your house.'

'Wow, thanks.' His kindness seemed to ease the pain in my leg.

Come morning, my knee was still sore, but I had to soldier on. A Facebook message told me that people would like to greet me in the nearby town of Athens – a township famous for its corn festival – and put me up for the night. I spent a solid day running and when I got there, no one was around to greet me. Every time I saw someone, I would think, *That's them, got to be* – but it never was.

I carried on, cursing the whole idea. 'I hate plans,' I said out loud as I ran. 'They build up expectations, and expectations can lead to disappointment – like now. Keep doing your hippy approach, Jamie, just go with the flow.'

That evening, a social media fan, Nadine from Ottawa, drove over 100 miles to give me a bag full of goodies. We went for a meal during which a lady came over to give me $20. Her deed was infectious: within ten minutes the entire restaurant had come over with cash gifts for SickKids, and $20 soon became $200. It was like a Mexican wave of donations.

As we were finishing our food, a six-year-old boy came to our table and handed me $10 but said nothing. His dad told us, 'My boy has a prosthetic leg. We used the hospital before and really appreciate what you're doing.' I knew at this point that the decision to run through Toronto had been the right one.

My phone rang as we were leaving the restaurant. 'Hi, my name is Rob McEwan from Argyle Communications, a PR company. I help people to get their messages out. I know you're coming to Toronto and with this being a town I know well, I wondered if you'd like support in getting media coverage? There's no catch – we just love what you're doing and want to assist you.'

'How can I say no to that?' I laughed.

That night I started to put my tent up in a green space around a cluster of houses. A resident popped her head over the fence and asked, 'Are you Jamie? My friend just shared one of your Facebook posts.' She invited me in for tea and biscuits, and introduced me to her six-year-old son, Lucas. 'He's recovering from ependymoma, a malignant cancerous brain tumour. Six months ago the tumour ruptured and he had to go through surgery at SickKids. The chances of Lucas surviving were slim to none. But after spending many months in that fantastic hospital, he did. If it wasn't for SickKids, he wouldn't be alive today.'

I noticed that the phrase 'I LOVE HATERS' was written on Lucas's hat. 'What does that mean?' I asked him.

'It means: don't be bothered by people who don't appreciate you.' Wise words from someone so young, but then he had experienced more than your average six-year-old. I also couldn't believe that someone sharing my Facebook posts had fanned the flames of inspiration.

I went back to setting up camp and was thrilled when two strapping teenage lads – one of them with shaggy hair and a surf vest on – stopped to give me a hand with it. What community spirit!

The following day, and 10 miles into my run, I stumbled upon a Foodland supermarket in Colborne, a leafy town about 90 miles east of Toronto. When I took fish, nuts, chicken and butter to the checkout, I realised that I didn't have my wallet. I guessed it had to be somewhere inside Caesar. I went outside, apologising to the cashier, and searched every inch of the chariot. No trace of it. I racked my brains. Then I worked it out: it must have been one of the lads who helped me to put the tent up last night. One of them would have had the perfect opportunity to take it while I was distracted, talking to his friend. Having been the victim of a con trick like that made me feel sick. After all this generosity...

How could I have been so dumb as to leave a wallet with $400 in open view? At least the cash came from my own savings rather than donations. Just as I was plucking up the courage to go back inside and tell the cashier that I couldn't pay for the food, she came out with a bag full of shopping. 'Hey, don't worry, I've covered it. I hope you get your wallet back.'

'Thank you!' I cried. 'That's so amazing of you. What's your name?'

'Cathy Allison.'

'Thanks again, Cathy Allison.'

I called the police. We went back to the green area where I'd slept and looked around for the wallet. Coincidentally, we saw one of the surfer dudes walk by. I pointed him out and the policeman strolled up to him. 'Come on, Fraser, do you have the wallet?' This guy was obviously a known wrong 'un.

'No, man,' protested the surfer dude. 'Of course I don't got it. I think it's a real shame he's lost his wallet.' He gave a big, possibly mickey-taking, grin. I had a strong hunch he had taken it because when someone smiles like that, it's usually out of fear.

'Let it go,' I sighed.

On Facebook I wrote:

If there's anything to take from this experience, it's that whilst there are people who'll seize any opportunity to make a quick buck, there are also those brilliant people, like the checkout lady, who will kindly gift me food when I need it. Those people are more precious than gold.

Getting near Port Hope, on the northern shore of Lake Ontario, I just didn't want to camp for the night. I called in at the Hillcrest Inn. 'Hi,' I said to the receptionist. 'Please don't think I'm crazy, but I'm running across Canada in a Flash suit. I was unfortunate enough to have my wallet stolen and I was wondering if I could have a bed for the night?'

'Yes, we do have beds available. Would you like to pay at a later date?'

I didn't know what to say. My survival instincts kicked in. 'I was kinda asking for a free bed for the night?'

She paused. 'OK then, come along and we can see what we can do.' It was one of the poshest hotels I'd ever seen. Robin and Alan, two other employees at the hotel, asked me what I wanted for breakfast. I had a feeling this was going to be a cut above tinned sardines. 'Anything, absolutely anything.' And it was damn good.

After the following day's run, another fantastic coincidence happened. A lady named Diane from my hometown of Gloucester drove up to me and invited me to go for a drink. Walking through the bar in my Flash outfit got me some odd looks. As I was sipping my favourite beer, a Corona, a man called Randy came to congratulate me for what I was doing. I wondered how he'd found out about me and it turned out he'd read my cape and decided to Google the website. 'So where are you sleeping tonight, Jamie?'

'Absolutely no idea, mate.'

He looked crestfallen. 'No way! So, talk me through it: from where you are sitting now, where are you going to sleep tonight?'

'I'm going to stand up, run out of here, turn right, head to Toronto and, when it feels right, I'll set up my tent in the dark.'

He stared at me for a while, deep in thought. 'There are people who talk about doing it, but you are actually doing it. Can you run another 6 km? I'm booking you a room for the night.' I refused the gesture because it felt too much considering that I'd only met him a few minutes ago. He insisted. I thought that if I refused him again, he might not ask a third time!

A few days later, racing through Toronto with my tracker on, I was excited to see if anyone would come out to find me en route to the hospital – and they did. Three families with kids showed up to say hi, and the dad in one of them was called Michal 'The Joggler' Kapral; he holds the Guinness world record of 2:50:12 for the fastest marathon while juggling three objects. The people you meet... He's also the founder of the prestigious *Canadian Running Magazine* and a great supporter of SickKids.

Time wasn't on my side so I rushed on. I accidentally clipped a bus driver with Caesar and we apologised to each other, even though it was definitely my fault. At a red light 20 yards down the road, I encountered the same bus a second time. The driver leaned out of the window and shouted, 'Ten dollars is missing from my bag and you're going to hell for this!' He was certain that I'd taken it after clipping him.

'I swear it wasn't me,' I said. 'Why would I do such a thing?'

He wasn't convinced and drove off, still furious. Welcome to the big city.

Before visiting the hospital, I dropped in to Global News *The Morning Show* for a live broadcast that would reach 100,000 people. Rob McEwan from Argyle PR met me just before we went on air. 'Jamie, you know, you are absolutely bonkers but I love what you're doing. I'll try to blow Toronto up for you and get you as much media coverage as we can.'

It was so surreal speaking to the presenters I'd seen on TV most mornings, as I woke up in random Canadian homes. I started the show with the Flash mask covering my face and I took it off to a torrent of laughter from the presenters. I was obviously coming across as the quintessentially eccentric Brit.

We soon turned to more serious topics. One of the presenters, Antony Robart, asked me if I was struggling physically.

'Yes, it is hard,' I replied. 'I'm running a ludicrous lot of miles.' I wanted to add more detail, but felt awkward about sharing my vulnerability with 100,000 strangers. I kept it light instead. 'Canada is just amazing. People have been taking me into their homes, although it doesn't always work out. In fact, one house I knocked on, some crazy person answered and told me to get lost.' All the presenters laughed.

When leaving the studio, my stomach was going round in circles. As I came up to the entrance of SickKids, a staggering five film crews were waiting for me (from CTV, CBC, Global, CP24 and CityTV), all shoving cameras in my face and barking questions at me.

I hugged and shook hands with doctors, nurses and a very special patient, Nico, aka Ironman. Nico had spent ten years at the hospital, due to a genetic condition that remains a mystery to every doctor who has ever studied him. However, SickKids have been there every step of the way to save his life and improve its quality.

Alongside dozens of people – including Nico's brother dressed as Spiderman – I did a lap around the hospital just to make those extra 13 marathons I had to run to get there worth it. I got so carried away, I'm sure I managed to run faster than the Flash, although Spiderman couldn't keep up and fell over. I went back, picked him up and sat him in Caesar. For the first time my baby stroller was being used as it should have. Nothing could have erased that grin from my face. As we reached the final turn, I looked round to see all the doctors and nurses smiling, Ironman laughing like a drunk hyena and Spiderman shouting, 'Weeeee!' at the top of his voice.

A doctor approached me and seized my hand vigorously. 'Wow, Jamie, going the extra mile really does make a difference.'

'Thanks, Doc,' I whispered in his ear. 'I really appreciate your kind words, but that wasn't just an "extra mile", that was 13 marathons.' We both chuckled. I wouldn't be forgetting this moment in a hurry. If this didn't propel me across the rest of Canada, nothing would.

That evening I Skyped Ed Archer. He was philosophical, as always. 'You've put the entire run in jeopardy, Jamie, but I'm going to be honest with you: even if you don't finish the rest of it, because of the winter or your visa, no one will ever be able to take away the experience you had, the money you raised and the difference you've now made. It was and will always be the right decision to do the extra miles.' There was nothing for me to do but thank him from the bottom of my heart.

At least 70 runners – a record for me, I think – from the Running Room club joined me on the jog out of Toronto. Slowly, each person reached a point where they had enough and dropped out. It was a last man/woman standing scenario. After 7 miles there were seven of us left and it was raining so hard that we all got soaked to the bone. We started singing 'Singin' in the Rain'. We were all loving it, but as it got near to the end of the day, we were still in the city – it really was that big. Once it hit 10 p.m. there was one last trooper named Steve by my side. 'I work all day in a goddamn office,' he panted. 'I need this.'

The following evening, after a good day's running, I saw people sitting outside the front of a house. I ran up the driveway and saw a woman staring at me. As I got closer to her, she continued staring at me, which was a bit disarming.

'Sorry,' she said. 'I thought you were a girl running up our driveway.'

'I'm a guy,' I smiled. 'Well, last time I checked.'

She introduced herself as Maggie Pearce and offered me a much-needed cup of tea. 'It must get uncomfortable sleeping rough,' she said. 'Why don't you have my sofa?'

That night, over more tea, Maggie told me she'd overcome cancer in 1986, the year I was born. 'It's funny,' she said. 'The moment I was told I was ill, I asked myself the question: what's life all about? The things I cared about most – like my career, house and possessions – stopped mattering so much. That was just *stuff*, and all of it revolved around money. Suddenly, I had new priorities: family, friends, love and how to make a difference to people's lives.'

As I was about to fall asleep on the sofa, I heard Maggie giggling to the 'I've Gone the Wrong Way!' YouTube video. In the morning, she complimented me for sounding just like her mother, who was also British. As we said goodbye, I had no expectation to see or hear from Maggie again.

A few mornings later, a man called Dave stopped me to ask if he could join me for a while. He was barefoot. 'It was only 40 years ago that humans started wearing running shoes,' he told me. 'Our ancestors evolved to run barefoot in order to hunt animals and they never had footwear.'

About 10 miles in, we hit gravel. I wondered how his naked feet would cope with this and got some sick pleasure watching him grimace over the harsh terrain. I asked him if he'd ever really hurt his feet.

'Oh yeah, many times. I've had a nail stuck in one. I've picked out glass from my sole. The list is endless. But for three years now, I've consistently avoided any injuries to the rest of my body. When I wore trainers, I was always hurting myself in my back, my knees, my groin...'

A moment after Dave left, passers-by started waving and honking their horns. A saloon car parked next to me, and a mother and a bunch of kids piled out. 'I'm Tracy,' she said. 'Can me and all my boys run with you?'

As we got going, I asked Tracy how she'd get back to her car.

'Don't worry about that,' she said in a relaxed tone. 'You should see the car move any minute now.'

'How come?' I said.

'I've left my 12-year-old in there to drive it along.'

'Very funny,' I said.

She wasn't joking. The car started edging along the hard shoulder. All I could see was this tiny head and eyes poking up over the steering wheel.

Some of Tracy's kids started dropping out, but nine-year-old Campbell continued with us. I was impressed when he reached 6 miles. 'Campbell, do you want a break?'

His head wobbled. 'No, let's keep going.'

I stopped anyway because he looked like he needed it. We sat on the grass and I asked him if he knew who Terry Fox was.

He nodded. 'Yes, we learn about him lots at school. We do a run every year for him, too. He was on one leg, you know? Did you know that?'

I loved that Terry Fox was known by a whole new generation.

An hour after I parted company with the family, my phone rang. 'Jamie, it's Tracy. Campbell won't shut up about you.' In the background I could hear him saying, 'Can I stay with

Jamie, Mom? Pleeeeease! I want to know what it's like to be an adventurer and a superhero!' Then Tracy added, 'Did you hear that, Jamie? What do you think?'

'Of course he can,' I said.

Campbell and his mum arrived while I was unpacking the tent from Caesar in the backyard of a local retiree. When he saw that a little boy would be staying the night, he offered us an upgrade: his garage.

Campbell and I lay down on the floor in our sleeping bags. I was exhausted, but I sensed Campbell wouldn't be sleeping too easily. 'So, Jamie, is this what it's like to be an adventurer?' he asked.

'I guess so,' I yawned. 'I mean, let's face it, when we were running together this morning I had no idea we'd be staying in this house tonight. That's what adventure is all about: having no idea what's around the corner.'

'Is it easy being an adventurer?'

'What do you think, Campbell?'

He lay back and stared up at the ceiling. 'I think it's easy. All you have to do is run a little and you get a nice garage to sleep in.'

———————

After half a mile the next day, I heard those dreaded words: 'When is Mom coming to pick me up?' Campbell's feet were dragging and his chin was buried in his chest. The poor lad was running on empty and I didn't want to stop, as I had a job to do. I tried the tough approach: 'Come on, Campbell, you said it was easy being an adventurer! Let's crack on.' He kept whingeing but, to his credit, managed a further 3 miles. I understood how he felt: that great feeling on day one, followed by having to run with tired legs on day two.

Tracy turned up and Campbell couldn't wait to climb into the car. I gave him a high five and ran on. Halfway through the run, I checked Google and realised I was midway through the time left on my visa but had only completed 2,500 miles. From now on, somehow, I needed to be running a lot faster. I then checked in on how the donations were going. They'd doubled in the last four days to $12,000 for SickKids and over £3,000 for the UK hospitals. I also calculated that I'd climbed a total of 58,023 feet so far, which was the equivalent of reaching Mount Everest twice. I knew I had plenty more Everests in front of me, as it were, especially with the Rocky Mountains ahead.

Later on that day, I was warmly greeted at a nice big house by Lenny, who'd contacted me via Twitter, and his two children, aged 12 and ten. There was something very different about Lenny, but I couldn't put my finger on it. Eventually, after the kids had gone to bed, he mentioned that he was transgender. I'm just a working class bloke from Gloucester so I'd never heard the term before. 'In short,' he explained, 'I was born a female but mentally I've always felt like a man. Two years ago, I went to see a doctor to explain my situation and he suggested the op.'

I couldn't help but look straight at his flat chest. 'What about, you know…?' I asked, awkwardly. 'You know… your breasts?'

'I've had them surgically removed. Wanna see?'

'Yeah, OK.'

He took his shirt off and revealed two huge scars underneath his pecs. 'I had surgery that cost $10,000 for breast removal and I've also been taking testosterone for over a year now.'

'How do your kids feel about it?' I asked.

'They still call me "Mom", but they have easily accepted the situation now that I'm happier being a boy, if that makes sense?'

That's another great thing about travelling: opening your mind to things you were previously ignorant about. In a sense, Lenny was someone else who'd had a dream and decided to pursue it, whatever the risk. As I waved Lenny and the kids goodbye, I thought, *A true Forrest Gump moment – you never know what you're going to get.*

My brain wandered off, as it usually does, focusing on the fact that I hadn't for a long while had any female attention, if you get what I mean. At least dreaming of women was a great distraction from the toil of my quest.

Then, by coincidence, a gorgeous blonde rocked up on the side of the highway. It was difficult not to stare at her and I knew she could sense my desire, but I didn't care.

'I'm Heather,' she said.

'You're hot!' I blurted out and immediately regretted it.

'Thank you, Jamie,' she blushed. I wanted her even more. Trying to change the subject, she pulled out lots of home-made badges from her bag. They read: GO JAMIE GO, JAMIE IS AN INSPIRATION and JAMIE IS A SUPERHERO. She couldn't stop any longer, as she had to go to work but said she'd come out again later to see how I was doing.

That night, I lay down in my tent in the wilderness and caught up on Facebook using my iPhone. I received this very touching message from a guy I'd met a few days before:

A couple of days ago, I was lucky enough to run with Jamie for the last few miles of his day. Never have I met someone so alive and in the moment. He faces an insanely daunting voyage yet every day is up and out the door at the crack of dawn, smiling and laughing at the madness of it all, putting one foot in front of the other, day after day.

Jamie, you have re-awakened a part of me that the work-a-day world has muted for too long and I can never thank you enough for that.

So thank you, a thousand times, thank you. From me, and pretty much everyone else along your journey.

I also got a message from Barb McDougall asking me to do a talk at the library in Sudbury, an old smelting town dating back to the 1880s. I had 24 hours to get there, which meant doing a marathon and a half in that time. I just about managed it and was joined for the last few miles into town by Chris and Gillian, where Chris took Caesar to the Outside Store for a tune-up, new tyres and all.

At the end of my talk somebody put their hand up to ask a question. 'Jamie, how are you *really* doing?' Ever since the breakfast show in Toronto, where I'd joshed around with the presenters, telling them everything was fine, I'd been storing up dark emotions about my adventure. I was anxious and afraid of injury, loneliness and failure. The burden of responsibility for raising money for the charities had been wearing me down. Now, in front of a hundred people and a CBC TV crew, those emotions brewed up to the surface and I wept uncontrollably. 'I just don't know if I can make it,' I sputtered. 'I'm hurting so badly.'

Barb walked up to me, crying too, and put her arms around me. 'You can do it.'

I felt strangely liberated after opening up like that. I guess it acted as a kind of therapy. Whatever it was, it turned out to be the perfect fuel for getting to the town of Spanish, so-called, according to one theory, because Spanish colonisers married into the local Ojibway tribe. I found a restaurant that was closed for the night, but I knocked anyway, and the manager gave me a monster club sandwich meal as well as a room for the night. The milk of human kindness was still flowing.

Before I set off from the restaurant, an old-timer called Kerry approached and gave me some words of warning. 'You're never going to make it through the Rocky Mountains, you know.' He handed me $5. 'Here, it's all I have. If I had more, I'd give it to you.' Shockingly, he began to cry. I put my arm round him.

A teenage girl called Melissa, Barb's daughter, joined me for the day's run and at the halfway point we stopped off at a lodge. The occupant was an old-timer and he welcomed us in warmly.

'Are you never scared of going into a total stranger's house?' asked Melissa while the old man was out of the room.

'Not really,' I said. 'I have pretty good intuition and he seems like a good man.'

Melissa and Barb headed off, and I ran on alone. A few miles later a woman called Cindy turned up. She'd been at the talk in Sudbury the other night. She was shivering from emotion rather than the cold. 'I feel like I haven't been able to express how much I love what you're doing.'

'Oh, don't worry,' I said.

'I have a wooden cabinet at home. Inside are some keepsakes related to my son Johnathan who died nine years ago. He was only thirteen years old.'

'I'm sorry.'

She pulled out a cute little alligator toy made from green, black and white beads. 'Johnathan made this while he was staying at SickKids Hospital. When he gave it to me, he said, "Here, Mom, this is for you so you'll never be alone."'

'Cindy,' I said, touching the lump in my throat, 'I can't take this—'

'Please, Jamie, I insist.' She also handed me a gold 'Starlight Hero Award' medal that the hospital had given Johnathan.

I couldn't find words powerful enough to thank Cindy properly. I hung both the mementos off Caesar, vowing for the sake of Johnathan's memory to finish this adventure and raise as much money as I humanly could for SickKids.

Before getting back on the road, I got an alert from Virgin Money Giving, the UK fundraising page, to tell me that the latest single donation had been £2,500! What? I'd never heard of a donation that big before. I wrote to Rich Leigh and suggested we publicly thank the donor, David Redvers – his name was all I knew about him. I emailed him:

Hi David, thank you – incredible donation along with a great comment. Can I thank you on FB/Twitter if you're OK with this? Do you have a Twitter name to tag you in? Would love to meet up when I'm back in the good old Glos, that's if I make it of course!

The reply from David was:

Jamie/Rich, to be honest I couldn't believe how little was in the pot and I was so moved by one of your YouTube clips that I wanted to do something meaningful.

I don't want any publicity out of the donation at all.

My ten-year-old son Charlie is your new biggest fan and frankly I'm delighted, as it's pretty inspiring stuff. If you fancy doing anything it would be brilliant if you would say hello to him in your next video update. Oh, and we'd love to buy you a beer when you're home. I guess you'll get a hero's reception at Kingsholm, as I discovered your antics through one of the Glaws lads on Twitter.

Watch out for the bears in the woods!

It was pretty obvious I was in bear territory when I saw a sign that read: DON'T FEED THE BEARS – DANGER. I felt a strange blend of fear and mirth – on the one hand, any rustle I heard gave me the shivers, but on the other hand I was tickled by the notion of someone just going up to a bear and feeding it. *As long as I don't feed one, everything will be all right*, I thought. Yeah, right.

At the back of an old derelict building I found a greenhouse and got my head down.

I woke up feeling like I'd been slumbering in lava, so hot was I. Having had only four hours' sleep, I dragged my feet for a few miles until a guy with long wavy hair and a round nose popped up on the side of the highway. He had spent the night watching my YouTube videos and his face was pinched with emotion. 'I was about to give up on this world,' he muttered. 'And here *you* are trying to help our country and you're not even a Canadian.' He introduced himself as Mike McCloud and handed over $100 for SickKids. He told me to go to Tim Hortons, a restaurant in the little settlement of Blind River (population 3,549).

I did as he suggested and met him again outside the drive-through section of Tim Hortons. Mike parked his pickup truck and put up a big sign that read: DONATE TO SICKKIDS. He must have asked every single customer for donations. In the space of an hour he raised another $100.

'Please, Mike, that's enough!' I said. 'You're becoming the Mother Teresa of SickKids.'

'No, it's not enough,' he said, almost aggressively. He was more passionate about his mission than I was. 'I run a roofing company and I promise you that for every roof I make until the end of your journey, I'll give 20 per cent of all my takings to SickKids.' That was a truly generous gesture and I was really touched by his determination to make a difference.

For the past few days I'd suffered from abdominal cramps. They'd suddenly got worse and the pain was making me woozy. I went to the nearest hospital. The doctor didn't have much of a bedside manner, but she did quickly diagnose musculoskeletal (MSK) pain. She wanted to dose me up with Ibuprofen to reduce the inflammation and, quite clearly, get me the hell out of there. I thought I'd push my luck a little. 'Could I possibly take a nap here for 30 minutes on the hospital bed?'

She looked at me as though I'd just pooed on the floor. 'No you cannot! This is a government building.'

I swiped my credit card for $400, hoping my insurance would cover it. Before leaving the UK, I hadn't found any companies prepared to insure someone running across Canada. No idea why. My only option was to take out some cheapie alternative. I didn't know if that would do the job – to be honest, I was frightened to find out.

Thinking more charitably about the doctor, I wondered if the lack of empathy was a good sign, meaning that MSK couldn't be that serious. I'd been contemplating the worst but I just needed to man up and crack on – so I did.

I received a tweet from Maggie Pearce, recommending good hearty food at the Bobbers Restaurant & Motel in Bruce Mines. I ran over 32 miles till 11 p.m. As I walked into the restaurant – which was technically closed by that time – the waitress, who had been chatting on the phone, quickly whacked the receiver down. She had an expression that said, *You weren't supposed to know that I've just been talking about you.*

'Was that Maggie on the phone?' I asked.

'Err... no, it was a... customer.'

I just knew she was lying. 'Come on... that was Maggie, wasn't it?'

She went bright red. 'OK, it was. But Maggie made me swear that I wouldn't let you know that she's been looking out for you because she knows how much you want to do this on your own. So what would you like to eat? Anything you like, it's all on the house. And here's a key to your room.'

I was angry with Maggie for caring so much, but I couldn't help but love her at the same time. It was nice to know someone had my back.

A few local joggers came with me the next day. I was struck by population signs that read 400. I love Canada for this. My run into Sault Ste. Marie marked the exact halfway point across the country. There were other milestones to celebrate: I'd now completed 100 marathons and it was my birthday. Hot Heather, who'd given me the badges, came back to run with me.

Theresa Mudge wrote a blog about what happened next:

As long distance runners, my husband Nathan and I were awestruck that someone would attempt a seemingly impossible feat. What captured our attention even more, however, was the degree of support from Canadians. Some were total strangers, others were people Jamie had previously met.

Anna Miltchev from Montreal knew that Jamie would be arriving in Sault Ste. Marie on his 27th birthday and wanted to give him a cake as well as nutritious food. Inevitably, we all draw the parallel to Terry Fox's Marathon of Hope.

At 1 p.m. we could see Jamie approaching – what a sight! It was 28 degrees, humid, and here comes Jamie running down the highway, beaming all the way. Following media interviews and photos, we went to the YMCA outside which was a surprise reception of a over hundred people, mostly children, all singing 'Happy Birthday'. He high-fived all the kids and choked up while trying to thank everyone. The birthday cake appeared. Before Jamie blew out the candles he said, 'I do have a wish and it's donations. I hope they will make the difference.'

We will remember Jamie not for his extraordinary physical achievement, nor for his wonderful generosity. We will remember him as an 'ordinary bloke' who dared to dream. We were captivated by his spirit and his message of hope.

Every day in Canada has been special, but I'll never be able to recreate the magic of my twenty-seventh birthday.

That night I was thrilled to learn that Heather was also staying in the hotel. We went to the bar, but I drank a few beers so my memory of what was said is hazy. After six months of running, I was officially a lightweight. It was lovely to have some company for the evening, but it turned out she had a boyfriend, so my crush on Hot Heather was brought to an end.

_____

My next destination was a tiny township called White River, seven marathons away. It was going to be tough and lonely. On the run, I could get no phone signal at all, which only added to my unease, but there was nothing I could do about it. I had to concentrate on putting one foot in front of the other and on the next bit of food that would enter my mouth.

I was seriously fatigued by midday so I flaked out behind some bushes. After an hour, I was awoken up by six excited kids. Their family gave me food, water and over $300 for SickKids from a cake sale they'd held.

Although the temperature was hitting 30°C, there was plenty of shade so I managed to squeeze out a full marathon. Rob, a chap from Bruce Mines, came to help me set up the tent that night on a dirt track just off the highway. 'You'd better camp a little off this road to allow the bear hunters to pass through,' he said. 'You do know it's bear season, right?'

'Cheers, Rob, I'll be sleeping well tonight.' While I wasn't too fearful of the black bears, the grizzly ones on the west coast would alter my camping strategy, I was sure.

The most epic boosts throughout these lonely days were Jami Burns popping over for a run every once in a while, and when a car paused beside me to blast out the *Flash Gordon* theme tune by Queen. I was roughly nine days away from Thunder Bay, where I could take a break and try to sort out my foot, which had been super sore.

The White River Motel put me up for the night. I dumped Caesar in the room and limped along to look for some food. Once I got to the nearest restaurant, as I was packing my foot in ice, a gruff old man walked in and glared at me. 'Get your shoe back on now – this is a restaurant.'

'I'm really sorry,' I said. 'My foot's killing me.'

'I don't care about your frigging foot. Get it back on.'

I did as he said. When the waitress came over to collect my plate and glass, I asked her who that guy was.

'He's the mayor of our town,' she shrugged.

Back in my room, I found some fruit and a card on the table that read, 'Unless someone like you cares a whole awful lot, nothing is going to get better, it's not – Dr Seuss.' Underneath it was a bulky envelope with this written on it: 'For SickKids, from the supervisor of the White River Child Care Program.' There must have been hundreds of dollars inside.

Late on, in my next run, I met an inspirational British couple who were riding motorcycles around the world for charity. I asked them how they came up with the idea and they told me it had come to them during a game of shithead. They promptly sold their house and off they'd gone. That takes a lot of courage.

I started the following day knowing it was going to be the longest leg of the journey. I was perked up when two Iron Men, Dave and Joe, met up with me. Iron Men are what I call 'super athletes', swimming 2.4 miles, cycling 124 miles and then running a 26-mile marathon all in one day. Having these guys with me so I could chat to them felt like a form of meditation – talking while you run is a brilliant distraction from the suffering!

With a few miles to go, I accidentally addressed Joe as 'Dave'. I couldn't think straight, my brain was starved of oxygen. Joe, however, was an old hand at this and kept talking comprehensibly. He had a really mellow and therapeutic tone of voice. We pushed on to 35 miles and bedded down in a helicopter hangar, of all places. We were greeted by a pilot named Danny who showed us to a fridge. 'Choose your weapon,' he said, flinging open the fridge door. It was packed with beer. He then produced a pile of hot pizzas. What a way to finish off a shattering day!

From the beginning of my odyssey, I'd been warned that the hardest part would be the approach to Thunder Bay. That's where Terry Fox struggled the most. As soon as I got outside the following day, I could see the foreboding silhouettes of the mountains. They may not have been tall, but there were plenty of the wretched things.

For the first 20 miles, a rainstorm thrashed me about like a rag doll. The steepness of the hills rapidly sucked the energy out of my lungs, legs and brain. I popped up my tent in the rain, hoping to wait out the downpour, but it only got worse. Each drop sounded like a golf ball slamming against the tent. I whacked on my soggy socks, drenched shoes and my one and only Flash suit, and went for it. Being higher up in the mountains, temperatures seemed to drop significantly. Another new addition to this nasty mix of weather conditions was a hellish headwind from the largest freshwater lake in the world, Lake Superior. Soon I couldn't feel my feet and my hands had turned purple, even with gloves on. I gripped Caesar so tight just to stop myself from shivering. Somehow I tacked two mile-high climbs one after another and finally completed 16 miles.

Mentally as well as physically, this was the darkest place I'd ever been. I clung onto the image of Terry Fox, picturing his dogged expression, tousled eighties hair and oar-thin artificial leg. 'He did this with cancer and one leg!' I yelled into the wind. 'How do you think he felt? Eh? Eh?'

I rarely paid attention to what date it was or even what day but, once I'd found an empty barn protected from the elements, I sat down with my iPhone and noticed that it was 1 September: the last day of Terry Fox's journey back in 1981. Here's what he wrote in his journal about it:

People were still lining the road saying to me, 'Keep going, don't give up, you can do it, you can make it, we're all behind you.' Well, you don't hear that and have it go in one ear and out the other, for me anyway... There was a camera crew waiting at the three-quarter mile point to film me. I don't think they even realized that they filmed my last mile... people were still saying, 'You can make it all the way, Terry'. I started to think about those comments in that mile, too. Yeah, I thought, this might be my last one.

That's the thing about cancer. I'm not the only one, it happens all the time to people. I'm not special. This just intensifies what I did. It gives it more meaning. It'll inspire more people. I just wish people would realize that anything's possible if you try. When I started this run, I said that if we all gave one dollar, we'd have $22 million for cancer research, and I don't care, man, there's no reason that isn't possible. No reason.

I couldn't wait for Thunder Bay and to see Terry's statue.

I woke up to clear cobalt skies and – thankfully – no rain. I got my wet gear together, did my marathon a lot more easily than I had yesterday and stopped to film myself saying, 'Today has been a much better day.' Then I noticed something bright in the distance. I carried on recording as it got nearer. I could make out green leggings. Who the hell wears green leggings unless they're as mad as I am? As the figure got closer, I spied a red T-shirt and a black face mask.

'No, it can't be!' I exclaimed. But it was. It was Kev, who'd come all the way from England to surprise me in his trusty Robin costume. We laughed while we put the tent up, laughed over dinner and were still laughing over breakfast the next morning.

Kev hitchhiked off to Thunder Bay, while I continued solo through endless rolling hills and small mountains in perfect conditions: sunny skies, a cool gentle breeze and the stunning Lake Superior on my flank. Every time I conquered another incline, I'd treat myself to a few minutes' viewing from the summit. It was as if hell and heaven coexisted within a mile of each other.

I took a break down a side road and heard a loud crack of branches. I thought back to the only wildlife I'd seen so far in Canada: two deers and a woodpecker. I hadn't even come across a bloody moose! I was beginning to believe that Canada had little in the way of wildlife.

There was another crack. Maybe this was the moose I'd been waiting for? I turned round and saw a bear about 20 metres away. I crouched, pulled out my camera and filmed the beast as it sloped off. My heart rate was higher than if I'd been running. I breathed so heavily that, when I tried to stand up, I nearly fainted. I ran off on shaky legs, thinking that bears do exist, they really do.

I scaled the tallest mountain so far, ranting like a psycho on the final mile. When I got to the top, the view was ruined by a gigantic black storm cloud drifting towards me. It was like a scene in a sci-fi film where the spaceship crashes into the earth, leaving a trail of destruction in its wake. As the cloud closed in, I scrambled around, looking for shelter. There was nothing apart from little boulders and flimsy trees, so I started to set the tent up on the side of the highway. Darkness slammed down on me. I felt distressingly alone.

It was then that, bizarrely, a school bus appeared, but with no children on board. Steve, the driver, had commandeered the vehicle to track me down, and give me a hot cheeseburger and chips for my tea. He had kept the food on the dashboard by the heater to keep it warm. Sarah, a passer-by, handed me a cold beer to wash it all down with. This was the last thing I could have predicted happening out here in such a remote place. Thankfully, my sturdy military tent protected me from the full wrath of the storm.

After a decent run, I found a campsite at 10 p.m. the following night. The reception was closed and there were no vacant spaces to put my tent up. The toilet was open so I bedded down in there. It was clean, dry and warm. The only problem was that it played loud music – I guessed so that people wouldn't sleep in there. I stuck some of my trusty duct tape over the speakers and slept like a baby for a few hours.

My alarm went off at 5.30 a.m. and all I could focus on was the statue of Terry Fox. I've never been a huge fan of any statue, but I knew this one would be different – and it was.

When I finally reached it, there wasn't anyone else around so I could have a quiet moment to reflect on this remarkable man. I considered how far I'd come in my own adventure and how hard it had been to get even to this point. I started to weep at the notion of Terry having come so far and then being forced to give up. But his feat and his memory have raised a whopping $700 million for cancer research to date. He touched a nation and the world. These facts will never cease to amaze me. Some people have said that I could be the next Terry Fox.

I could never ever be Terry Fox. In my eyes, there will never be another individual like him.

People who'd heard on social media that I'd be at the statue started to gather at 3 p.m. Hundreds of people showed up and a vast number of kids were dressed as their favourite superheroes. Erinn DeLorenzi, a cool mother who wore a lot of gold and had big curly locks, had been instrumental in getting them all together. Music pumped out until Mayor Hobbs made a lovely speech. When he was done, he handed me the microphone, which made it all feel very official. I related how difficult the challenge had become. 'This is a really inspirational day. I've been motivated to get to the end as much by you guys getting out here for me as by Terry Fox.' A woman near me burst into tears, so I added, 'It's getting bloody tough for all of us now.' The crowd laughed. Afterwards, everyone greeted me personally to thank me for what I was doing.

At Thunder Bay I had the privilege to meet the Investors Group, one of the biggest investment companies in Canada. I lightened the mood from the start by strolling into their HQ at 8 a.m. dressed as the Flash. 'Is it your birthday?' I asked one of the women. 'Cos I'm your stripper!' Each and every person came over to show their appreciation for what I was doing. After

I gave a brief talk, they made large donations and a great guy called Larry Lovis pledged to give me $10 for every marathon left for me to do, or $900 for SickKids if I made it all the way.

Erinn had more fundraising plans. She organised the 'Sleeping Giant Brewing' party day, which involved lots of fun games such as beer pong. Then we headed for the Thunder Bay market where so many stalls promised that all profits would go to SickKids. I lost count of the people who were dressed up as superheroes and striking poses at me.

The most affecting moment was meeting a small boy named Samuel who was battling cancer. 'He's doing really well though, and it looks like he's going to beat it,' his mum Carolyn said, and Samuel smiled ear to ear. We raised $1,000 in the space of two hours. Superhero powers indeed!

I entered the Terry Fox Annual Run, comprising a couple of 2-mile laps. I paired up with a very obese man who was panting hard and asked him why he was there.

'Cos of Terry's inspiration. You can see for yourself I have a weight problem and there are so many days when I want to give up on everything. Then I think of Terry and I suddenly have perspective again. Running these 4 miles is like a marathon to someone like me, but I'm going to give it my best shot and never give up.'

I was taken to Ogden School, which is attended by a lot of Native Canadian kids from troubled backgrounds. All the staff and students were dressed up as superheroes and chanting, 'Jamie Flash!' The children had been learning all week about my run across Canada. In maths class they'd been answering questions like, 'If Jamie runs 200 marathons at X speed, how many days will he take to reach his final destination?' After watching all my YouTube videos they'd been writing essays about my adventures. One kid must have seen the one entitled 'One Wrong Turn' because a teacher handed me a comic strip of me dressed as the Flash, screaming, 'I've gone the wrong way!'

I was treated to a buffet breakfast during which a teacher put her arm round me and said, 'Let's get Jamie fat.' When it came to my presentation, I burst through a plastic banner into the gym and high-fived over 200 kids. How could I refuse this opportunity? During the presentation there were plenty of giggles and I felt I managed to reach out to every single child in the room. I wanted them to take away messages about having adventurous fun, about being inspired and inspiring others, and about making a difference through fundraising. I told them an interesting fact about Terry Fox. 'If he'd had the same kind of cancer today, the chances of Terry Fox losing his leg would have been extremely slim and the chances of it spreading and killing him very low. All his hard work for cancer research has helped so many people avoid what he had to endure.' The room went silent. I was presented with a $600 donation to SickKids. For a school that size it was an astronomical achievement.

We finished off what had been one of the best days of my life by doing an epic run around the school, all still dressed as superheroes.

———————

Leaving Thunder Bay, I was anxious about the challenge ahead: I had to complete 90 marathons in 100 days. To kick-start the run out of town, I had to burst through a 15-foot sign that read GO JAMIE GO, before a dozen runners braved it in the pouring rain to come with me. To psych us up we had two enormous speakers on the back of a four-wheel truck, blaring out classic tunes like 'Don't Stop Believing'. We took singing in the rain to another level. After the runners were gradually picked up to go home, I was soaking wet again – a familiar sensation by now – and found another old barn to sleep in. It was dark, draughty and the floor was sodden. I couldn't help but envy all the runners that had gone home to a hot shower and a cosy bed for the night.

I put on my head torch and located a dry spot, plus a wood stove, magazines and a cardboard box full of wood. Bonanza! I lit a fire, hung everything up to dry, ate some sardines, rolled out my mat and sleeping bag, and nodded off. I was startled awake by the box of wood on fire. I'd stupidly left it on top of the stove and it had been set alight. Screaming hysterically, I picked it up and tossed it outside in the rain. In the process, I melted my Flash belt. Before going back to sleep, I put out a cheeky Facebook post:

I left a pair of my trainers, signed by me, in Thunder Bay. Let's put them up for auction for SickKids and start the bidding at $30/£20. On the 25th of September I'll announce the winner and get them posted out to you. Place your bids in the comments below. Good luck!

Many bids came in: $100, followed by $300 and then $500. Maggie Pearce said she had a 'special home' for these shoes and trumped everyone with $800.

I did another 15 miles the following day and at Savanne River Resort a few people welcomed me with gifts. Larry gave me a luminous orange hat so the hunters wouldn't shoot me by accident and two ladies offered me a horn to scare off the bears. I was glad – but also troubled as they all imagined worst-case scenarios for me. The final present was a fluffy toy moose, because I still hadn't seen one on this trip.

The Resort treated me to a massive turkey dinner with home-made raisin pie, prepared for me by the Native Canadian Chief White Cloud of Lac Des Mille Lacs First Nation. Quentin, another Native Canadian, kept topping up my water and making sure I felt right at home.

Although all was going well, for the first time I started to think about the finish and about how far there was left to go. This is a bad habit to get into. What had worked for me so far was living in the now, in the moment. But, mile after mile, I couldn't take my mind off the distance and how bloody long it was: 80 more marathons away!

What snapped me out of it was an oncoming car that was edging closer and closer to the hard shoulder where Caesar and I were running. With just a few yards between us, the car didn't swerve – it came straight at us. I leaped onto the roadside, tugging Caesar with me. I guessed the driver must have been drunk or tired – or maybe both. I didn't think I'd become famous enough for someone to want to assassinate me.

I made it to a church in Upsala, a little way north of the Lac Des Mille Lacs, where the locals fed me a delightful picnic. I told them my personal philosophy on life: 'I don't plan anything because a plan becomes an expectation. And an expectation can lead to a disappointment.' A woman called Melissa gave me extra food to take away, plus a brand new handmade Flash belt to replace the one that had perished in the fire. 'My husband's driving this way at 6 a.m. tomorrow,' she said. 'What do you want for breakfast?'

'Anything but tinned fish, Melissa. Thank you so much.'

With no plan and nothing at all in sight, I carried on running. At sundown, Melissa and her kids drove up to me with a cup of tea and a margarine tub full of hot beef stew. A little further on was a cabin on the roadside. I ran over and found the lock to be broken, and inside there were a stove and a store of wood. Was this too perfect? Maybe. It was as if someone had set all this up for me. I was tucked away from the frost that had been building through the day, wolfing down the beef stew that wasn't unlike my mum's recipe.

After reading everyone's encouraging comments on my Facebook page, I felt like I had propellers attached to my legs. Even the signs counting down the distance didn't bother me much. I've always wondered: what's the point of those? Are they there just to torment drivers? And a bloke running across Canada, possibly. It's like staring at the clock at work – the time will pass that much slower.

That night I camped under two shooting stars. Camping can be cosy.

I awoke with a bad head cold and dosed up on extra vitamin C tablets, which didn't shake it off. It would take a lot more than a stuffy nose to stop me running, anyway. The sun rose and cast everything in a golden hue, especially the leaves. This was like Eden.

During lunch I noticed that my belly button felt sore. I checked it out and found it was oozing brown discharge. I didn't even know your belly button could get infected. I guessed my immune system had to be really low and the five hours of sleep I got were not giving me enough rest. For the sake of my health, I took a break.

My spirits were lifted when I received an audio file in a text message from a teacher at Ogden School. It sounded like a whole classroom of kids was in the background. 'Keep running, Jamie. Ogden loves you. Don't give up!'

With those words still ringing in my ears, I ran fast to a town named Ignace where I had a talk booked, stopping only to clear out my belly button and douse it with Manuka. This honey quite literally saved my infected, blistered butt after cycling 12 days on a static bike, so I hoped it would do the same job now.

During the talk, I showed the scene from the 'Bangkok to Gloucester' video, when I cried over a loaf of bread. 'The poor people who gave me the bread,' I said, 'would have given me the shirts off their backs.' I was introduced to the mayor, who told me that Ignace was my oyster. I felt terrible when I met a kid who was wearing a Batman outfit because I wasn't wearing my Flash suit, as it was in the wash, and I could see the disappointment on his face. I showed him my YouTube clip

'Superhero cycling', in which Kev and I cycle through the city of Batman in Turkey, dressed as Batman and Robin. It cheered him right up.

At the end of the talk, the audience had gathered some money together, which they wanted to give to me for food, clothing and medicine to help clear up that cold. I thanked all of them, but said, 'I would really prefer it if you gave this money to SickKids. I've been disconnected from society for over two years now. I've had no fixed abode, no bills, no commitments as such. All I've needed money for is to travel from A to B and to buy food along the way. Although I don't own anything, I feel I have everything.'

As I left, Chantal Moore, the principal of Ignace High School, invited me to address her students. I love being spontaneous and letting everything click into place organically. Having over 150 kids in one room in the hope of inspiring them is priceless. I have to believe that at some point in their lives – which I will never personally see – they will choose to make a difference, and this talk, this moment, might well trigger that. It flowed well and, when the bell for break-time went off, the kids didn't flinch. Principal Moore told me afterwards that she'd never seen that before. At the end, the kids walked over to chat with me. One boy aged only ten spoke in such a mature tone, as if he were a teacher. 'You're doing really well at inspiring the young.' I couldn't help but grin like a village idiot.

By morning my head cold had moved to my chest. Jamie Richards messaged me:

Mate, you have two choices. Find somewhere warm and dry, and sit out the illness – ideally with hot lemon, honey, etc. etc. – or crack on. But if you crack on in these conditions, you risk a lot. Two or three days now might be a cheap price to pay in the long run.

I knew I wouldn't be able to mope around feeling sorry for myself, drinking lemon tea for too long, so I got back on the road, certain that I'd heal over the next few days. I started off a dribbling wreck. My feet were dragging, everything ached and I could barely focus. After a few miles, I didn't want to stop. The illness wouldn't beat me – it was a matter of pride. Reaching mile 13 – which would normally be when I'd take a break – I kept on going and I ran a whole marathon without stopping. By mile 23 I was yelling, 'I'm an animal, I'm an animal!'

I came across a picnic area, tried the men's toilets, but the stench was too bad. Instead, I set up my bed on the floor of the ladies'. A pastor named Jonathan King showed up with food and water. Good man. Apart from the odd mouse in the toilet, it was a roof over my head and that was enough.

The day had come when I finally had to announce the winner of the trainers auction: it was my great supporter Maggie Pearce, of course. What was even sweeter of her was her decision to give the trainers to Ogden School. As she said in her Facebook message, 'You're their superhero!'

Ever since I'd left Maggie's house, she'd been my number one follower on Facebook, Twitter and the tracker. Often when I walked into a restaurant, they'd know who I was simply because Maggie had called them ten minutes before my arrival. She didn't know I was aware of this, because she told every person she talked to not to say anything. But most of the time they'd say, 'I'm not supposed to tell you but a lady named Maggie just rang and she wants to make sure we give you a good feed and look after you.' It was so selfless of her.

Running on and making some further calculations, I knew I had to run 27 or more marathons every month if I was going to make it before my visa expired.

Nearing Manitoba, I got a phone call from a random number. If you're in the fundraising game, you have to answer every call, as you don't know where it might lead. 'Hi, who's this please?'

'Hi Jamie, my name is Peter Turkstra. What I'm about to say may be a little difficult for you, but I feel the need to let you know.' My heartbeat sped up. 'When you cross that border into Manitoba, your fundraising is going to stand still. No one will donate.'

'What the hell do you mean? I'm raising money for children's hospitals – kids for goodness' sake. Of course people will carry on donating. Who are you anyway?'

Then another voice: 'Jamie, I'm Peter's friend. Listen to me: Peter is trying to help you; he's a good guy.'

I considered ending the call, but decided to hear them out. Peter came back on. 'Jamie, I'm not sure if you know Canada well, but Ontario is not liked out west; there's a huge rivalry. In fact, I could go as far as saying that we're hated out west. Therefore, I think you should raise money for one hospital in each province you run through. That'd be a better strategy to maximise donations.'

'Look, I really appreciate your help but I just can't do that. I feel loyalty to SickKids in Toronto.'

'I'd really like to make a donation to two children's hospitals: $5,000 each to McMaster Children's Hospital Foundation and St Joseph's Hospital Foundation under your name. I have a connection with these hospitals, as they've helped people I know. Do you mind if I do that, Jamie?'

I was so astonished I began stuttering. 'Of c-course you c-can. Listen, Peter, I'm gonna go. I obviously need to have a think.'

'No problem,' he said calmly. 'I hope to speak again. I know what I've said is a lot to take on board.'

I didn't realise there was such rivalry between the provinces. It seemed a bit silly to an outsider like me. I Skyped Rich Leigh for some PR advice. He was only 25 years old, but he's always had a wise head. 'We'll have to be very clear with the messaging when we announce what you're going to do,' he advised. 'Most importantly, what do you think of the new idea of raising money in each province?'

'I guess I just wanna have the biggest impact possible.'

'If you raise money for specific hospitals in each province, it will help you to connect with the families that have had treatment from each one. I'd imagine communities would rally around even more.'

'It's a tricky one,' I said.

'Jamie, whatever you choose, you know everyone will back you.' Maybe a few runs would help me to find a solution to the puzzle.

I was on a mercifully shorter run to Dryden, a small city on Wabigoon Lake. It was only 12 miles into town, which was a cakewalk compared to my previous days. 'Let's just get this job done,' I said. And I did, in Flash time. Shaw TV came out to do an interview with me; the presenter, Tommy, asked all the right questions to try to get the donations rolling in, and he even donated $20 himself.

Knowing that two out of my three pairs of trainers had deteriorated, Pastor Jonathan King met me at the Four Seasons shoe shop. They gave me a 50 per cent discount and Jonathan paid the rest. I've always found it hard to accept such kindness directed at me. I gritted my teeth and shook my head. 'Please, Jonathan, you really don't have to do that.'

'That is true, Jamie,' he said in his grave, dulcet voice. 'It is more blessed to give than to receive. But for me to give I need you to receive.' The theory was convincing enough. I smiled and shut up. We went out for dinner that evening with his amiable family and I got my own back when the bill arrived. 'What did you say earlier about giving and receiving?'

I stayed the night in his church, had a bash around on the drum kit and nodded off before 9 p.m.

I left knowing that, after the next marathon, I'd be in the pleasant-sounding Vermilion Bay. My brain disconnected with my body and the first 13 miles flew by. The rain and cold were back with a vengeance, though. I checked to see how far I had come. 'Nineteen miles?' I shrieked. I carried on ranting to myself. 'Why did you check the watch so early? Why? I'm not even close. How could you think you were nearly done?' Foolish me, I kept checking every five minutes, hoping to see 28 miles on my phone, but that moment never came and time grew sluggish.

I tried hard to get back into 'the zone', where I'd been during the first half-marathon. But that's the problem: as soon as you will or try to think yourself into the zone, you've lost the battle. Not really being conscious of the fact that you're running seems somehow to ensure that your technique is perfect, that you feel relaxed, that your eyes are paying attention to the traffic, and so on – but you're not even thinking. The best runs are when you arrive at your destination and ask yourself, 'How long have I been going for? Where am I? How many miles have I done?' It's not an easy notion to put into words, but all runners will know what I mean. Anyway, after 20 miles I was banished from the zone and I wouldn't be able re-enter it that day. It was a hard, horrid slog to Vermilion Bay.

I was met there by Shirley and her fellow members of the Vermilion Bay Lions Club, a volunteer organisation that helps the local community. They'd put on a pot luck night – in which everyone brings their own food – at the town hall, and I got to show some videos and discuss my adventures. The club handed over $250 to SickKids and promised to pass my name to other groups in the province, in case they wanted me to talk to them too.

After I left Vermilion Bay, I decided to change my daily routine. Instead of split runs – a half-marathon in the morning and the same again in the afternoon – I was now doing a whole marathon in one go. There were three reasons for this. First of all, I wanted to run in the daylight: the nights were drawing in, and starting and finishing in the dark was just too depressing. Secondly, I might be able to sleep more than five hours a night if I got to finish earlier and, finally, if I could finish around 4 or 5 p.m., I'd have the evening free to give talks to help with fundraising.

After three days under the new regime, my calves, Achilles tendon, ankles and feet were hurting way more than usual. Not only did I feel more at risk of injury, but I'd also picked up another niggle, this time in my ankle, which had obviously come from not getting my usual few hours' break in the middle of my run. The slopes on either sides of the road – intended for drainage, I thought – in this part of Ontario weren't doing me much good either. One leg had to work harder than the other, and the feet and ankles were under a lot of stress to keep the rest of the body running in a straight line. The trick, I found, was to run on the side of the road, so that one foot would tread lightly on the pavement while the other would stamp down hard on the slope. I also preferred to move facing the traffic and see what was coming rather than have it zooming up behind me.

With the side of my ankle in eye-watering agony, I got my head down and just pretended all was well. The hills were my arch-enemies. I knew there were prairies beyond and I wanted them!

After encountering no one for hours, a small group of kids on the roadside cheered me, and banged pots, pans and rolling pins. That was the tonic I needed to get me to the Comfort Inn, where a complimentary room from the Lions Club awaited me.

'I cannot express the deep gratitude that sits in my heart for you,' said a woman named Sherry, who met me in reception. 'Neither the doctors in our hometown nor in Winnipeg could figure out why our little girl had acute liver failure. We sent her to SickKids, which had some of the best doctors, not just in the country, but in the world. For 51 days they fought so hard to make her better, but in the end she was chosen to become an angel. She is one of the angels who will guide and protect you on your extraordinary journey.'

'Thank you,' I said. Sherry's loss must have been traumatic and I couldn't imagine how difficult it had been.

As I neared the border, the decision about whether I should raise money for a hospital in each province was still weighing on me. I sat down that night and bashed out this message on Facebook:

Legging it 30 miles every day is hard enough and I've been doing some thinking about the best way to do it. Here's my plan: I'm going to raise money for one children's foundation or hospital in each of the provinces I am yet to run through. By doing this, I'll be giving the people of the province the opportunity to donate back into their own community (if they wish to). Also, as I meet people in each province, they will more likely have a connection to their local children's hospital and I think that connection will raise more

money and change more lives in the process. I want to do what's best for children both here in Canada and at home in the UK.

I hoped Peter Turkstra was right. It was hard to fight the pangs of guilt about letting down Toronto's SickKids Hospital, but I hoped that distributing the money more widely would make a more significant difference.

I spent the night a few hundred yards from the border crossing with Manitoba. It darkened as quickly as the temperature fell to –15°C. Winter was coming and it would only get colder from now on. Over four days I'd done five marathons with a bad ankle and on a very sore foot. I should have stopped to heal but I couldn't, for time's sake. Before I went to bed, I collected wood and put it in my tent, so in the morning I could light a fire. Even at below freezing, the fire kept my hands warm while I packed everything away.

MANITOBA

For some reason I imagined Manitoba to be flat, but instantly I was faced with two big climbs. After those, the terrain soon levelled out into a barren, treeless prairie with a long snaking road running through it. One final push of 34 miles and I'd be in Winnipeg, the elegant capital of the province. At 8 p.m. a family who had found me through my tracker stopped in their car to offer me food. Ten minutes later, another car pulled over and did the same, except that this family escorted me for the final few miles. I crashed right at the end of the run, scorching pains going up and down my legs, but I had to keep going. All I could do was plod dizzily, my eyes closing against my will. Every step I took, I screamed, 'No!' The last 100 yards were slightly eased by the presence of a seven-year-old kid running by my side, but he fell over so badly I was convinced he was going to cry. Instead, he stumbled back onto his feet and said, 'Man, that was a bad wipeout!'

Knowing that the 15 miles into Winnipeg would be my last run – at least for a few days – made it all the more enjoyable, although I was limping for the last part of it. Melissa, an ultra-runner with long, dark, flowing hair and a personality as bouncy as a space hopper, joined me. Her dedication blew me away, given that she'd run a 24-hour race the day before.

I often dreamed about Canada as a child, although I'd be lying if I said it involved crossing the country on foot. Aged six, I was addicted to *NHLPA Hockey*, a computer game based on Canadian ice hockey, and my favourite part was starting fights between the players. It's what young boys are like, I guess. From that age I'd dreamed of seeing a real-life NHL game and, most importantly, a fight. Another great supporter of my adventure, Gary Rozak, scored tickets for a Jets game in Winnipeg, which is no easy feat; I felt privileged. Maggie Pearce arranged a pool of $600 to go either to Manitoba Children's Hospital (the new charity for the province I was running through) – if the Jets, a Canadian team, won – or to my cousin Kev's charity, Paddling the Mississippi, if the American Anaheim Ducks won. Kev was paddling the Mississippi River at the time, from its source in Northern Minnesota, near the Canadian border, to the Gulf of Mexico: 2,350 miles through ten states. He was also raising money for Gloucester Children's Hospital so Maggie's competition really was a bit of fun because, whichever the result of the game, the money was going to a deserving place.

The game had the drama of a great movie and the noise of an ear-splitting concert. Sadly, the Jets lost and there were no punch-ups, but it's a typically Canadian experience. So Canada, so awesome.

I'll let Judy Otto's blog sum up the story of my time in Winnipeg:

The highlight of the week with Jamie was his visit to Teulon Collegiate. The staff and students got into the spirit of things: they raised money for his charity, hung up great posters in the hallways, and wore red clothing to support the Flash. It was a truly heroic effort. Melissa took us on a tour of the school and we could feel the excitement building everywhere we went.

Melissa had pledged to shave her head if her students raised over $1,000. They were about $100 short, so they sent the bucket of money around the room once more during Jamie's presentation. This time another $600 was added to the bucket to make a total of $1,500! Jamie was overwhelmed.

A teenage student, Kristopher, approached Jamie after all of the pictures and autographs. He apologized for having taken so long, but he had run off to a bank machine to take some money out for the charity. He seemed awkward as he fished in his wallet for the cash and Jamie tried to put him at ease, saying, 'It's OK! You really don't have to do this.' The school had already been extremely generous, but this kid was on a mission!

'No,' he said. 'I really *do* need to do this.' Then he told Jamie that he'd conquered cancer when he was young. He apologized again as he tried to explain how much it meant to him that people like Jamie wanted to help kids like him. Kristopher's bravery was the perfect ending to our visit to Teulon Collegiate.

The next day Jamie had a bone scan at the Medical Arts Building. He had a little nap during the last stages of the scan – you have to grab some sleep whenever you can. I just want to add here that Jamie has this crazy effect on people – whether it's his inspiring mission or his charismatic personality – that makes them bend over backwards to help him. I called him a 'people whisperer' because of this rare skill. Occasionally, there are people who are immune to his charm, such as the receptionist at the Medical Arts Building. 'What do you mean you don't have a Manitoba Health Card?' she asked him, as if nobody foreign had ever been to this hospital. Jamie still treats these people with the utmost respect. The great news later that day was that the scan showed no stress fracture and no bone spur. More likely he's either bruised his bone or done some minor damage to his ligament.

I rested in Winnipeg, nursing my foot, and I was anxious about my visa running out and the Canadian winter setting in. I had two options: I could get going with the foot not fully recovered and hope to complete the 60 marathons before the pain got too much; I could try to manage the injury as best as possible – and I knew my pain threshold was good. If necessary, I could limp my way to the finish line. The alternative was to stay put until the foot was fully healed, but how long would that take? I could attempt a visa extension – as I'd done in China during my monster bike ride – and pass through the Rockies in January. It would be slow going, roads would be closed and I'd have to battle through −30°C temperatures.

'Sod it,' I said, putting my costume on. 'It's option one – I'll go mad if I stay off the road too long.' As was becoming the norm, some other superheroes escorted me out of the city. We ran 10 miles until the darkness came. Judy and Melissa stayed with me as I approached a row of houses on the prairie. 'Come on, Jamie, we want to see how you work the magic.' I rapped my knuckles on the heavy oak door and, before I had even finished my spiel, the owner invited us in. 'I'm Ron. You have a bed tonight and, lucky for you, it's our pizza night!'

It was great to be back on the friendly road of surprises.

In the morning, Ron's wife, Debra, cooked me some porridge. I was whisked straight back to boyhood and my mum saying, 'Here, J, get this into you. It will stick to your insides and warm you up.'

A mile and a half into my run that day, the ligaments on the inside of my knee flared up and I couldn't bend my leg, which makes running tricky, to say the least. I locked my leg in a straight position and limped, placing one foot gingerly in front of the other. This technique put less aggravation on the knee, but I couldn't move fast enough to keep warm. As I shivered, I threw every layer I owned onto my body. The bitter prairie headwind didn't stop, stripping the heat from me bit by bit. I limped for two long hours and it was only the sight of a solitary house with a FOR SALE board on it that started to warm me up. The garage door was swinging open so I set up camp immediately inside, just as it started to hail. A door led into the main part of the home, where I could see an inviting red carpet, but I suspected it was alarmed. The last thing I wanted was to set it off and have to try to hobble away from the police.

Once I sat down on my thin, blow-up mattress, waves of doubt washed over me. 'Can I make it?' I kept asking myself. I needed a pep talk from my dad. 'Jamie,' he said, his voice distorted on Skype. 'Stop beating yourself up! There isn't a clock and this isn't a race. I imagine you're thinking about the finish, but go back to basics: focus on the moment you're in, just like you have throughout this whole journey. If you need to heal, shorten the runs. Stop if you have to and keep picking away at those miles when and where you can. Before you know it, the finish will be in sight. I promise it will. You're impacting lives. You have to keep going.'

At 5 a.m. I did yoga to ascertain the state of my knee. I thought it best to stay put in the garage for the day and let it heal properly. If I moved on and the same issue flared up again, I'd most likely be in the middle of nowhere and without shelter. I could continue limping but compensating with the other leg would place all the strain on it. I didn't want to end up with neither leg operational. By spending one extra day in that garage, my chances of running out of there and making up the mileage at a later date increased.

Sitting, waiting and not moving was one of the roughest challenges throughout my odyssey. I kept telling myself that being on my own and vulnerable in a glacial garage was in itself a challenge. I applied masses of Arnica gel, and ate lots of fish oil and curcumin to help with the inflammation.

Suddenly, the garage door opened with a bang. I assumed it was an estate agent who had been instructed to move on the squatter but it turned out to be one of those delightful Canadian families, carrying a hot hamburger for me.

I left the garage at 6 a.m., when it was still dark. Given that running in the dark with hundreds of cars whizzing towards me was dangerous, I ran on the gravel roads that ran fairly parallel to the highway. Another advantage was that the gravel had a softer impact on every stride, and plenty of farmhouses were coming up in case I needed to take a break.

My fresh legs felt magnificent and I clocked up 15 miles before reaching the hamlet of Oakville. It was so empty I thought it had been evacuated. When I finally found a woman out walking, I shouted, 'Oi! Please wait, I have a question for you.' She speeded up, possibly trying to get away from me. This could be the one and only person I was going to see that day so I wasn't going to let her escape. I repeated myself, louder than before, 'Oi! I need your help.' The wind was so strong that it felt like being shot at; the sleet was falling in a wall and there was no bloody way I was taking my midday break outside. I got to within arm's length of her.

'Hi, my name is Jamie. I'm currently running across Canada for children's hospitals dressed as the Flash.' I pointed down at my silly costume, which was now iced with sleet. 'I'm looking for a place that will keep me out of the elements for a few hours. Do you know where I can go?' Only then did I realise how weird and desperate I must have come across.

Her body language was saying: *Get away from me, you nutcase*, but what she actually said was, 'Do you want to come back to mine? It's a lot warmer and I have soup.' She introduced herself as Grace and led me to her modest home where I met her husband Chris.

'I've seen you on TV with that suit, right?' said Chris.

His recognition of me seemed to lighten the tense mood. I stuffed my face with soup, did some yoga and strength training, and snoozed in front of their roaring fire.

Soon it was time to leave their cosy house and I plodded off, unsure of where I'd be sleeping that night. Melissa pulled up in her car. She was wearing a costume in the shape of a giant can of Coca-Cola, her limbs sticking out. 'I dressed up so you don't have to feel so alone and stupid,' she said. I thanked Melissa for her unreal effort. My confidence was back up, so we got running and I was glad of the company. The sun went down, the temperature fell below zero and more sleet pinged off our faces as the wind grew stronger. Our reaction was to run faster and talk louder.

'This reminds me of the "fuck it" moment,' yelled Melissa. 'You know, when everything is against you, you can't get any lower, and the only thing left to do is start screaming, "Fuck it!" Here, try it Jamie.' I didn't take her up on it, but from a woman who's ran 100-milers and 24-hour races, it was sound advice indeed. It might be a useful weapon at a later date.

A lot of farm dogs prowled the country roads west of the Assiniboine River. Most would come and bark at me. I'd either bark back or simply give them a stare, and either response would make them cower off. But one particular Alsatian only got more vicious when I barked at him. He bounded towards me, baring sharp teeth and showing me fiery eyeballs. I tugged out my Canadian flag and waved the stick in Fido's face. I love dogs, I really do, but at this point it was either him or me. He wouldn't be moved. I cautiously wheeled Caesar up the road, holding the stick in the dog's direction as I went. He followed me up the road, howling, before losing interest and hurtling off back to the farm.

When the darkness set in, my thoughts turned gloomy too. I started to think of friends and family back home in Gloucester – Kev, Keiran, my mum, dad and brother – and questioned whether they really liked me or if they thought that I was stupid and selfish. I hadn't called or made much of an effort in months. It took a while to realise that I was in a state of paranoia and that none of those thoughts were rational. I reassured myself that I wouldn't feel like this forever. I just had to ride out this wave of fear.

Two headlights were shining in the middle distance for ages and when I got close enough, I could see it was another familiar face from Facebook, Chris, who had arranged my stay in MacGregor, a town of 20,000. Chris couldn't wait to get out of his car and give me a bear hug. He behaved as though he were reuniting with a long-lost relative after 50 years. 'Jamie, come here. Don't worry, it's only a little way from here, man.' He pointed down the road to a light glowing amid the darkness. It was a target to aim for while Chris drove behind me.

We arrived at MacGregor Motel and the manager, Wendy, was in an animated mood. She told me that she'd been following my progress for a good while.

'I'm sorry,' I yawned, 'but I'm absolutely knackered.'

'What?'

'I mean really tired. I'm broken, to be honest.'

'No worries at all,' she said and took me to my room, which was full of goodies. Chris stayed with me while I ate his home-made chilli and pumpkin pie.

Another day down, another day closer to the impossible.

Warm-up exercises are essential when everything around you is frozen. For the first time I cracked open my pack of hand and feet warmers, which reminded me of tea bags. I gave them a gentle shake and placed them inside my gloves and trainers – they worked a dream.

Heading towards Brandon, the highway was brutally boring. Everything began to hurt, the wind was bashing me backwards and my energy depleted fast. I played a game where I'd pick out a tree in the far distance and say to myself, 'Once I get there, I'll take my break behind *that* one.' But before I came to the tree, I'd quickly pick another one further ahead. This stopped me from taking a break too soon. When I eventually did pause, around the 19-mile mark, I sat on the highway with no choice but to be out in the harsh winds, spooning cold, tinned sardines into my mouth.

I did a second talk at the Investors Group; throughout the journey they kept asking me to give a speech at each of their local branches and contributed with donations. It was always difficult to take time out from running, but on this occasion a mum presented me with a cheque for $500 with a tear in her eye. A woman called Wendy came up to me as I was heading out and told me that Terry Fox was a second cousin of hers. 'I was thrilled that someone was more or less literally following in his footsteps in support of a great cause. It's also great to see the bright side of the world we live in, as we all too often forget how many people in the world are willing to offer a helping hand. There's all this negativity in the media; it's like they want us all to distrust each other. Seeing the teary look on that mother's face when she thanked you for your dedication is enough to make anyone want to do good in this world!'

After saying my goodbyes, I went on to the Blü Kitchen & Bar for supper. Wearing my Flash outfit had become so normal that I no longer even noticed it, but in a place this posh, heads were turning.

The next morning, after 10 miles, I said hello to a lady in her garden. She replied in a thick Scottish accent, 'Oh, you're that boy that's running across Canada. Shall I get the kettle on for a cup of tea?' It had been over seven months since I'd heard our famous British saying: 'Get the kettle on.'

I let out a huge breath and replied, 'I'd love one.' I spent three hours with Elma and her Scottish husband, Charles. I tried to do some yoga, but my sore back wasn't having it so I just spent more time listening to this older couple chat away while I ate cheese and bananas, and drank more tea.

Later I found myself running on the edge of a rainstorm with winds of nearly 30 mph. I felt like I was fighting a battle, forcing all of Caesar's 60 kg along a gravel track on which the wheels kept slipping. On a steep downhill stretch, I let go of him to go for a pee. When I turned back, the wind was shoving him uphill. Step by step, mile by mile, with all my weight leaning into Caesar, I at last made it to a village named Alexander.

———————

Leaving Alexander around 7 a.m., I decided once again to hit secondary roads through farmers' fields. For the first time in days I felt happy, running alone with not a single distraction apart from my footsteps crunching on the dirt track. After 11 miles I was at a Sioux Valley reservation, an area dominated by the Dakota tribe of Native Canadians.

As I neared it, people must have been watching my tracker: I got many messages on Facebook and one in particular read, 'It's a native reserve, Jamie. If I was you, I'd run around it. It's really dangerous.'

I decided to ignore those warnings and keep going. I came upon an enormous tent in someone's garden. It looked ideal for a break. I was anxious as I rapped my fist on the door, as this was the first time I'd been on a reservation. I wasn't sure what they'd make of me. A tall Native Canadian man came to the door, a fierce expression on his face. 'Where are you from?' he asked.

I told him I was a Brit from Gloucester, where everyone chases cheese, breaking their arms and legs in the process.

He still kept a stern look on his face and I started to think about the messages I'd received. Then, he smiled. 'I'm Tony. Take the teepee and feel free to light a fire in there.' He then told me about the history of the teepee and how his ancestors lived in them hundreds of years ago.

'I can't imagine what it might have been like to survive in a tent during winters of –50°C,' I said.

By the time I'd lit a fire, blown up my mat and rolled it out, the whole place was pretty toasty. Teepee engineering was obviously attuned to cold climes. As I lay back on the mat, it deflated under me; I noticed that little hot ashes had spurted out of the fire and made holes in it. It was a hard lesson learned.

Tony's wife, Leaha, came in with an apple and cinnamon tea, which helped to swill down my somewhat dry tinned tuna lunch. I felt drawn to the Native people and their shy, spiritual ways but I had to keep moving, so I thanked the charming couple for allowing me in their teepee and was back on the road.

As the sun faded, it was enthralling to watch the colour of the sky shift from bright blue to brown and then black. I found it a sweet diversion from the tedious plod along the winding gravel roads through acres of meadows.

I found a shed to sleep in but at 2.30 a.m. an old farmer woke me up. I was so out of it that I swore at him for interrupting my rest. 'Hey, son,' he said. 'Why don't you sleep in the house?'

'Oh,' I said. 'Sorry for—'

'Don't worry,' he replied.

After that little exchange I must have fallen asleep again and when my alarm went off at 5 a.m., I was still in the shed. I've been wondering to this day whether the farmer's visit had all been a dream. I put four layers of clothing on, put on the head torch and set off into the moonless gloom. A few miles in and it was still dark but I could see headlights like gold buttons heading in my direction. As they got nearer, I noticed that they were wide and high, and belonged to a truck. The vehicle got to within 30 yards of me and was driving at 80 mph. I yelled at the top of my voice and jumped out of the way with seconds to spare. The adrenaline was too much to handle at 7.30 in the morning.

I sat down and took stock. How undignified would it have been to have died like that at such a late stage of my adventure? It didn't help when I realised that the lights I'd attached to Caesar were switched off, so it was all my fault. After that, I lit myself up like a fireworks display.

As I clocked up the miles, my feet went numb from the cold but luckily for me the Burr family showed up in their SUV. I gratefully got in for a hot cup of tea and to put my feet over the heaters. It felt like a dream to be able to wiggle my toes again.

At mile 15 I came across a few cottages. No one was at home so I stood in the blustery weather, unsure what to do. Further on I could see a church with its door wide open, so I went in and explained who I was to the people there. 'We're sorry there's no heating,' said a teenage girl, 'but you're welcome to stay here, if you like.'

'It's better than freezing to death,' I said, my teeth chattering. Finding protection from the wind in the exposed landscape of the Prairies is more precious than finding money trees. I crouched down and spooned sardines, salmon, nuts and coconut oil into my mouth. Before I went back into the hell outside, another woman in the church handed me $20 for the hospital.

Not long after, I could tell that each time my sole plonked down onto the concrete, more internal damage was being done. Also, I could no longer feel my face, fingers or feet. Trudging in through the front door of the Toders' family home, the warmth got rid of the numbness, but unfortunately the agony in my foot returned.

I chose to stay with the Toders. I spoke with Ed Archer via Skype. 'If you continue running on a damaged foot,' he warned, 'you may injure it long-term and this will affect your future challenges.' After we hung up, I thought, *There he bloody goes again with his 'future challenges'*. All I cared about was getting through this one. As usual, I felt glum because I wasn't out there running, but there was plenty to entertain me at the Toder household for my few days' rest. I referred to it as 'the man pad', as it was home to five men, one of whom was named Chance because he'd nearly died fighting an illness while in a children's hospital. I played computer games and got into play-fights with the lads. The camaraderie was good for my soul and Jolene fed me up like I was her firstborn.

I saw Coral at the CDI Injury Recovery Centre in Moosomin and she told me that I had chronic tendonitis in my foot. I also received reiki treatment by Kim Flannery and LeeAnne from the Virden Oil Capitals ice hockey team. Infuriatingly, the foot didn't improve much but the manager, Lindsey Gullet, gave me the honour of attending a Caps game and 'dropping the puck', which means literally being the VIP who places the puck on the ice at the start of the game. Quite the accolade.

I spoke to kids from Moosomin Elementary, Elkhorn School and Virden Junior High. At Virden I noticed a troubled teen at the back of the room who was trying to get attention from the teachers by repeatedly opening and closing a cupboard door. He was trying to show us all that he didn't want to be there.

I wanted to engage with this boy. He reminded me of myself at that age. I asked if he wanted to be part of a little play I'd devised wherein I get one kid to pretend that he or she is smoking a cigarette and another to pretend that he or she is running. Eventually, the smoker stubs out the fag and joins in the running – it's a fun way to show kids the value of inspiration. 'You can join in,' I said to the kid, 'providing you do it properly.'

'No, I don't want to,' he replied, but in a shocked and surprised tone of voice. At that moment I saw that something had changed in him. He was now resting his hands under his chin and his legs were crossed, watching everything. He sat and focused on me for the rest of the presentation. I hoped that a small seed had been planted in his brain.

The following morning, I sprang out of bed at the 4.30 a.m. alarm and smelled some gorgeous coffee. Jolene and Chance were up to see me off for the 6 a.m. run. 'Jamie,' said Jolene, 'do you know how cold it gets out west? You're going to die, you know!'

'Shhhh will you,' I replied. 'I'll be fine.'

It was time to face the road once again. To set off pain-free was a pleasure, but I doubted it would last. I'd become more accepting of the inevitable deterioration that happens when you push yourself to the extreme. Such resignation is a bigger psychological hurdle than blocking out pain.

Once I reached a warm farmhouse to sleep in, I picked up an email from my dear old mum:

Hi J, I hear your foot is taking over your head, so you need to get mentally strong. Music will help you to do this, it will feed your soul and restore faith in yourself. Think about it, your brain is more powerful than your foot. Don't put too much pressure on yourself – if you feel your foot is too bad then rest it. I don't want you to have permanent damage. The pressure is off, it's stunning what you have already done and if you wanted to stop now we would all be proud of you. If you want to finish, that's great too – either way you have done great. Please keep your chin up J.

Now and then it's nice to have a mum asking you to stop just because she cares. However, I was trying to show people, especially kids, that we can do anything. That meant that the journey would have achieved nothing unless I finished. Also, since my mum has never run a day in her life and smokes a lot of fags, I'm never going to listen to her on this matter, but it was a lovely message all the same and that's what was important.

I reached a huge milestone when I crossed the border between Manitoba and Saskatchewan. I'd smashed six provinces and had three to go. Manitoba will always occupy a special place in my heart – so short, yet so sweet. On every vehicle plate I'd seen it said: FRIENDLY MANITOBA – and that's truer than true. I'd love to go back there someday.

Jolene greeted me at the border and congratulated me on entering the next province. She handed me some beef jerky. 'Happy Hallowe'en,' she said. I'd completely forgotten – but at least I was dressed for the occasion.

One hundred and thirty-five marathons down, only 65 to go.

SASKATCHEWAN

Fleming, a minuscule settlement of 75 people, was 17 miles in. I'd learned from Twitter that the Fleming Windsor Hotel had offered to put me up for the night. When I walked into the bar, it just so happened that the mayor was there, having a beer with his friends. I suppose, with the population being this small, the odds of that happening were pretty good. I joined them for a few Pilsners. Almost everyone in the bar at that time donated cash. A bit tipsy, I said to the mayor, 'What a great start to Saskatchewan!' I wasn't sure whether beer was great for inflammation but, like music, it is good for the soul.

The time difference in the new province caught me out. Before I realised that I could have had an extra hour in bed, the alarm went off at 4 a.m. Both the bitter rain and gale force wind slapped my cheeks, as I used both hands to haul Caesar along, straining my upper body like never before. Since the start of the trip, I'd probably done 1,000 push-ups to try to keep some kind of upper body strength, but the reality was that I was getting weaker, losing my muscle and wasting away. It wasn't just the legs that I needed to get me to Vancouver – it was the whole body.

Gradually, and with each mile, the old pain was setting in. It wasn't fazing me just yet, though. As it got dark, with no signal on my phone, I started to panic because the only directions I'd been given to the farmhouse where I could stay were: 'Take a right after the white fence.' Just as I was about to scream again, Alex the farmer drove onto the highway and signalled to me.

His wife, Brenda, fed me like I was royalty, with pork chops, apple sauce, potatoes and gravy. We had delicious pie for afters, which they called 'impossible pie', but I was so tired I instantly forgot its name and spent the rest of the evening in bed, trying to remember it. As I drifted off, I made my own name up for it: possible pie, because I felt full of possibility.

By the morning, my inflamed right foot was so swollen it wouldn't fit into my trainer, so I grabbed a pair of scissors and made a cut on each side of the shoe, which became too loose. So I found some duct tape and began wrapping it round the shoe to tighten it up, while still leaving enough space to fit my ballooned foot in.

I didn't mention it to the older couple, as I didn't want to worry them. I left the farmhouse after a huge fry-up and ran just over a mile, when I noticed that I couldn't find my phone. I checked Caesar and when I couldn't see it anywhere, I grudgingly hurtled back to the farm, only to find no one at home.

'Alex!' I yelled. 'Brenda! Hello?' I knocked on all the doors and windows several times and finally opted to carry on – I could get the phone later, perhaps with the aid of a Facebook message. Feeling like a maniac, I ran back the way I'd come, muttering to myself, 'How the bloody hell are they not home? They couldn't have even washed the dishes in that time.'

A few miles later, at −10°C, I was rummaging through Caesar for some more hand warmers and… There was my phone! More screams. The great thing about the more remote parts of Canada is that no one can hear you shout.

It was a perfect day for running: pristine cloudless skies, a comfortably warm sun and a vague chill in the air to keep me cool. I found a hut on the edge of the railroad tracks and built a fire to stay warm. As I rested, I looked over my travel visa. For the first time, I noticed that it expired on 30 November and not on 18 December – there was no way I could make that. My knees went weak and my stomach churned. I dug out my phone and called immigration to see what I could do about it. I explained my predicament and the officer sounded baffled. 'We haven't had a situation like this before, but leave it with us and we'll try our best to find a solution.' I couldn't wait for them to call me back.

A chubby security officer loped over to me, saying he'd received some concerned calls about someone in the area who might be an arsonist. I told him about my quest and explained that my fire was purely intended for warming me up. In typical friendly Canadian fashion, the officer didn't have the heart to tell me outright to leave, but I picked up on his troubled body language nonetheless.

'Do you want me to move along?' I asked him.

Like a politician, he wasn't going to give me a yes or no answer. Instead, he warned me of the hazards of being so close to the track. I stamped the fire out and packed my bags, smiling at his tactful approach. As I left, he introduced himself as Ed Bond and gave me $20 to pass on to the Children's Hospital Foundation of Saskatchewan. He was a bit shocked when I hugged him.

I took a back road from Whitewood to Broadview, simply because it would take me off the highway, which was starting to bore me. The tailwind on my back speeded me up, but it couldn't stop the inevitable creep of foot pain.

At mile 10, blobs of watery snow cannoned down from the sky and softened up the dirt track, meaning that I was pushing big, cumbersome Caesar through sludgy sand. At mile 16, the physical exertion added to my lack of sleep the night before made me go a bit delirious but I eventually made the marathon distance.

The following morning, I could not have predicted that I was about to face one of the toughest runs of my life. I downed a litre of lukewarm water, three cups of coffee and two bowls of corn pops, then did some stretches, and added feet warmers and hand warmers to my usual outfit. It was still dark as I set off at 7 a.m. – another sign of the impending winter season. After a few miles on the open highway, white fragments of ice were flying into my eyes. Was it snowing lightly or was the breeze dislodging frost from the road? Whatever it was, I was far from comfortable. As the headwind blew stronger, the road got whiter and my face began to freeze. I could barely keep my eyes open, and having eyes that work is kind of essential to running. I placed a balaclava over my head, remembering the Canadian who'd given it to me saying, 'You're gonna need that out west.' I put my ski mask on to protect my eyes and I found watching the bits of ice pinging off the lenses as I trudged on to be almost hypnotic.

By mile 4, I'd tucked my head down to try to make myself as streamlined as possible, but Caesar was getting more and more sluggish. Although I never checked the weather, it was clear to me I was in a storm. Everything was white. I couldn't see more than 20 yards in front of me. Although my running shoes were parcelled up in duct tape, the cold found its way in, numbing my feet like lumps of meat in a fridge. The feet warmers were useless in these climes: my hands were *almost* warm, but I couldn't seem to cover up the gaps between the sleeves of my jacket and the gloves.

Needing a pee, which was always problematic while wearing the Flash outfit, was even more difficult in these conditions.

I took my right glove off and immediately knew it had been a bad mistake. Once I'd 'made my deposit', I was unable to get the glove back on. For some reason, it just wasn't going to fit and I lost all sensation in my hands – they were frozen stiff. I could feel the frostbite setting into the fingers. Worse than that, I could feel the rest of my extremities going numb, probably because I'd paused for too long in the cold.

I tried to flag down every car that came past, but the drivers would smile, wave back and drive on. Were they crazy? Did they really think I was having a joyful time in this –5°C snowstorm? Possibly risking my life, I shuffled right into the middle of the highway to try to stop cars on either side. My hands were taking the full brunt and I knew I didn't have too long left. At last, a man called Brian Urschel pulled over and gave me a whole hour in his car to bring my fingers and toes back to life.

Soon after Sheri, Jolene's friend, appeared in a BMW with a big bag full of Oreo cookies. I knew I ought to stay away from sugar, but this would give me the energy for the next 8 miles before the inevitable sugar crash. I wolfed all 12 biscuits as if I were taking part in an eating competition.

Brian joined me in the mayhem for the last 6 miles. The snow stopped, but the 70 mph wind didn't. We formed a strong partnership quickly: one would push Caesar, taking the brunt of the headwind, while the other ran behind, slipstreaming to build up energy and later on take over at the helm. We developed this strategy without a word being exchanged – we were two single-minded men on a mission, striving to get the job done. Brian squeezed out words through his face mask, which I could only faintly hear amid the howling winds, 'With the wind chill, it's probably more like −20°C right now. Welcome to the Prairies!' Every half mile, my arms would start to give way, and Brian would pat me on the back and relieve me. After a similar distance, I'd notice Brian's back bending forward, which I took to be a sign for me to pat him and, in turn, take over Caesar. Near the end of the run, my tender tendons were seriously holding me back and Brian took the reins for the last stretch.

In the morning, I got an email from immigration:

Mr McDonald, unfortunately you cannot extend your Working Holiday Visa. However, you may apply for a Visitor's Visa before the expiry date of your current visa (November 30th). You will then have implied status and can continue doing what you have been doing to complete your journey. We wish you all the best.

'Who is the man!' I whooped. 'The dream is still well and truly alive!' I couldn't get complacent, though – I'd only bought myself a few days. A cruel Canadian winter in the Rockies – my next destination – could still mean I wouldn't get back to my family for Christmas.

I cracked on to finish off the rest of the run in one go and, while doing so, I noticed something different within myself. It was a sensation I'd felt on my cycling adventure, but had not yet experienced on this one: loneliness. It was funny to be meeting so many people but still having an emotional gap that couldn't be filled. Beer, close mates, a few giggles – this was what I was missing.

Jenna Parker, a massage therapist from Wolseley, and her husband Dion met me at a motel and kindly paid for my stay. Jenna also gave me a first-rate massage, breaking up as much scar tissue in my foot as she could. As she got to work on me, I got depressed about the food I'd dumped in my room. I really didn't fancy more nuts and tinned fish.

'Do you fancy having supper?' asked Jenna. She must have read my mind. 'It's my two-year-old's birthday party tomorrow. There'll be plenty of steak.' How could I turn down the opportunity to eat meat and cake, sing with nippers and watch some of the funniest attempts at armpit farts I'd seen since I was a toddler? All of this cheered me up enough to motivate me for another day's running.

After the now familiar cycle of feeling my limbs freeze and then finding different methods of thawing them out, I put on a tune that I knew would get me through to the end of the day: 'I Heard It Through The Grapevine' by Marvin Gaye. This Motown classic got me singing and shaking my bottom as I made my way along the prairie.

Soon I realised that my watch had been a kind of cold conductor, so I took it off my wrist and attached it to Caesar. As I ran, I checked it every so often to get a feel for how freezing it actually was. It read −5°C and then, a mile later, −9°C. I swore it was colder than that, but I trudged on, reminding myself that I'd already handled far chillier conditions.

For the first time in the Prairies there was absolutely no wind, just an eerie curtain of pallid fog hanging over me, as I made my way. I had my ski mask on, which was slightly tinted, and I could barely see anything that was 10 yards ahead.

I looked down at my watch once more and it read: −18°C. The wind chill factor had no role in this. 'What the hell am I doing?' I shouted. An hour later, I had so much ice clinging to me that it was like I'd added an extra layer of clothing. My feet felt like they had ice blocks strapped to them, making my trainers, duct tape and feet warmers utterly useless.

With the fog thickening, I waved my head torch at all the oncoming vehicles just to make sure that they could see me along the highway. Getting run over would not help me to get to Vancouver on time.

I reached Sintaluta, a remote village of just 98 people. I went into a Co-op food store and discovered they had no heating inside. A clerk gave me a stool to sit on so I could try to manually warm up my feet. I took my shoes off and rubbed them with my hands, but I couldn't even feel them. Once back on the road, Sheri showed up on the fringe of the highway. Feeling fairly deflated, I climbed into her car to get out of the freezing cold. Sheri looked at me and said, 'Jamie, I'm not supposed to tell you this because Jolene knows that you want to do this alone, but you're going to be all right for the rest of the run.' I must have given her an incredulous look because she replied, 'Yes, Jamie. Jolene has started a secret Facebook group and the number of moms that are on it is growing fast. We're all going to network and call ahead of you in the towns you're running to get people involved so that you get food and shelter.' I thought back to Jolene's words before I left her house: 'You won't survive a Canadian winter; you're going to die, Jamie.' My face must have looked perkier. Sheri said with a huge smirk on her face, 'Jamie, the Facebook group is called Stalking Mamma Bears.'

Sheri had picked me up some Tim Hortons chilli, and a bit of spice was exactly what I needed to keep me going. I took my socks off and placed them on the heaters in the car to thaw them out a tad. Sheri presented me with some new Ski-doo gloves that managed to keep my fingers toasty when I was back on the road.

Now the sun was out, I tried to squeeze some sunblock out on my massive schnoz (it always seems to soak up the rays the most), but it was frozen. Sheri drove along with me, acting as my 'warm-up escort'. Every 3 miles or so, I would get into her car and inject some life back into my extremities. 'I just can't see you get cold again like that,' she said.

———————

In the morning I received messages telling me that the Children's Hospital Foundation of Saskatchewan was in the process of being built. I was surprised that this province didn't already have its own children's hospital and was extra-motivated to raise as much cash as possible. We'd raised over $10,000 for Manitoba in less than a fortnight – I wanted to do the same for Saskatchewan.

The road was so icy it was like running across a hockey pitch. If I was going to make it to Regina, I'd have to run 28 miles in a day, which was going to be no mean feat given my chronic tendonitis. The promise of a rest for a few days egged me on, though.

For a few of those miles I was distracted by a phone interview with Claire Carter of BBC Radio Gloucestershire. It felt pretty cool to be racing down a Canadian highway while all my mates 4,000 miles away in Gloucester were listening. I can't put into words how much pride I felt, knowing that my hometown was behind me.

As the miles accumulated, so did the cars that parked up beside me. A lot of the drivers had seen the CTV news clip which showed my running shoes being held together by duct tape because they were in such bad shape. One motorist said, 'Here, split the money between you and the cause – get yourself a new pair of running shoes, for God's sake.'

'Thank you,' I replied, taking the money. 'I really appreciate the offer, but I'll be giving it all to the new hospital that's being built.'

'Well,' he said. 'I guess you're right but I still think you need some new sneakers.'

I thought – but didn't say – that, whichever way you look at it, a hospital is more important than a pair of shoes.

By mile 8 I was tired earlier than usual. A Native Canadian couple stopped on the busy highway. We held hands while they spoke in their own language, with eyes closed, in a delicate and rhythmic tone. I had no idea what they were saying, but it was beautiful. They handed me some 'sweet grass' – a healing medicine, nothing illegal! – and a $50 note for the hospital. 'You're going to make it,' said the woman.

'I hope so,' I winced, my foot playing up again. 'I'm going through hell.'

The Native man took off his puffy jacket and placed it over me. 'Keep warm,' he instructed sternly. Again, I was reminded of the time I almost starved on my cycle ride in Tajikistan, before being taken in by that desperately poor family who gave me more or less their only possession in the world: a loaf of bread.

I ran on to the Diner restaurant in Balgonie, a spacious and quiet town. The manager took care of the bill and all the punters donated to the hospital. One lady in her sixties came to ask for an autograph and an excited social media supporter, Elodie, showed up in a Saskatchewan Roughriders football team kit. 'Jamie, you're invited to the game on Monday. The CEO, Jim Hopson, personally wants you to come.'

'Wow, that sounds amazing,' I swooned. It was a bit like Alex Ferguson inviting someone to see a Manchester United match. As it was Friday already, I knew I'd better get a shift on if I was to make it to Regina for Monday.

She pulled out a tin of green paint, green gloves and green boxer shorts.

'What's all that in aid of?'

'Green is the team colour. It'd be great if you could be green too, while you make your way to the game.'

On the highway I must have looked like a flying Christmas tree. I got plenty of toots for that. At mile 15, I grew dizzy, as the pain surged through every inch of my body. It was like being struck down with flu. Elodie showed up in her car as dusk fell and she could see how far I had deteriorated in the space of just a few hours. She insisted on being my escort into Regina. I plodded along in front of her car while she drove behind me with her headlights on.

At mile 20 the headwind was up to 25 mph, and I had a crisis of confidence. 'I'm not gonna bloody make this,' I said over my shoulder to Elodie, but she couldn't hear me. Why was I so down? I'd previously easily run 35 miles so why today, of all days, was I done for at mile 20? I jumped into Elodie's parked car. I said nothing – I didn't need to. 'Shall I get you a hotel? There's one right on that street, right there!' That was certainly near and it would have meant no more running for the day, but I got out, determined to push on a bit longer and reach her apartment. I kept telling myself, 'I've done this a million times before... Just keep moving! It's only a few more miles.' I squeezed out another 2 miles in −7°C before getting back into the car.

My entire body was screaming at me to stop but a few minutes later I got back on the road. I have no idea how I managed another 2 miles, but I did. I then got back inside Elodie's car and she suggested eating something. I felt so sick that the very thought of food made me want to puke. Elodie was trying every ploy she could to get me to eat. 'Here's a banana. Some chocolate? Come on, Jamie, you need to eat *something*.' But I just couldn't face it. I asked her to turn up the music. Elton John blared out of the speakers. 'I'm still standing. Yeah, yeah, yeah.' Elton was the man to get me back out there to face more miles.

I hit the streets of Regina, ramping Caesar up every curb and causing even more agony to my arms. My mind was just telling me, 'No more, please no more.' I looked down at my phone to see a load of supportive tweets, including those from Gloucester rugby players Shane Monahan and Jimmy Cowan.

With 2 miles left, Elodie asked if I was hungry again. 'Anything and it's yours.'

I still felt awful, but I knew I needed something. 'All I want is meat that drips with fat.'

Her reply was instant. 'I have just the place: Tony Roma's, famous for their ribs.'

I got out of the car again but I had nothing left. Voices in my head shouted, 'This is too much suffering for one human.' I screamed for the remaining couple of miles until I made it to Elodie's apartment. That was my limit.

I lay crumpled on Elodie's sofa, wrapped up in a heated blanket while I slowly ate racks of ribs. 'That was like running two marathons in one go,' I mumbled. 'I must be ill.'

'You could be ill,' said Elodie, 'or it might be something to do with the fact that you're running across the second largest (and most probably coldest I might add!) country in the world.' She looked on my Facebook page and read out a note that Michael Bennett had left on my wall:

I have been following your progress since your arrival in Kenora, Ontario. I was one of the runners that escorted you from the eastern

outskirts of Winnipeg to The Forks located next to the Canadian Museum of Human Rights. As our little delegation of runners stood next to this gorgeous museum, I considered the connection between your vision and that of the CMHR.

If the CMHR represents a beacon of hope for all humanity then you, my friend, are surely the flame that ignites that beacon. It's the beacon that builds community and opens hearts and minds to the concept of goodness on a micro-scale. To change the world takes one painful step at a time. To believe that each step, each mile, each day brings you closer to your dream of goodness inspires us. You, the Flash, superhero that you are, have come to represent the flame... and we do not have words to express our gratitude.

Jamie, this is what I promise you: when you reach the Pacific Coast – and you surely will – I will run silently to the statue of Mahatma Gandhi at the foot of the Canadian Museum of Human Rights. I will pause and I will think of you and what you have accomplished. I will think of goodness and hope. I will think of flames and beacons and superheroes. Then, my friend, I will drape a Flash cape over Gandhi's head and tie it snugly. This small gesture is to honour you, Jamie. You see, Gandhi was another individual that ignited the flame of hope, the beacon.

After Maggie Pearce left a $500 gift card with the Running Room in Regina, I bought warmer gear and new trainers. I told Maggie how much I appreciated her help, but also how guilty I felt for spending it because this journey was all about giving. Anyway, I now had Gore-Tex runners that were more waterproof – and, more importantly, windproof – than my old shoes. I bought heated insoles that came with a remote control to set the level of warmth I desired. I wondered if James Bond himself ever had kit this cool. That said, I was anxious in case my feet might sweat, which could be disastrous because sweat freezes. It can get a little chilly 'downstairs' too, so the guys at the Running Room included some essential windproof boxer shorts. A shop named Cabela's supplied a new insulated sleeping mat that would reflect the heat when I camped outside.

I was soon bored of shopping – it's not my thing – so I was happy to move on.

I then spoke to Garret Woynarski, a massage therapist, over the phone and my intuition told me that he would be the man to aid my recovery. 'If you want to fix this injury,' he said, 'you have to take a holistic view. The nerve tissue that stimulates the muscles, tendons and ligaments in the foot can get as irritated as the muscle itself. With neurofunctional electroacupuncture we can calm the excessively irritated nerve tissue at the hip and in the ankle to relieve the nervous system hyperactivity, calm the pain sensors and relax the muscle tissue.'

'Okey-dokey, Garret,' I said. I had no idea what he was talking about, but he sounded like he knew what he was doing.

I agreed to three sessions of Gua Sha – a tool-like instrument used to scrape the muscle tissue at the bottom of my foot – to find out whether my scar tissue was being disrupted. If the procedure is successful, the muscle fibres are realigned, blood flows more easily and inflammation is reduced. Lying on Garret's massage table, it was so soothing just listening to him speak – his voice is so calm and smooth. I started to talk about the pressure I was under.

'There are two different kinds of people in this world,' Garret said, as he got to work on me, 'the "planners" and the "naive". When the planners go food shopping, they make a list, take the shortest route, buy everything they need and make it back home stress-free. The naive don't make a list, get lost and don't find everything they need; the journey takes longer and it's more stressful, but they eventually get the job done. See, Jamie, you're the naive type. The planner will continue to plan to stage one, two, three, even eight, but when they reach stage 12, they get scared. That fear stops them from pushing out of their comfort zone. The naive person hasn't thought about steps two or three, let alone step 12. This short-term vision approach allows you to live your heart's passion and take unimaginable steps.'

He placed his hands over my body, looking for areas of treatment. 'The knots in your stomach are validation that you're still human. We all have a fear of change, be it starting a new journey or continuing on one. As we accumulate years, we reflect on the moments of change throughout our lives. If we are in tune with our intuition, we will recall that all change is preceded by huge knots in our stomach. Herein lies life wisdom. Ask yourself how you would feel if the person next to you had the exact same knots in their stomach and they continued on, but you didn't.'

Those words really struck a chord and I reflected on them for a long while after I left Garret.

I spent the afternoon glued to the computer, trying to sort out the online visa extension. Immigration don't make it easy – it's like they don't want you to get one – but I shouldn't have been so naive to think it would be simple. I didn't get it done, but I felt another few steps closer to knowing how to sort it out.

At 5 p.m., when the sun started to go down, I began packing. It was late in the day, but I needed to continue running to maintain my progress. I hit a back country road which was leading to my next destination, Grand Coulee, where a family were waiting for me. I noticed something new about my feet: even in the rain at –1°C they were warm, which was a first. My new socks and Gore-Tex trainers had passed their first test easily. By mile 6, Elodie appeared and drove the route I was on to ensure that it was clear.

Looking out of the window from inside the warm cabin, all I could see was white snow: the trees were white, the houses were white – if Batman himself were outside, he would have been completely white too. I've visited many countries and I can honestly say I've never in my life seen anything like I did that day. As the snow fell, I kept thinking that there should be more noise but the surroundings were silent, or rather eerie.

As I neared 7 miles, the foot was giving me grief again – Garret's physio didn't work, but his story did help. At Pense,

I was pleased to meet Chad, a keen runner and Facebook follower. He invited me back to his to warm up and eat turkey soup for lunch. His two daughters, seven and nine years old, started watching my YouTube videos in front of me and I had to laugh when I saw them laughing at my tomfoolery. Both of them donated their wages, earned for walking dogs, and Kolbi, the younger one, pulled out an extra $5. 'Here, Jamie, this is my tooth fairy money.'

Chad wanted to run with me to the next town of Belle Plaine, 9 miles away. 'We're on the highway,' he said. 'The conditions are pretty bad out there, so having a tail will help other trucks and cars see that we're out there.'

I called Elodie and she agreed to be our escort again. The snow continued to fall, making the Prairies look like something out of a fairy tale. Chad demanded to push Caesar and made it look easy; he must have had a lot of upper body power. We clocked up a few miles more quickly than usual thanks to the wind on our backs.

We passed a truck apparently crashed off-road and Chad didn't bat an eyelid, as if it were an everyday occurrence. 'Touch the road, Jamie,' he said.

I thought it an odd suggestion, but did as he asked. It wasn't like touching a regular road at all – this was as slippery as a sheet of glass and smoother than an ice rink. 'How do tyres grip on to this?' I asked Chad.

'They don't,' he frowned. 'That's why you get *that* happening.' He pointed to the crashed truck. When we had a break in Elodie's car, I was apprehensive about another vehicle sliding into us.

I'm a man of odds. Every time I'm up against it, I ask myself: what are the odds? I remember being scared silly of sharks while swimming in the Great Barrier Reef. I drew a breath and asked myself the same question. The fear soon evaporated. I can overcome any obstacle so long as I imagine – and come to terms with – the worst-case scenario. Now, I was aware that getting smashed up by a car was unlikely to happen, but I *had* nearly been hit twice on this trip, so I knew it was possible. Twice in 200 days is a 1 per cent chance. With the kinds of conditions I was running in that day, I was sure the odds would dramatically increase, easily to 2 or 3 per cent. But it was still only a tiny percentage – you have to keep these things in perspective.

I continued to face the traffic so I could see the cars and trucks coming. I was ready as I'd ever been to make a giant leap off the highway should a vehicle fail to spot us.

Chad was a screamer too. As we passed signs and other milestones, he'd let rip and that would have a knock-on effect and have me screaming too. It was always good to release some testosterone and alleviate the fear of being hit by a truck. We finished up and had a beer in Chubby's Bar. The Saskatchewan special is Pilsner, which I love. It went down easier than water. A young red-haired and red-cheeked woman came over to me. I could smell the booze on her breath. 'I've seen you on the TV!' she cried. 'I *love* what you are doing for our children.' She made such a scene that the whole bar heard what she was saying and gave me cash for the charity. One beer turned into a $250 donation to the Children's Hospital Foundation of Saskatchewan.

Elodie found a couple called Bruce and Diane Wight in her phone book and rang them to see if they'd put me up. They were more than willing. Di made possibly the best lasagne I have ever tasted in my life. With a seriously full stomach and lack of motivation after a tough day, I still managed to do strength training, practise some yoga and blog before hitting the sack.

After my five hours' sleep, I got back to running and was thrilled to find that the trusty snowploughs had cleared the highway well. I had to move onto the road because the snow was too deep on the hard shoulder. My technique changed to a sort of shuffle wherein each time my foot landed, it would slide a few inches. It was a surprisingly efficient approach that resulted in less impact on my feet. I 'did the shuffle' for a good 6 miles.

A police car parked in front of me, lights flashing. The window rolled down and a bearded mouth said, 'Don't worry, son, you're not in trouble.' I must have had that expression on my face that said, *It wasn't me!* He added, 'We've received over one hundred phone calls from people who said they'd seen a guy running on the highway, in a snowstorm, with a baby.' He demanded to look inside my pram only to find that there was no infant. I told him what was really in there and we both had to chuckle.

'OK, Jamie, I think facing the traffic like you are is a wise idea. Thank you for what you're doing, best of luck and be safe.' A few more slides, a few more miles and I really wanted to capture the icy road for posterity. I set up the camera and filmed myself as I took a run-up and did a massive slide. As I came to the end of it, I lost my footing and fell onto my arse. If I hadn't been holding onto Caesar, I'd have cracked my head open or broken my neck. That was enough larking about for one day.

At the midpoint of the run that day, Elodie turned up with two Tim Hortons chilli pots and cans of coconut water, which had become without a doubt my new favourite drink. It does the same job as water, but it also has super powerful nutrients and a sweet taste. 'If you need anything, Jamie,' said Elodie, 'I'm a phone call away. I mean *anything*.'

A short while later the same police officer was back. 'Sorry, Jamie, we've had so many phone calls since the last time we spoke regarding your safety.'

'What? I'm fine. I'm facing the traffic, as you agreed I should. I know it's icy, but if there are cars taking up both lanes, I move right out of the way. Anyway, it's usually only one lane being used so there's plenty of space for both of us.'

He nodded. 'I understand, Jamie, but people out here are really worried for your safety, so I'm going to escort you into Moose Jaw.'

The officer put on his flashing lights – very appropriate for my Flash suit. I attracted a lot more attention than before, which prompted motorists to give me 'drive-by' donations out of their car windows. By mile 12, though, my tendonitis went chronic. Adam Pasquet, who'd been following on Facebook, showed up in a car to accompany me into Moose Jaw. This was the first time I'd had two vehicle escorts – I felt like the Prime Minister of Canada himself!

I gritted my teeth as we came up to mile 15. The pain was getting unbearable, but I knew treatment awaited me if I pushed on. I looked over my shoulder, behind Adam's car, and saw that the police car was still tailing. 'Canada has my back,' I said confidently. At mile 16, I tried my shuffle technique again but this time, for some reason, it only exacerbated the pain.

'Jamie,' Adam shouted over to me. 'Would you like me to push Caesar for the last mile?'

'No, I'm all right, thanks.'

'Come on, man,' he insisted, more firmly. 'You're only ever running here once. Let me do it with you cos I want to push Caesar.'

'If you insist, Adam. Get out here then and take the strain!'

Adam took me straight to his workplace, the Turtle Island Health and Wellness Centre. He and therapist Rebecca Parker gave me a much-needed massage. I drifted in and out of consciousness for a full hour while four hands rubbed me down.

I ran out of Moose Jaw the next day, with Adam still driving behind me. The roads were so slippery I had to shuffle carefully along the backstreets until I got to the highway. In –15°C the tailwind was at my back and the sun was starting to come out. The cold didn't bother me much; maybe I was getting used to the temperatures – or more experienced at dressing myself properly.

Everything started to thaw out. I'd been running in my Gore-Tex shoes but they had become stiff and hard on my feet, so I decided to switch over to my regular road running trainers. I no longer had to keep my balance on the snow and the runners felt so lovely – it was like putting on a pair of slippers.

At Caronport, Yvonne, another Facebook supporter, greeted me. She said she hadn't been expecting to see me so soon at her house and she wanted her kids to be able to run with me.

'Bring them out of the house right now,' I said, 'and we can do a lap around the block.'

'You sure, Jamie? You must be so tired.'

With approximately 40 marathons left to go, it was kind of a celebratory victory lap for having come this far. At any rate, what was an extra half mile on top of 5,000?

Two of Yvonne's children, Drake and Ethan – as well as the latter's seizure response dog, Texas – came out to run with me. When we started on our lap, I asked Ethan about his dog. 'I have epilepsy; it kind of sucks.'

'I know what you mean, I had epilepsy too.' This little exchange brought back all the unhappy memories from my childhood. I recalled lying in bed, sneakily putting the TV on – as kids do – and making my mum panic because of the noise. She'd come rushing in, terrified that I was having a seizure. Obviously, I don't remember any of my episodes, but I can still picture the bad, twisted never-ending dreams and the pure exhaustion when I came back round. 'I can't believe you have a cool dog,' I said to Ethan as we finished the lap.

'Yeah, I know I do.'

I wasn't allowed to pet Texas because he wasn't permitted to receive any love from anyone else. All of his attention had to be on Ethan at all times.

Back at the house, we ate a succulent beef dinner and I had an uplifting chat with my dad over the phone. 'I've given this some thought, for quite some time...' He paused.

'What, Dad? Don't leave me hanging.'

'I really want to come to Canada and see you finish the journey.' I didn't jump for joy, but deep inside I felt a pang of pride. If I could make it to the end of this wild adventure, having my dad at the finish would be the stuff of dreams.

Sadly, my mum would not be coming, as she was looking after three foster children.

Yvonne served me a very special breakfast, labelled 'home-made holy crap cereal'. It comprised the good stuff: chia seeds, nuts and whatever else holy crap cereal contains. Ethan skipped school because he wanted to run with me. Any mum who grants their kid the day off school to do something crazy like that is one cool mum. Yvonne tailed us while Ethan and I hit the highway. She kept trying to drive slightly in front of us, in order to block the 20 mph wind.

A few miles in, Ethan became really inquisitive, asking question after question. One of them was, 'If you could actually be a superhero, which one would you be?'

I didn't want to be the Flash because that meant I'd have to continue to use my legs and we all know they're buggered! 'Superman,' I said, 'because he can fly. Now my turn to ask a question. If you were to be a superstar for a day, who would you be?'

He thought about it. 'Well, I wouldn't want to be a celebrity because they seem to make bad decisions. I'd like to be an athlete – they really inspire people.' Wise kid.

Yvonne and Ethan drove ahead to the next town, Mortlach, to try to get me a room somewhere. In the meantime, I tackled the frozen hard shoulder using one of the two-way lanes, while big trucks and cars whizzed past. The force of the wind was so strong that I'd often put my elbows on Caesar to take the strain off my arms. This way I could make my body go lower and tuck in behind my chariot to avoid the wind.

Every hour Yvonne would pull in with soups, beef sandwiches and cups of tea to fortify me for the next battle with the elements. At mile 7, Ethan got out of the car to do another mile with me. By now, the wind was so powerful that lumps of snow were blowing across the terrain. On the final stretch into Mortlach, the duct tape (which I was still putting on my new shoes as it was such a good windshield) peeled off my runners and the feeling in my toes was dead within seconds.

I stopped in the Country Garden Cafe, which was awaiting my arrival. It just so happened that it was British fish and chips night. I murdered a fish supper as well as a large piece of chocolate cake. The owner, Shannon, told me they'd organised a raffle whose proceeds were going to the Children's Hospital Foundation of Saskatchewan. She then said, 'Come for your free breakfast in the morning and at the same time collect the donation.' You have to love these small, good-hearted Canadian communities.

Over breakfast, most of the locals told me I must be mad running in wintertime. I said nothing back but thought, *If everything went according to the schedule I'd planned at the start, I'd be on the home stretch running into Vancouver right now*. But, as I'd figured out on this trip, I wasn't a natural planner: I was a naive idiot.

Everyone waved as I headed out into the coldest temperature so far: −28°C. This was no longer a run, it was an Arctic expedition. The first 2 miles were comfortable – thanks mostly to my fancy heated insoles – but my nose was starting to tingle, and not in a pleasant way. Although I had my balaclava on, the wind was biting through the pin-sized breathing holes. I put on another balaclava over that one. While my face got warmer – especially my nose – breathing through two layers of material, with fewer holes, was demanding. I tried to run as rhythmically as possible, but this wasn't easy given that the terrain of the hard shoulder would, every few yards, switch from rigid ice to slushy snow.

A guy pulled over to offer me a bed at his house 10 miles away. I wanted to run further than that. 'Thank you for the offer,' I said, 'but I have to push myself extra today.'

'There's absolutely nothing past my house,' he protested.

I was feeling almost Zen-like. 'That's OK, I'll keep running and it will work out.'

'What do you mean it will work out? It's −30°C outside.'

'It will work out... It always does.'

The trucks kept blowing me back as I tried to press on. A slight gap between my balaclava and my collar gave me the sensation of a knife slicing my neck. A guy named Denny turned up at the 10-mile mark, offering me his friend's camper van for the night. As much as I wanted to finish after 10 miles, I knew I had no choice but to continue. *Something always comes up, it always works out*, I thought. Denny produced some hot soup. I thought my sandwiches would go well with it, so I grabbed them out of Caesar, but they were frozen. I dipped them in the soup to shake off the ice and shoved them into my mouth. The bread was soft but the mustard, ham, cheese and butter were rock-hard. I still ate them.

I ran on, the wind blowing shafts of thick snow across the road and onto the hard shoulder. The sun went down at 5 p.m.: winter was biting and the days were getting shorter. However, one of the most brutal environments in the world during sunset turned out to be aesthetically pleasing – it's heaven amid hell. I could see snow-capped hills – a first for me in these flatlands – turning orange so that they looked like Egyptian sand dunes. As I moved, the orange morphed into magical reds, greys and purples.

I decided that, for my safety, I'd start running with the flow of traffic. Elodie came back to tail me with her hazard lights on. I started to feel guilty – not only was I putting myself at risk by running in the dark on the icy, blustery highway, but now Elodie was too. Gargantuan trucks were flying past at breakneck speed. At one point, she honked her horn to warn me to move in lest a truck plough straight through me. The thought of putting Elodie at risk persuaded me to run harder. I scaled a steep hill, which made everything hurt. My tendonitis pains were coming in five-minute surges, forcing me to bite down hard on the inside of my balaclava and go even faster. I needed to get myself and Elodie off this bloody road.

I was convinced that I'd run the remaining mile, so why were we not there yet? I jogged back to Elodie and asked her the same question, the anger boiling in my ears and cheeks. 'How long to go? How long, Elodie?' I was sweating so hard that I couldn't slow down; I had to keep going fast enough to keep my blood pumping and stay warm, as I didn't want my clothes to freeze. We finally made it to the farmhouse's driveway. I conquered a series of steep inclines by taking baby steps and forcing all my weight onto Caesar.

We were welcomed into a cosy room by a farmer called John. I was disappointed to have covered only 18 miles that day, 8 short of a marathon. Elodie checked her phone for the weather forecast. 'Jamie, can you guess what the temperature is out there right now?'

'Hit me.'

'It's −35°C. You were running in that!'

The frostbite had made the tip of my nose brown and scabby. I don't like frostbite one bit. I'm not vain or anything, but I really like my schnoz and I want to keep it.

Before I left, John's wife, Rhonda, insisted that I feed the cows.

'Don't cows feed themselves?' I queried.

'Did you forget about the snow outside?'

I hopped into a tractor and sat next to John. The cows must have known that we had hay with us because they followed us everywhere we drove. It was like the Pied Piper at work. I always think of farmers as 'wise men', since they spend so much time alone, thinking. I asked John about his future plans.

'We're not expanding our farm cos bigger ain't always better. We all need to grasp the difference between greed and need.

We're losing connections with people cos of that greed, losing that community sense. Once everyone got TVs, they stopped visiting each other.' To an extent he was right. I spent nearly a year cycling in countries where most of the population couldn't even afford TVs. The poorest places seem to have the strongest communities. I watched the cows huddle to keep each other warm while they ate the hay. They too had a sense of community.

It was time to get back to my adventure. Some social media supporters who'd read about my nasal frostbite brought with them a hockey helmet that was meant to protect the entire face. Unfortunately, it didn't fit my head. At any rate, wearing a hockey helmet *as well* as the Flash outfit might have looked too ridiculous, even for me.

More seriously, my nose was constantly cold – even when I was warm indoors. This was not a good sign. I cut the nosepiece off the hockey helmet and taped it onto my ski goggles. I hoped it would block the –30°C wind chill.

I noticed a sign that said: MOOSE JAW 52 MILES. 'Look Jamie,' I said to myself, 'look how far you've come in a few days.' It's always hard to reflect back and appreciate what you have achieved when you're always driving forwards towards a goal.

At mile 12, nothing mattered. High on endorphins, I continued to plod out the remainder of the stretch, almost pain-free. The basement of the next farmhouse I stayed in housed a wonderful surprise: a diving board, a slide and a huge swimming pool. Yvonne and her children drove out so the family and I all jumped in. I wrestled playfully with Emmett, the youngest kid. His brother Ethan shouted over, 'Jamie, check this out!' and leaped off the diving board. He had such vim and confidence that I imagined him running across Canada some day. Drake, another brother, doggy-paddled up to me. 'This is the best day of my life,' he beamed.

For the first night in months, I opted for a full eight-hour sleep. It wasn't easy to wake up from that, but I felt more healed than usual. Ron, the farmer, and his wife Brenda gave me everything I needed for the morning: plenty of coffee and even more meat. It was a humongous amount of food, a breakfast of farmers more than a breakfast of champions. 'If you leave here hungry,' said Ron as I made my way outside, 'it's your own fault, kid.'

Although it was around −25°C, I have to say that the going was good. The sun was blazing down at me, which solved the major problem I'd been having lately: fighting off the cold. Moreover, there was no wind. I was waiting to see a pig fly past.

A few miles in, a car pulled over and it was Yvonne and the kids – they were back for one last show. Everyone got out to run at least a mile to demonstrate their support. Yvonne also dropped a huge surprise on me. 'We were planning a winter holiday to see our favourite NHL hockey team, Edmonton Oilers, play the Arizona Coyotes, but now we're going to Vancouver to see you finish.' We had a huge group hug – it wasn't a 'goodbye'; it was a 'see ya later'. Now I was assured that people – including my beloved dad – would be at the finish line, I really hoped I could make it to Vancouver.

As they drove off, I realised that theirs was going to be the last vehicle I could warm up in for some time. I still had 11 miles to go. My focus was less on my body than on my face. The ski goggles kept steaming up on the inside. Every time I exhaled, the hot air hitting –25°C turned into liquid, making everything wet. I took the goggles off, pulled down my woolly hat as far as it would go and wrapped my scarf around the front of my face, leaving just my eyes and the bridge of my nose open. It was the best I could do.

As the sun vanished at mile 13, the cold reached a whole new level. I watched in awe as the tips of my hair froze and my fringe bounced around, poking my eyeballs as I ran. Yet again, my nose was taking a battering in the cold. I was scared of the oncoming cars in the dark, so I put the pedal to the metal, as it were. I ran my heart out, knowing that there was a bar and a bed up ahead in a town named Morse. I didn't stop until I reached it.

I sank a Pilsner and ripped apart some spare ribs while a guitarist played Johnny Cash in the background. Pat Bakus took care of my bill and prepared a blow-up bed at the community hall. She even left out some fruit for a midnight snack.

From the community hall I headed straight over to Morse Cafe to demolish a stack of pancakes and to speak to anyone who wanted to listen to my adventures in their fine country so far.

These days, the first few miles of my runs were always enjoyable. I was no longer waking up stiff. My legs stayed fresher for longer and the more movement I did, the more mental pressure about the expectation of finishing was released. The wind was surprisingly faint again and the sun was shining brightly.

I heard a loud reversing noise behind me. It was Denny again. 'Do you wanna get in?'

I sat with him for a bit and then got out. 'Will I see you again?' I asked.

'Damn straight. I'm staying here with you until you find a place to sleep.'

'Denny, you really don't have to. I'll be fine out here.'

'I know, but I don't have anything better to do.'

We laughed and shook hands. 'OK, Denny.'

At mile 15, I spotted a few hills in the distance.

'Give me your camera,' said Denny. 'I'll film you here. These are the foothills of the Rocky Mountains.' I didn't know how to react. Was I happy that I was nearly at the Rockies? Did that mean the flat terrain was over for good? What I did know for sure was that I was frightened of the Rockies.

The wind howled and battered Caesar, as we struggled our way uphill. Pushing that big chariot had never felt natural and never would be. I got into Denny's car to warm up and, even though I needed another break with 3 miles to go, I wanted to get the job done before it was dark.

We were greeted by Richele at the community hall by Rush Lake. She handed me coffee and showed me to a portable bed.

Next to it was a lamp – a really nice thought. A large hall had been converted into a cosy and homely room.

Denny stayed with me for a beer to celebrate the end of the day, while Richele brought over two home-made beef meals, complete with lots of mashed potato. Denny was being too kind when he refused his meal, as he was well aware that I could easily devour two. 'How do you think people perceive you?' he asked.

It was a tough question. 'Well, I hope people see me as just an ordinary bloke who enjoys a beer and *a lot* of food.' I thanked Denny for being such a top man and he left me to it. I was by myself with my own thoughts and loneliness seeped in. To take the edge off I played the *Forrest Gump* soundtrack on my laptop and put the volume up to full blast. 'Fortunate Son' by Creedence Clearwater Revival came on and it has since become the song that plays at the start of all my YouTube videos. I praised myself for how far I'd come and my fear of the Rockies faded. My fingers clicked, my knees gave a little turn, my hips started to wiggle: before I knew it, the rest of my body followed. I wouldn't call it a dance, more of a freak-out.

As I was gathering my things, half asleep in the community hall, Mary Robinson surprised me with a hot bacon-and-egg breakfast. This was great preparation for the day's run, which was going to be a bit of a race. A reception was waiting in Swift Current, including a very special girl called Amisha, who was the champion child for the Children's Hospital Foundation of Saskatchewan. One problem I had was that the Roughriders were playing at 5 p.m., so if I didn't make it before that time no one would be there, as they'd all be at the game. It was the Grey Cup final, the equivalent of the FA Cup final in England. Even those who weren't football fans would be watching. I didn't want people missing this major event just to see some broken Englishman running into the city dressed as the Flash.

I received a tweet from Erinn DeLorenzi that read: '@MrJamieMcDonald Swift Current by tonight? Wow Jamie, you're flying. Any special requests? I know someone in the "greeting party" waiting for you ☺.'

'@delorenzifrenzi a new pair of legs & a pilsner beer please,' I replied. 'If you can't deliver, don't bother contacting me again.'

By mile 6, a cheery guy called Warren joined me. He was beaming and wearing luminous shades that made him look like a pop star. 'This is awesome, just awesome,' he said, bouncing about beside me.

The climate was definitely warmer, but there was a catch: high westerly winds. Staring at Warren's bubbly, excited face was a great distraction from the windy conditions. Another car stopped and three ladies dressed up in green got out, screaming, 'Go Riders!' Finally, I didn't feel so silly in *my* green pants. Warren and I jumped into their car for a warm-up and another fantastic Tim Hortons chilli. Then the ladies offered us the ideal finish to the day's race: a cold beer. Warren and I looked at each other. 'Why not?'

Minutes after we left, Denny was back. He handed me a hot chocolate and cookies. I thought about the sugar intake for a second, said 'Sod it!' gobbled up all the cookies and necked the cup of hot chocolate in one.

High from both the beer and the sugar, Warren and I picked up the pace. We knew how important it was to make it on time. Warren offered to take Caesar for the rest of the way. Not sure if he was up to it, I handed over the reins as we hit a slight incline and soon Warren couldn't speak, as his breathing had increased so dramatically. I felt his pain. 'I've been there a thousand times, Warren,' I said to him by way of reassurance. I don't know whether it actually did reassure him. You can't underestimate the difficulty in pushing a 60-kg baby pram uphill against a malevolent 35 mph headwind.

At 3.50 p.m. we passed the SWIFT CURRENT sign. Journalists were filming us and taking photos as we met with Amisha. She was smiling away, holding a WELCOME sign. Looking at Amisha's ear, I could see that it was deformed. I high-fived her and as we got chatting, I asked if her ear caused her problems. In a cute and innocent tone, Amisha replied, 'I have microtia which means I was born with only one ear. I only got out of hospital yesterday. I've had all kinds of problems because the ear is connected to the heart, kidney and spinal cord. I've already spent most of my life in hospital.'

It was no surprise to me that Amisha was the 2013/2014 Champion Child for the Children's Hospital Foundation of Saskatchewan, representing all the sick children of the province. I then met her family, Mike, Veena and Krishin. They were as lovely as she was.

Constable Borges of the Royal Canadian Mounted Police (RCMP) presented me with a donation of over $500 from the local detachment. Erinn took my tweet earlier in the day literally and as I turned around, a representative of the citizens of Swift Current presented me with a giant pair of stuffed legs.

I jogged on with Constable Borges tailing me in his marked car. I was highly amused when he halted traffic on busy crossroads just so I didn't have to pause my running. People were tooting their horns and waving at me. I felt like a member of the Royal Family, even if I wasn't dressed like one.

At the plush Best Western Hotel I was warmly greeted by the receptionists with a $25 gift card for Original Joe's Bar and Restaurant. Not only that, but they were also putting me up for free in the Jacuzzi suite. I'd gone from royalty to rock star!

As there was so much non-running stuff to be done, I stuck around in Swift Current for a while. I visited Dr Van Der Berg at the Medical Arts Clinic, who gave me a free prescription for a strong anti-inflammatory gel. I was then whizzed off to receive two very professional treatments from chiropractor Dr Kevyn Kristmanson and massage therapist Jaelynn Ens. The royal treatment continued. The support was overwhelming.

I made numerous attempts to get the visa application online and failed each time. It was time for the 'old-school' way: the post office. I was able to pay for the visa and get a receipt to say that I'd applied. I was now officially in Canada on 'implied status'. Immigration would get back to me within 82 days to tell me if I'd been accepted for the new visa. Hopefully, I'd be done before then, but with much of the Rockies still to go, who could be certain?

I spent the afternoon doing a talk at the local school. The staff and students had done sterling work, gathering over $200 for the foundation. After I mentioned my previous achievements, including the 14,000 miles of cycling and my world record, I asked a simple question: 'I was never properly trained as a cyclist or a runner, never practised much either, but now I have achieved all these things – what does that tell you?' I really thought I'd got my message across. A nine-year-old boy put his hand up and, with a deadpan face, said, 'That you're crazy?'

If I'd had a prize to give, I'd have given it to him.

A late start, a short run and a few more miles closer to the Pacific Ocean. That night I stayed with Cathy and Archie, an older couple. Their age may explain their good advice. 'Make sure you take advantage of being inside when you can,' said Cathy. Archie added, 'For goodness' sake, cover up all that skin. Eventually, that wind will get to you.' Their wisdom was welcome, but I thought to myself, *After running for the past month straight in sub-zero temperatures, I think I'll be all right.*

As I was putting my kit on, Archie said, 'You've got more spunk than I've got, kid!' I gave them both a big wave and headed out to tackle the day.

I was barely ten minutes into my run at −30°C and I could feel a tiny cold spot on the mesh of the shoe that wasn't covered with duct tape. That little gap eventually felt like a huge door opening to freeze my foot as I went along. I thought back to Archie's advice: 'Eventually, that wind will get to you.' It had.

I made a strategic decision to keep trudging on my frozen foot instead of taking the risk of removing my gloves and pulling the tape out of Caesar. I'd only numb my hands doing that. After looking at the map, I knew I had to cover more than a marathon, with approximately 28 miles before the famous wind turbines of Gull Lake would materialise.

By mile 5, I'd had an interesting experience, though not one I'd care to repeat. My nose was runny and the snot froze, like an icicle dangling from my ski mask. This brought home the reality of the conditions I was travelling in. Being caught in the serious cold the other week had made the end of my nose go brown and blistered with frostbite. Seeing the freezing snot made me wonder whether it was happening all over again. But there was no time to worry too much about it – I snapped off the 'snot-sicle' and ran along.

I kept on running while my foot got colder. Right then, a big yellow school bus full of kids drove past. The passengers waved at me and I waved back. Then I saw a police car in the distance do a U-turn and speed towards me. Would I be arrested for running against the traffic? Quite the opposite. Constable Bennett and his partner, Officer Summer, allowed me into their car to get warm and gave me yet more of that lovely Tim Hortons chilli. I knew for sure I wasn't in trouble when Officer Summer gave me the front seat while she climbed into the back to take what would normally be the suspect's place. As I thanked them, Constable Bennett gave me $240, which they'd raised from their colleagues, one of whom had been the friendly policeman who'd escorted me earlier on in Saskatchewan.

It was wonderful having people from earlier on in my journey connected to people I was encountering now. The dots were joining up everywhere, even if they were miles apart. Constable Bennett asked me about my expectations for the rest of the trip. I told him I was daunted by the Rockies, which promised to be the biggest challenge of my adventure.

'You've inspired a lot of people along your journey,' he said. 'Our entire detachment are just a few of many. You have no idea the people you are touching. Just think about all the money you're raising, the lives you're changing and the people you've met – and that is what is going to get you over the mountains. Remember: you're bigger than the Rockies.'

Bigger than the Rockies. I liked the sound of that but deep down, I knew I wasn't.

It had warmed up to –10°C – a veritable summer's day. I saw a grain elevator about 5 miles away and it struck me as good enough shelter for a rest. Once I sat down in it, the rest of my body went into shutdown mode, a bit like a computer does when left alone. My phone ringing jolted me awake.

'Hi Jamie,' said Debra from the studio in Rogers. 'We're about to go live on air.'

'What? Oh, OK.'

She introduced me to another guest, Carion Fenn, who'd set up a new foundation for people with syringomyelia, the illness that had almost wrecked my childhood. I offered an upbeat message about how you *can* get over the illness – you just have to believe you will. In my case, movement, especially tennis, was my distraction and, I think, eventually what helped me through.

As I finished the phone interview, a burly employee of the grain elevator came in through the door. 'You can't stay in here,' he said, 'but you can sleep at mine if you want.' He introduced himself as Taylor and directed me to his place in Gull Lake, 7 miles away.

Jogging off into the darkness with my tinted goggles on, I felt as if I was trapped in a big, black bubble, out of which I could see very little. Luckily, I could see enough to get to Gull Lake. A crowd of over 30 well-wishers met me. It was 8 p.m. and I really didn't expect that kind of reception. One of the young kids came up and said, 'Jamie – did you see us earlier?'

'I don't think so, sorry.'

'We were waving at you from the school bus.'

Those dots were joining up again.

Sara, one of the people in the crowd, asked if I'd like to stay in her spare room. When you're aching all over, it's hard to turn down an offer like that. That night, I received a lovely text message from Officer Bennett: 'I will say to you as a police officer we are at times tagged as heroes. I spoke to a class in the past week and when they asked who I think of as a hero, I said you.' From a brave public servant who may have to risk his life to protect people, his message blew me away.

Plenty of bacon, eggs and coffee later, Sara ran out of town with me. There was an intense wind coming from the south at a ludicrous speed of 30 mph. Sara and I would often be blown sideways and forced to shout through the howling wind. After 5 miles, Sara's dad came to pick her up in his car. I joined them for a bit to warm up and noticed that the vehicle was rocking, so strong was the wind. I was dreading the thought of getting back out there, but I had to.

With 8 miles to go before my destination, the duct tape unfastened from my feet and flew off into the prairies. At −15°C I couldn't take any chances, so I located some fresh tape inside Caesar and tore some strips off. It was too late, though: my foot was so cold that there was no way of warming it back up. I stood in the middle of the highway, giving a Mayday wave. After at least 30 cars had gone by, one female motorist stopped and rolled down her window. 'What's the problem, son?'

'It's not a huge issue,' I winced. 'I could do with warming my feet up. Running on like this might cause me some permanent harm.'

'Sure thing, hop on in!'

I grabbed my phone and my food. The lady sat with her son and we made small talk while I ate sandwiches and nuts. The food warmed up my core but sadly not my foot, so I rubbed it hard to try to get the blood circulating again.

Once I left the car, being able to feel my toes again, I packed Caesar and it dawned on me that I never got those kind people's names. I always try to ask and I was a tad annoyed at myself for being so rude.

They drove off, waving, and I carried on running as the sun was starting to set. A couple of miles went by and I went to grab my phone to tweet – but it was gone. My stomach churned and I felt faint. I tracked back through my memories and was certain I'd left it in the car with the people whose names I didn't even know. I realised then how dependent I was on my iPhone – it was my life. All my numbers were on it, as were the fundraising opportunities and help networks. What I'd lost was more precious than gold.

I sprinted towards the spot where I'd got into that last car. Something about running east, in the wrong direction, just broke me every time. I wasn't even slightly hopeful that the phone would be back there; I knew I had left it in the car. 'How can you be so stupid, Jamie? How?' I nearly turned back on several occasions but I had to rule out the possibility that I'd dropped it on the roadside.

Only when I reached the spot where I'd got out of the car did I see a black object on the floor. Was that it? Was it? It bloody was! I went into another frenzy, this time motivated by joy rather than wrath. 'Yeeeees!' I took a deep breath and composed myself for the rest of the journey. With the endorphins multiplying, I was happy to see the sunset, making my last 4 miles running in the dark way more bearable. It was worth losing my phone just for the elation.

I was greeted by Patty Sloan at the only hotel in the area. With machine-like efficiency, she handed me a Pilsner, turned the fryer on and cooked up some spare ribs. Everyone in the bar – even the sober punters – made a donation, which added up to a whopping $200.

I couldn't believe I had yet another nice place to sleep in. At the start of this journey, I'd spent more than seven months sleeping rough in ditches, toilets and tents, but over these recent months in the harsh winter, people had been way more generous with their offers of shelter.

Before I got going the next morning, I drank six cups of coffee and ate a shocking quantity of bacon and sausages at Barry Aiken's newly opened restaurant. I'd lost so much body fat from running over 4,000 miles that I was always craving meat, especially fatty meat. Barry explained that a storm was coming in a few days. 'You better get as many miles in as you can – it's looking real bad.' For a Canadian in Saskatchewan to say that the weather's going to be 'real bad' is akin to announcing that the end of the world is nigh. I recognised that I was at the mercy of a merciless weather cycle: a storm would come and then clear up, until the next one struck, even bigger and colder than before.

For the time being, conditions were the best they'd been in weeks, possibly months. The temperature was around the zero mark, which was perfect, as I love that slight chill when I run.

My main motivator that day was fear of the storm coming in, so I ran and ran and ran, and then ran some more, channelling all my energy into every step. The hills were zooming by. Nothing was going to stop me.

After 7 quick miles, a station wagon parked up next to me. Leanne Hughes and her daughter Amber presented me with my Canadian favourite: beef stew. We chatted away, and Leanne asked me whether I had a wife and children. 'No, I don't have either. I don't think I could even hold down a girlfriend while I'm doing these kinds of adventures.' Her question did make me wonder about the next ten years of my life and whether it was practical to keep doing what I was doing. Whoever she will be, my future wife is going to have to be a very understanding woman.

Later on in the day, Leanne came back, this time looking worried. 'It's getting dark – I'm tailing you.' It was an order, not a request. She followed me with her hazard lights shining the way west. I must have stopped three times, just to quickly check if we had arrived. I was like the petulant child in the back of a car who keeps asking, 'Are we there yet?'

After the day's marathon, we made it to the famous Piapot Saloon and Guesthouse, which was founded in the 1920s and still has that Prohibition vibe to it, even though these days it serves 50 different types of whiskies. I was greeted by the amiable owner Glenn Bonnett, who didn't stop smiling and laughing from the minute I walked in. Locals Carolyn Beveridge and her husband joined me for dinner. 'Did you hear someone this morning shout "good luck" to you?' she asked. 'That was us!'

I had to confess that I hadn't noticed anyone shouting that to me. They didn't seem offended – they may not have paid for my meal if they had been. As I left the Piapot the next day, Glenn wanted to take a photo of me on a rough dirt track that looked straight out of an old Western movie.

I was surprised to be sweating for the first few miles of the next leg. Unusually, the sun was out, the wind was non-existent and the temperature above freezing. It'd been so long since I'd sweated that I perversely enjoyed it. I'd take the heat over the cold any day. If you're hot, you sweat and cool down quickly, but if you're cold, you have to pile the layers on and even then it can take hours to warm up.

By mile 4, Pastor Ed Dean of the Salvation Army showed up with a hot chocolate and a biscuit from nearby Howard's Bakery. Ed had grown a lustrous handlebar moustache for Movember, the facial hair-growing season in aid of cancer charities. Appropriately, the biscuit was in the shape of a handlebar moustache. 'Come stay at mine,' Ed said, almost casually, and I was happy to accept.

On the next stretch, everything went smoothly until mile 5, when my stomach started to cramp up. I needed to 'drop some friends off at the pool', but there was no spot out of sight. I ran faster to find one, the disadvantage being that my stomach was shaking around more. After a couple of miles, still nothing. Damn these open fields as far as the eye can see! I tried to focus on anything and everything to switch off from the cramps. I sang, 'There's nowhere to run, nowhere to hide'. It worked because I made it to the next hotel in time.

Ed met me there and drove me to Healing Hands, where the adroit Kathy Schneider treated me to a reflexology session free of charge. As soon as I sat back in the comfy chair in that tranquil, low-lit room and Kathy had started to massage my feet, I was fast asleep. I woke up to five of her daughters all coming in to say hi. We laughed at the fact I was getting attention from six women, which was all part of the therapy, I suppose. Before I walked out, Kathy offered me a $100 bill for my own expenses. I was extremely grateful, but explained that the money would have to go to the work in progress that was the Children's Hospital Foundation of Saskatchewan.

We moved on to dinner at The Star with Ed, his son David and Monique Massiah. Despite the good craic, I was bitten by homesickness again. I'd been on the road too long. When I checked the menu, it was time for a taste of home, so I ordered a chicken curry and a pint of Guinness.

When my alarm sounded at 5 a.m. the following morning, I knew something wasn't right. I felt defeated, broken, completely wiped out. Worst of all, I had no motivation to get on my feet. I played some music on my phone to try to lift my spirits, but that just upset me more. I couldn't even get inspired to write my blog.

Right then I received a call via Skype from Jamie Richards. It was a godsend.

'My anxiety has been through the roof,' I told him. 'A lot of things have been coming up lately that I can't seem to accept.'

'Such as?' asked Jamie.

'Realising that there's no physical way I can complete my journey in time to be home by Christmas. I want more than anything to spend it with my family. I've missed Christmas at home many times before but this time it's different. Over the last eight months I've done nearly 170 marathons. I've been on the road too long and I can't take any more.' My voice cracked with emotion. 'I'm having anxiety about finishing this quest too.'

'It's understandable to be feeling this way,' said Jamie. 'You're in a huge and beautiful country on the other side of the world, alone for much of your time. Try taking ten minutes each day to take some time and reflect on your family and your friends. Try to remember what they mean to you and how lucky you are to have them.'

I did precisely that, there and then, and the tears began streaming down my face. I pictured sitting with my nan after Sunday dinner, watching an old, bad black-and-white film. I imagined being with my parents, popping crackers at the Christmas table. All the little things that I'd taken for granted all these years now made me maudlin because I was missing them so much.

Once Jamie went offline, I tried to pack my gear into Caesar, but I couldn't. I sobbed some more. I moped around the room, staring out of the window from time to time to get my head around what I'd be facing. I walked over to the mirror to try to give myself a talking-to. That didn't work either.

I decided to look at the money I'd raised online. Canada: $66,265; UK: £9,346. I kept telling myself that a lot of good was coming from my trip but when I looked at the totals on my computer screen, I felt no emotion. They were just numbers, meaningless numbers. And if they were meaningless then what I was doing didn't matter at all. I was psyching myself down rather than up.

After several hours of crying, I said to myself, 'Jamie, you have to pack this in. Pull yourself together, man, you have serious work to do.' I finished loading Caesar, put my outfit on and got outside. After my first few steps down the road, I received a phone call from Amisha, whom I'd met in Swift Current. I'd tweeted about my morning tears and her mum suggested she call me. In the sweetest, most angelic voice ever, she asked how I was.

I was stuttering, trying to hold myself together. 'I-I'm al-all right, Amisha, th-thank you.'

I sensed that she knew I was lying. 'I hear you're sad? Don't be sad,' she said.

I was about to cry once more so I had to get off the phone quickly. 'Thank you, Amisha, I'm really touched. It means a lot. I'm going to have to go.'

'OK, Jamie, just know that everyone loves you.' I couldn't get the words out of my mouth to say what I wanted to say to her: that she was a massive inspiration to the world. I hung up and the water pistols in my eyes were firing again. Then I grew angry with myself for giving in to these emotions. 'You think you can beat me?' I yelled. 'You can't beat me!' I didn't even know who I was SHOUTING at.

As hard as it was, I had to share the journey. I tweeted: '@MrJamieMcDonald: 2 miles in, floods of tears continue... I'm totally breaking.'

I can only imagine what passing motorists made of this crazy British guy in a Flash costume sprinting down the highway with a baby stroller, yelling at himself...

About 5 or 6 miles into the day, a man pulled over to offer me a donation. I was in such an unsettled state that I couldn't even look him in the eye. I didn't want anyone to see me that way. It was such a dilemma: I didn't want to make him feel uncomfortable, but I didn't want him to see me crying either. I thanked him for the donation and told him that I had to keep on going. I could feel the shame burning my temples.

Ed appeared at mile 8, at a point when I thought I'd calmed down a bit. As I opened his car door, he took one look at me and said, 'How are you doing, Jamie?' I said nothing. My throat ached and my lips were quivering.

'Jamie?'

I nearly collapsed into the driver's seat, making a desperate, wounded sound as the tears flowed afresh. He did what any amazing person would do: he offered me food, and he listened.

Running was all I had left; it was all that I could fall back on to fight the depression. I didn't allow myself to fret about being cold, tired or hungry. I repressed all feelings, physical and spiritual. I was a kind of robot.

When I stopped for a break, Twitter proved to be excellent therapy, too. It was cathartic to keep my followers updated on my state of mind. I studied every single word of every single reply. I needed all the love I could lay my hands on.

Al Humphreys, a highly respected adventurer, wrote: 'What you're feeling is completely normal on big trips. Keep on, my friend.' Marcel Garvey, an English rugby union player, posted: 'Jamie, keep going mate and think of it as trying to help kids see more Xmases.' From Steve Black, who was Jonny

Wilkinson's mentor, I received: 'You deserve huge spiritual and emotional support for your sterling efforts for such a worthy cause. Reward beyond this life.' Rugby player Mike Tindall of England and Gloucester said: 'Mate, you are truly a special bloke, what you are doing is incredible. Stick with it pal!'

The next stretch was truly barren and isolated, and seemed more so once it went dark and started raining. The Saskatchewan–Alberta border was the next obstacle – as much mental as physical – that I needed to overcome. My earlier near-breakdown was bringing on the exhaustion far too early.

Lyle showed up on foot. He'd contacted me on Facebook to offer me lodgings for the night. He pointed to a light in the distance. 'I'm up over there, son.' I took off towards the light with the anticipation of conquering another province. Saskatchewan had been so good to me but the last day in the Prairie province had been one of the worst of my life. As I crossed the invisible line, I whooped for joy about how far I'd come – seven provinces done with only two left to triumph over. I took a picture of a sign that read: THANK YOU FOR VISITING SASKATCHEWAN. PLEASE DRIVE CAREFULLY.

ALBERTA

As I arrived at Lyle's house after a few more miles, I staggered like a zombie around the place, trying to piece together the tearful day. Lyle had to be really direct with me: 'Here's a towel – take a shower here. That's your bed for the night.' I went to the bathroom to freshen up. In the mirror my eyes were half-closed and bloodshot, like a criminal's.

Lyle's wife, Carol, came through the door and gave me a bear hug. She then put her hands on my waist. 'Oh my, you're so skinny. Your mom must be so worried.' She made me a big bowl of medicinal chicken soup.

I woke up the next day scared stiff that I was going to be in the same tearful state as before. But I didn't cry and nor did I feel like crying. As I got ready to leave, Carol's maternal instincts were on show once again. 'There's almost a blizzard outside,' she warned. 'Stay here for as long as you like.' While I appreciated her offer, I had to move onward.

Lucky for me, the wind was coming from the northeast rather than from the west, meaning it wasn't so biting. Charging around in a blizzard gives you no time to be weak, so I put my head down and ran, taking careful steps in the perfectly straight, snow-caked road. It looked as the Prairies always do: daunting. I stared at my hands, pushing Caesar along, and repeated this mantra: 'Nothing can stop me.'

At mile 7, a stranger was there to warm me up in her car. 'I'm Tracy Russell,' she said and pointed to a stack of supplies on the back seat: a cup of tea, a burger and her kids' monkey quilt.

As I ate and drank, I reflected on key moments over the past two years: cycling Turkmenistan in 50°C heat, sleeping in a ditch in Turkey... And now I was running in a snow blizzard. This was quite a graduation from anything I'd done previously. I then recalled a conversation with Kev back in Gloucester who said that people there kept asking him how I was coping in these atrocious conditions, day after day. 'Jamie is comfortable with being uncomfortable,' he'd say to them.

Although it was a shorter run that day, I was proud all the same to have chipped away at the miles to edge a little closer to Vancouver. I was warmly welcomed at the Irvine Hotel by a lady named Claire, who seemed to laugh at everything I said. Claire had been born in the UK but moved out to Canada seven years ago. It was nice to hear a Brit talk and I especially enjoyed her first few words, spoken in a proper London accent: 'Do you want a cuppa tea then?'

It was no cinch to leave Irvine, given that I had to do more than a marathon – about 16 miles more – if I was going to make it to Medicine Hat, which I'd been told casts a picturesque reflection over the South Saskatchewan River, in the same day.

I checked the weather forecast as soon as I woke up. I buried my head in my hands when I saw −26°C. I procrastinated to delay the inevitable. I called this person and that person, and checked my emails and social media messages. I even started to clean Caesar, and I'd never even thought before about cleaning him! Nearly six hours had passed before I got dressed and finally resolved to leave the hotel. I took off at the absurdly late time of 1 p.m.

Everything was a glorious white again, which is as pleasant on the eye as it is tiring for the body. I trudged in deep snow until I made it to the highway, where the snowploughs had worked their magic. Once I got some miles under my belt and began moving, I said to myself, 'This ain't that bad; it's just putting one foot in front of another.'

By mile 5, my right foot was getting too cold for comfort, as it always did compared to the left one. I hadn't put enough socks on or my electronically heated soles in. Then again, it may not have mattered, as my tendonitis was constricting the circulation there, which caused almost constant inflammation. The foot was so cold that there was no way of warming it back up again, at least not while running outside.

I hoped that one of the passing cars was going to stop to say hi, so then I could jump in and catch some heat. Sadly, that didn't happen so I ended up running with a freezing foot. But I had no choice.

When it became unbearable, I stopped in the middle of the highway and waved my hands like a maniac. A car pulled in and I introduced myself. 'Hi, I'm running across Canada for kids' hospitals... don't know whether you've heard about me?'

'No,' the old man frowned.

'Well, my hands are ice-cold, my feet also, and there's no way I can heat them back up out here. Can I use your car for ten minutes?'

He stared at my Flash outfit, looked down at his watch and hesitated. 'The thing is, kid, I have a really long day driving—'

'It's no worries,' I interrupted. 'Honestly, I'll find another car.' He drove off.

The next car that parked up beside me was driven by a guy who looked exhausted. He could hardly keep his eyes open but had the energy to berate me for being out in a blizzard. 'You must be the craziest bastard I know. Get in!'

This legend of a man had been working away for three weeks on an oil rig and was heading back to see his family. He told me his name was Liam and I thanked him for letting me in. 'No sweat, man. I know what it's like to be outside in this. These conditions can kill.'

After a little while, my extremities were warm enough for me to run again. Liam told me once more that I was the craziest person he'd ever met. 'Just please don't die out in this. It's perfectly possible, man.' I knew he wasn't kidding.

With Liam's words of warning still in mind, I ran facing the traffic and was submerged by huge clouds of snow kicked up by the cars and trucks. I was more or less blind and, more hazardously, the vehicles behind me couldn't see me. As I was edging closer to the hard shoulder, a snowplough materialised from one of the snow clouds and was heading straight for me. I shoved Caesar into deep snow and jumped onto the roadside. Yet again, I'd cheated death.

I stopped to tweet about this experience, and two followers – Tammy and Keith Vanderloh – and their 13-year-old son, Tanner, arrived within an hour of reading it. The magic of modern technology! I sat in their car, eating the soup they'd brought me, and talked about my feelings. 'I don't know what's wrong with me lately, but my motivation has disappeared. I feel like giving up.'

'You should do motivational speaking when you're finished with this, Jamie,' said Tanner. 'And you can tell everyone how much you wanted to give up, but didn't, and then tell them how you kept going.' I opened up the car door and started to run, stronger than before.

The daylight was disappearing fast. Another Twitter follower, Mandi Campbell, drove up to me with the intention of tailing me with her hazard lights on. 'Dark and snowy?' she gasped. 'You won't survive without my help.'

I punched the air when I reached Medicine Hat. It had been a serious battle these past few days just to motivate myself but I'd got through it... just. I stayed at friendly Tracy's house that night and Skyped Rich Leigh. He'd had a bright idea to help with fundraising. 'I think you should ask people on Facebook to change their profile pictures to the Flash symbol, saying "supporting JamieMcDonald.org".' I loved it, so did as he advised. Little did I know that this meme would infect tens of thousands of people around the world. The legendary rugby players Mike Tindall and Freddie Burns were just two of those thousands who changed their pictures. Donations for all the children's hospitals rocketed. If that couldn't motivate me, I didn't know what would.

With the Canadian winter at its harshest, I decided to call Marvin, a member of the Mad Hat Running Club, to ask him if he thought it was in any way inadvisable to run in −40°C. 'Sure you can,' he said. 'But maybe you should wait until the warmer part of the day and leave about 1 p.m. And try to pick a route that's better sheltered from the wind.'

I'll let Marvin's blog take up the story for a bit:

Me and my fellow runners Tom and Mathew met Jamie at the lodge. The sun was shining and the wind was on our side, which was great. In no time we were all working up a sweat, even in −26°C.

Things were going well and when we were almost at the halfway point, my friend Bonnie met us with some hot chocolate. Whilst drinking, all of our faces started to ice up. Jamie was amused by this and I think he felt comfort in not being the only one out in these conditions, as he usually is.

As we were running the next stage, Jamie said he had some masochistic tendencies, given some of his previous endeavours. He didn't deny it, but jokingly suggested that maybe I and most other runners could be accused of the same thing. I think most runners are just endorphin junkies.

We headed up out of the river valley to find that the wind was coming at us from the side and we were losing our shelter. However, we only had about four miles left, so we picked up our pace and carried on. This was quite tolerable until we got to the last mile. We then made a turn and had to go directly into the wind. With it being later into the day, the sun had been down a while, making it a lot colder. We were now running into a wind chill factor of −40°C or possibly even colder. Things got worse quickly – like really quickly – and a few cheeks were frozen almost solid. Luckily we were at our destination before any of our extremities got too bad.

Personally, I don't think the weather will get that cold again before the completion of Jamie's run, although with Canadian weather, you never really know!

That night the Mad Hat runners and I ended our run at a farmhouse where the farmer's wife, Mandi, gave us hot drinks around her table. We all discussed how ridiculous it is to run in those kinds of temperatures. After everyone left, Mandi gave me a sumptuous farmer's meal: chicken, carrots, sweetcorn and, of course, mashed potato.

Over dinner, we heard the news of Nelson Mandela's passing. I was grief-stricken because he's been such a huge inspiration to me – and to the entire world, of course. I've read his very moving book, *The Long Walk To Freedom*, at least six times. He's inspired so many people. When I first read his book, I asked myself how Mandela kept motivated to carry on with his journey, especially after serving 27 years in prison. Once I'd finished it, I got the answer: making a difference to people's lives. We can all take this wisdom away with us and use it how we like in some small or big way. Having been through the hardest week of this challenge, I realised that exactly the same motivation was driving me.

I was still daunted by the Rocky Mountains, so I phoned Anna Sanford, a Major in the British Army Training Unit at Suffield, Alberta. She spoke quickly and directly. 'Yes, Jamie, text me your address. I'll meet you here at this time and this is what we are going to do...'

I'll let her blog continue the narrative:

It's safe to say that no day is routine at the British Army Training Unit Suffield (BATUS), but this one was as different as they came. Running across Canada! That in itself is extraordinary, but to go east to west at this time of year and stay in a tent on the side of the road is even more extraordinary. It was clear that BATUS and CFB Suffield might provide some assistance to Jamie and, within hours, a group of experts was assembled.

Early on Monday 9 December, Jamie found himself standing in front of a theatre full of British soldiers at the BATUS Health Fayre. They were treated to Jamie's humour and humility as he explained who he was and why he was doing this – as well as how he was feeling about the Rockies.

The Senior Medical Officer did a presentation about non-freezing cold injuries. Everyone in the room was thinking, 'Don't go running outside in this weather!' The SMO happened to have a spare neoprene face mask which he generously gave to Jamie. This should stop his nose getting frostbitten again.

Jamie was whisked away to see the Royal Army Physical Training Corps Rehabilitation Instructor. Then Jamie met the Commander of BATUS, who gave him a prestigious award: The Commander's Coin. Very few people receive this.

Fuelled with a cup of tea – Tetley's of course – Jamie was ready to visit the resident Army Air Corps Flight for a quick lesson in meteorology and weather radar interpretation. Aircrew are trained in Arctic survival, which isn't far from what Jamie is having to do these days. At times, Jamie's face dropped when he realised what he had let himself in for, but he quickly composed himself and went back to his usual jolly self.

Everyone tried to be as confident as possible about the next stage of Jamie's trek, but no one in the room could hide their fear for him. One General said, 'Jamie, once you leave here, we are all going to worry about your wellbeing. Going over the Rockies at this time of year is ridiculous. You're mad.' He shook his head in disbelief.

Jamie was whisked off to meet up with a fellow Gloucester boy, Major Dan Taylor. Jamie's face lit up at the chance to talk about home. Another home comfort: Jamie got to meet Santa, who was on his way to the Forces Post Office to collect his letters from the local schoolchildren.

Moving onto a high protein lunch – specially prepared by the Regimental Catering Warrant Officer – at the Junior Ranks Mess, a huge surprise happened. After Jamie had chatted with the catering staff – subjects included why on Earth he was wearing a Flash outfit – they presented him with a $300 donation to the Alberta Children's Hospital Foundation.

Officer Jeff Zimmer from Alberta Wildlife and Fisheries had kindly given up his afternoon to come and tell Jamie about the local wildlife in the Prairies and up into the Rockies. He explained the threats and how to deal with them. There was a slim chance that Jamie would come across grizzly bears and wolves.

Other colleagues explained to Jamie how to cope in the extreme cold, how to layer his clothes properly and how to generally keep himself warmer with correct use of specialist equipment. There'd be no hotels, homes or shacks in the Rockies. Jamie loved it when he was shown how to build a snow cave.

We gave him some extra equipment: a cooking stove, some gas canisters, a special harsh weather sleeping bag, a poncho which can be used to make shelter, and a thick water and windproof cover for the sleeping bag. We also instructed him on how to melt down the snow before drinking it.

Everyone at BATUS was hugely impressed with Jamie's dedication, resilience and strength of mind. At the same time, we were horrified at his lack of preparation. His approach to his expedition is about as far away from military planning as you can imagine. However, the fact that Jamie has got this far is testament to the incredible drive and perseverance of a single man and the huge warmth of hundreds of Canadians.

The first 20 miles of the day were straightforward, as it was still flat prairie land. Although the last thing I wanted to do was put up my tent, especially in −15°C, I could see for miles and miles and there was nothing. Luckily, I received a text to say that somebody would be bringing me a heated portable office to sleep in. They'd be driving out with it on the back of a trailer. That was how I met Julie Jenkins, Tanya Trembecki and their kids. Tanya's son, Cody, is the Champion Child for the Alberta Children's Hospital Foundation. He was born almost four months early, weighing just over a pound. His lungs were so underdeveloped that he needed a ventilator to breathe. He was so fragile that he required around-the-clock intensive care. He soon needed a tracheostomy. While the external breathing tube helped to keep him alive, it also brought risks of blockage and infection. When he was five, the hospital's ear, nose and throat (ENT) specialists built Cody a new permanent airway, using cartilage grafts from his ribs. After 2,365 days of living with his trach, Cody was able to breathe on his own through his new windpipe. Today Cody was living it up: running, swimming and monkeying around in the playground. He was so grateful to his care team that he'd raised $16,000 to help other kids like him.

Julie and Tanya, the Mamma Bears that they were, had decked out the office with a lamp, a bedside table and even a kettle for making tea. I will never forget the home-made lasagne prepared by Jody Trembecki! Although we were in the boonies, there was a nearby toilet. I joked that, if it hadn't been for the office they'd brought me, I'd have been sleeping in that toilet. I'd done that often enough on this trip. After messing about with the kids and chatting away to their mothers, they all left me to it.

Seconds into the next day's run, I noticed that this was the warmest day in weeks at −5°C – scorching! I received a Facebook message that read:

Hey Jamie, enjoy your chinook experience today – no it's not a helicopter, but a warm prevailing wind from the west coast. It's a very happy day for many Canadians and I'm sure it will be for you. Keep running!

I dare say I enjoyed it. I was becoming more and more Canadian by the minute.

A few miles later, Julie's sister, Kaley Broersen, turned up to drop off Rhonda, a small ultra-distance runner who bounced alongside me with every step. Time flew by as we shared stories. 'You know I once ran a marathon with my baby,' she said.

'No way!' I giggled.

'I had to stop a few times to breastfeed him, and that's not easy after an intense run.'

'How long did it take you to finish the marathon?'

'Under three and a half hours.'

I high-fived Rhonda. Now, that's what I call determination.

Every few miles Kaley would show up, trying to force-feed me but I kept replying, 'I'm like a caveman now. I'll hold off until I'm really, really hungry – usually at the end of a run, before I demolish lots of food in one go.'

Julie called to invite me to stay in her farmhouse which, she said, was just a half mile off the highway. My back started to knot up and get sore. It's frightening how pain can narrow your focus and strip all your happy thoughts within seconds. A bunch of kids who showed up to run with me became the first distraction from the back pain. Their smiles were most welcome. The second distraction was five girls showing up later. They were CrossFit enthusiasts who wanted to join Rhonda and me for a bit.

We exited the highway to try to find Julie's. 'It's about half a mile from here, isn't it?' I panted.

'More like two and a half,' one of the girls laughed.

My spirits plummeted and I grew angry. Why, oh why had Julie said half a mile? Why lie to me like that?

By then it was so dark that the cars driving by were unable to see us and there was no pathway for us to step aside onto, only deep snow. We had a few close calls when cars had to swerve out of our way just before colliding with us. My fellow runners were as anxious as I was about being run over. We all wanted to get off the road quickly.

I ranted mentally at Julie. What a complete and utter bitch! How dare she lie like that.

We finally made it to Julie's farm in the middle of nowhere. I opened the door and was faced with a huge lit-up Christmas tree, with plenty of excited kids frolicking around it. One child was holding a sign that read: KEEP GOING JAMIE.

'We have a surprise for you!' exclaimed Julie.

I said to myself, *It had better be good after the way you stitched me up*.

'I'm dying to tell you what it is. Everyone gather around.' She was trying hard to fight back the tears to continue her speech. 'We find what you are doing so heroic and we are forever grateful, so we've been up to something. We've been running an online auction. People have donated items and other people have bid for them. So on behalf of Team Bumblebee, we would like to present you with a cheque for $10,025 and growing.'

All my rage dissipated. 'All is forgiven,' I muttered as I hugged Julie.

After a four-hour sleep, I had to leave. I was buzzing, especially as I was joined by Julie and all the kids I'd met the previous night. Mile by mile, people dropped out, thanking me for what I was doing before they left. Once we reached mile 8, more runners joined us: Carmen Powell and her sister Tara Stogre. Now the pack was down to five: me, Carmen, Tara, Devon and his 11-year-old son, Russell.

Lucky number eight wasn't a lucky mile today. My back tightened and fired bullets of pain down to my hamstrings. My leg went into evil cramps. As I looked down at the almighty Russell, I could see he was fighting his own battle, panting like a dog and sweating profusely. I couldn't be bothered to worry about my pain anymore. Seeing a child overcoming an immense challenge like this motivated me to repress my own suffering. I wondered if I was looking at yet another future cross-Canada marathon runner.

We made it into the car park of the church in Brooks, which came to prominence as a bison hunting centre in the late 1800s. Despite Russell being so fatigued, he had that proud look in his eye. I knew that look well. Best of all, his father proudly wrapped his arms around him. This made me think of Vancouver, with my dad at the finish.

I tended to kick off all my Canadian talks with the YouTube video of my last foreign adventure, cycling from Bangkok to Gloucester. During one scene I shout, 'Jesus Christ!' When I played it in this venue, the Trinity Church, the God-fearing crowd gasped. I placed my hands over my face. But by the end they were applauding. As good Christians, perhaps they'd forgiven me.

Pastor John Theiss stood up and said, 'Thank you, Jamie, your message of hope and inspiration is very touching. I for one know how important it is for the children's hospital to have the best facilities possible.' He turned to the crowd. 'Could you please stand up if you have a connection to the Alberta Children's Hospital, whether you've been in there or you know someone else that has.' I was astonished to witness all 48 people getting to their feet. Children's hospitals are connected to all of us in some way or another.

Carmen and Tara ran with me out of Brooks. A half mile later, an unfit-looking guy called Jay joined me, gasping for oxygen.

'My buddies will never believe me when I tell them that I got off the couch to do this.' Once Jay dropped out, the baton, as it were, was passed to Devon, Candice and Monique for the final stretch to a farmhouse where I'd be staying the night. We all giggled at Monique as she clung onto her trousers to stop them from falling down.

I stopped and looked around the wilderness. It was hard to fathom that I was only a couple of days away from Calgary, the largest city I was due to visit since Toronto a few months ago.

I stayed the night in a farmhouse with an older couple named Val and Ed. He had been fighting a battle against cancer. 'I'm the kind of guy who's a born extrovert,' he told me. 'Though when I was ill, I became introverted. I had to fight to get back to being my old self, and it's working. I feel a lot better now.' Someone like Ed had found the cure to any illness or negative situation. I could have sat and talked with him all day, but I had to keep on moving.

Just before I left, I had a conversation with Jamie Richards, my nutritionist. I told him about how the tendonitis pain had receded once my back had started bothering me. 'Isn't it amazing that we can't be in pain in two different places at once? Maybe that will tell you everything you need to know,' he said.

Monique, Candice, and a girl I didn't know – Lindsay – showed up to run with me for a while. Each of the girls took turns pushing the chariot for me. We started joking about how Caesar was acting like a hussy and cheating on me with other runners.

The hills in Alberta were starting to get steeper. Sonja and Adelena accompanied me for the last mile up a particularly nasty incline. The wind was like an artillery bombardment and the new army equipment inside Caesar nearly drained all my energy.

I made it to the R&R Motel Inn in Bassano, almost 100 miles east of Calgary. The sympathetic staff gave me a Jacuzzi suite for free. Although I didn't have time to use it, I loved looking at it.

It was a bit late to head out of town at 2 p.m., and I was dreading running in the dark, but I went for it anyway, without knowing if I had a place to sleep at the end. A pair of girls stopped on the other side of the highway. They ran across the snow towards me and then suddenly disappeared with a scream. It was like a magic trick. When I got closer, I saw that they'd face-planted into a ditch that they hadn't seen coming because it was covered with snow. Once they were back up on their feet, they continued to fight through the snow to come and see me. They gave me a big, wet slushy hug. When they left, they made their way cautiously around the ditch, not wanting to make the same mistake twice.

As the night and more snow fell together, I was only 8 miles in and the air was bitingly cold. It got under my skin and into my bones so quickly that it was too late to get more clothes on to chase it away. It was my good fortune that Monique parked up nearby. I demolished a tray full of slow-cooked, marinated beef with loads of dripping fat and sweet potatoes. Getting a hot food delivery in the boonies is better than finding water in a desert.

I left Monique and continued to run through the dark. A bold full moon reflected off the snow, lighting the way ahead. This not only eased my anxiety, but also made the last stretch quite thrilling.

At 8 p.m. I received a call and heard the sweet voices of two female strangers. 'Hi, we are your new Mamma Bears, the Stacys. Can you chat for a minute?' I told them I had no idea where I was or what was near me, and that I was just going to keep running like Forrest Gump. They outlined what they called 'the hillbilly plan', whereby I'd sleep on a mattress in their car. I told them I wanted to keep running until 11.30 p.m. in order to clock up as many miles as possible until I met them.

I gritted my teeth through the dark and the suffering, knowing that the extra distance I covered now would be worthwhile if I made it to Calgary on time. I ground out another 10 miles over hilly country until I reached Cluny Hilltop petrol station.

Minutes later, the two Stacys and their friends Melodie and Lindsay pulled over at the station. 'You want to keep going?' Melodie asked, fully prepared to run with me.

'No way,' I yawned. 'I'm done for the day.'

I got in the SUV, ate warm food, drank cold beer and chatted with the ladies. Drinking beer after a marathon tended to get me tipsy these days, so I climbed into the back of the car to sleep on a mattress for the night. Sweet.

The only problem was that the car was so hi-tech that I couldn't find the thermometer gauge to adjust the heat. It was either too hot with the heaters on or too cold with them off – not the greatest start to one of the longest runs of my entire journey.

In the morning, after three hours' sleep, I ventured out to the petrol station to get hold of my natural medicine: one big, black coffee. Afterwards, I was in no mood to deal with a police officer who was disturbed about my running in the dark in the direction of oncoming vehicles. He made a few calls and insisted he escort me 'with the traffic'. I knew his heart was in the right place.

As I approached Strathmore, a group of about eight runners – mainly women who were all mothers – stood on their marks. As I went past, they set off and followed me. By mile 31, I was belly-sick and unable to speak. I'd done way too much and suffered in silence while the mothers chatted excitedly to one another. I considered how helpful the maternal instinct had been to me on this adventure. They were also savvy networkers, who'd helped my fundraising campaign no end by Facebooking, tweeting, speaking with friends, calling ahead to other towns and generally spreading the word. I supposed that, more than anyone, mothers would naturally feel for sick kids and want to help them. At 9 p.m., and 35 miles in, I heard cheering at the end of the road. I'd made it. After rolling Caesar into the garage of Brett and Jan Hart's house, I tried to take off my shoes while standing up but couldn't, due to my right foot being painfully swollen. I sat down in the kitchen and took an age to peel them off, wincing the whole time. Everyone had gathered round, but

I wasn't in a talking mood. I felt as guilty about that as I did about turning down Jan's tremendous spread of food. I still felt so sick that all I could manage was a beer.

People called Dr Derek Pyper, a chiropractor, to try to sort me out. My foot was so tender to the touch that I whimpered every time he tried to manipulate my bones, which were locked up from inflammation. After the treatment, I forced myself to eat some spare ribs and vegetables. The life force seeped back into my body and brain. We chatted for a little while during the meal and I told some adventure stories to everyone. I went to bed questioning whether I'd reach Calgary or not.

When I woke up, I couldn't put my tendonitis-stricken foot to the floor. I doubted I could walk out the door, let alone jog to Calgary. There was another sound reason for not travelling that day: a new blizzard had caused fatalities on the road just west of Strathmore, as well as inside the city limits. But even so, I simply had to get going. When I met with the group that was due to run off with me, I said, 'I'm so sorry but given today's weather, I don't want to put anyone else in danger so I'm gonna run alone.' The looks of disappointment on people's faces would have melted a frozen heart. Thinking about it, my heart was about the only part of my body that hadn't frozen yet.

I popped outside to check out the blizzard. It was −29°C and I would truly have to be insane to start running in this. Around noon, the two Stacys showed up at the house with a surprise for me. They had spent the last few days gathering donations for a 'Helluva Basket', as they termed it. All the local businesses chipped in some amazing prizes for a raffle which had raised over $3,000 for the Alberta Children's Hospital Foundation.

One of the Stacys, Stacy Schuett, told me that she had given birth to a baby girl called Tatum exactly 11 years ago on that day, 20 December. Tatum was born with gastroschisis, a grave condition that affects the abdominal wall. She fought courageously for 19 days until her kidneys gave out. The anniversary of Tatum's birth and the news of me running towards Strathmore had motivated the Stacys to get the 'Helluva Basket' together.

At 1 p.m. the snowfall had died down enough to convince me that some runners, including Corinne and Stacy, could accompany me on side roads out of town until we reached the dangerous highway.

An hour later, a lady hopped out of her car, sobbing. I hugged her and told her that everything was going to be all right. 'I've been following you for months,' she said. 'I just wanted to show you how passionate I am about what you're doing.' Her name was Michelle McDonald and her baby brother's name was Jamie McDonald, same as me. 'He was born with a congenital heart defect,' she said.

'How old is he?' I asked.

'Well, he passed away aged five.'

'I'm so sorry.'

She handed me a $50 note and thanked me again for what I was doing.

That was another memory for life, I was certain. The group ran with me to the next intersection and said their goodbyes.

I was running solo – as scary as it was, I was happy that I didn't have the responsibility of other lives taking such risk in the storm. The wind blowing the snow at such breakneck speed was going to make this a tricky and dangerous run. Each passing car left me looking like a snowman. Often enough, I couldn't even see the vehicles. I was pretty sure that they couldn't see me either. The dark would only make the already poor visibility worse.

I didn't want to ruin anyone's Christmas by becoming their speed bump. For the first time in this whole run, I made a call and asked for an escort. Shaun, Preston Rusnak and Josh Knapp obliged. A police car approached, blue lights flashing, 30 minutes later. The officer's eyes and mouth were wider than flying saucers. 'I'm here to talk some sense into you,' he said. 'What are you doing running on a highway in a blizzard in the dark? Have you lost your mind?' I tried to reply, but couldn't get a word in. 'What is wrong with you? Do you have a death wish?'

These were fair questions. I regaled him with my story so far. 'I don't want to be out here any more than you want me out here. I've called for an escort and one should be coming any time soon.'

'I'd like to stop you, but legally I can't.' The policeman then seemed to simmer down. 'I have to tell you, I think it's amazing what you're doing, but you *are* outta your mind.'

My escort came as soon as the policeman departed. 'Let's go to Chestermere,' said Preston, turning his lights on for me. As we proceeded, I couldn't help but concentrate on running, which is the worst thing to do psychologically. I also couldn't pull my mind away from the pain in my foot and back.

I was in this horrible state until 13 miles in, when I heard people chanting, 'Go, Flash, Go!' over and over. I couldn't see anything but highway and snow. Was I aurally hallucinating? Then I slipped my tinted goggles up onto my head and there they were, right in front of me: Kelly and her three kids holding bright signs: CANADA LOVES YOU, GO FLASH GO and, my favourite, SUPERHEROES ARE HOT.

I hopped in their car for a quick warm-up. All my extra layers had buried my Flash costume, prompting the kids to start whispering, 'Is he really a superhero?' I lifted my shirt up to reveal my Flash symbol. 'Shhh, it's a secret. No one needs to know.' They put their hands to their mouths – they obviously believed me.

Reaching the 17-mile mark, I focused forward and spotted red flashing lights. Maybe *this* was a hallucination. But no, it was the Chestermere Fire Department, ready to follow me for my last mile. As I came into the town, people lined the road to shout, 'Keep going, Jamie!' My body may have been beaten, but my mind was smashing it.

At the fire station the crew played their sirens, even though it was 9 p.m. I was told I could stay there for the night, amid the fire engines and under the poles where the firemen slide down. I had to unpack Caesar immediately, before all the snow melted and soaked everything I owned.

The firemen woke me up with an enormous breakfast and asked me to do a little presentation for the locals. When

I asked the head firefighter who told him to come to my rescue the previous day in the storm, he said, 'Your Mamma Bears did.'

Calgary, here I come!

CALGARY CITY

There was an extra incentive to reach Calgary in time – I was due to be awarded an honorary White Hat, sort of like being given the freedom of the city. It was quite an accolade, and the last British people to get White Hatted were Prince William and Kate. But it all seemed a long way off as I moaned and groaned around the fire station on my bad foot. It was time again to be twisted and turned by the latest chiropractor to offer their services. Dr Shannon Farnel from Optimum did sterling work on me. At one point, she even cracked the joints in my nose. Whatever she did, the pain subsided enough for me to press on.

I ran out with my ostentatious escort: a fire engine! Some of the firemen ran by my side, too. Other cars piled up behind the truck and it was like having my very own parade into the city.

Soon I could see the 'Welcome to Calgary, Heart of the New West' sign and hear the distant cheering. The day was brisk, sunny and clear. It allowed me to see, for the first time, the albatross that had stalked my daydreams and nightmares for months now: the Rocky Mountains. There was nowhere to hide from their brooding, overbearing presence. Once again, I felt insignificant and at the brutal mercy of Mother Nature. The Rockies were the biggest obstacles standing between me and victory.

Arriving amid horns, screams and flashing lights, I addressed the crowd that was waiting at the sign and spoke of my fear of the Rockies. 'You know, Jamie,' said one girl, 'you don't have to run over the Rockies, just *through* them.'

'That's a nice philosophical way of thinking about it,' I said. Inwardly, I thought, *Nope, I'm still scared shitless*.

One British family offered me a packet of Wotsits crisps. Then another British woman approached me. 'I'm Jane,' she said in a rich Gloucester accent. 'We used to play tennis together.'

I remembered. 'Wow! That was 13 years ago.'

'And here we are in Canada together. Who'd have thought it?'

Everyone cleared off and James Fell, a writer for the *Calgary Herald* newspaper, joined me on the final leg. I thought, *How cool would it be if every reporter could interview me and run at the same time?*

Next I headed to the City Hall with Paul, Laura, Robin and Aletha, all from the Athlete Factory. I was warmly greeted by Mayor Nenshi and councillor Giancarlo Carra. To start the ceremony off, Nenshi raised the White Hat up in his left hand and discussed some of its previous recipients. It was surreal to be mentioned in the same breath as the Dalai Lama, Prince William, Oprah Winfrey, Arnold Schwarzenegger and William Shatner. So was I now in the same category as Captain Kirk and The Terminator? I could have died a happy man there and then.

'You have to abide by the rules and the ceremony that I am about to take you through,' said Mayor Nenshi. 'So, here we go. You will notice that inside the hat may look half empty, but it is in fact half full. And the people of Calgary have filled it half full with their very best wishes for you. Your job is to fill the other half with your great memories from the rest of your journey. Now, take it in your left hand, raise your right hand and repeat after me: I, Jamie McDonald, having visited the only genuine western city in Canada – namely Calgary – and having been duly treated to the exceptional amounts of heart-warmin', hand-shakin', tongue-loosenin', back-slappin', neighbour-lovin' western spirit, do solemnly promise to spread this here brand of hospitality to all folks and critters who cross my trail hereafter.'

'I certainly do!' I roared.

'On the count of three, we will raise our hands and give a loud "Yahoo!" One... two... three... Yahoooooooooooo!'

I was given a tour of the Alberta Children's Hospital to see where the money raised was going. From the outside, the hospital looked like a building made of colourful Lego. Meghan Kociuba, events manager for the foundation behind the hospital, explained how all the kids, parents and friends had a huge say in designing the hospital. They voted overwhelmingly for plenty of bright colours and play areas. I also noticed that this place didn't have that distressing hospital smell – you know the kind I mean. It was quiet, tranquil and fun. I was fiercely proud that, so far, we'd raised well over $30,000 for this, the best kids' hospital I'd ever been to.

Somehow I managed to score a ticket for a Calgary Flames hockey match. The Stacys called Tanya Glencross, the wife of Curtis Glencross, a superstar player for the Flames. Curtis then invited me to breakfast with his teammates. The equivalent in Britain would have been breaking bread with a top Premiership football team.

In Curtis's kitchen, the team were probably being too polite, grabbing bits of food here and there. I wasn't so polite: I ate more than all of the other players put together – even more than 6 foot 4 Brian McGrattan, the fighter of the team who looked stronger than a gorilla. They were bantering all morning, taking the mickey out of each other as sportspeople will. I laughed as much as I ate.

Just to add to the experience, Corinne's dad picked us up in a limo to take us to the game. We drank champagne and after one glass I was predictably tipsy. I was getting to be a cheaper and cheaper date. For the first time on this adventure, I was able to switch off from the mammoth job in hand and just enjoy myself. I was only briefly reminded of why I was there when my face came up on the jumbotron – the big screen – in front of nearly 20,000 people. At half-time some of the players gave speeches, asking for donations.

The Flames equalised with four seconds to spare and then won a penalty shoot-out. The game was a thriller, the arena electric. At the end, Tanya Glencross said, 'After hearing your story, you've made me look at myself and question whether I could be doing more in this world.' The media in Calgary totally got what I was trying to achieve. Global, CBC, CTV and all the breakfast shows covered my run. They were instrumental in raising $40,000 for the Alberta Children's Hospital.

Running on Christmas Day – why not? In the morning, I wrote my blog and was touched by all the Christmas wishes. At lunchtime, I cracked open a can of chilli tuna fish and spooned it out with beef jerky – I convinced myself that the beef jerky was kind of Christmassy.

I no longer cared that it was Christmas. About a month ago I'd broken down and accepted that I wasn't going to be home for the big day with my family.

As soon as I hit the highway, there were no hard shoulders because 2 feet of snow was packed up over them. The traffic was surprisingly heavy, though. Why were people out on Christmas Day? Shouldn't they be eating dinner or pulling crackers?

I had used every muscle in my body to keep throwing that chubby bugger Caesar up onto the snow bank. Then I'd find a little pathway in the snow, take Caesar back down and race with him before the next wave of cars came through. I covered a pathetic 4 miles in the space of two hours.

I'd had enough of this strategy of sprinting and stopping, so I started trudging through the snow on the median – what Canadians call the island that separates the two directions of traffic.

Some motorists would slow down and yell, 'You fucking idiot! What are you doing? Get off the highway.' What had happened to 'goodwill to all men'?

I wished them all a merry Christmas and sang the John Lennon Christmas song that was stuck in my head all day.

Eventually, a car pulled off to the side and the driver's window rolled down slowly. 'Hey, how are you doing?'

I was concerned for their safety, as there were cars hurtling past at what seemed like 100 mph. I waved him on and shouted, 'Keep going!'

'OK, I'll see you again.'

Sure enough, five minutes later he reappeared. He got out of the car and walked over onto the median with me. He wished me a merry Christmas – preferably one when I wasn't all alone – and gave me a $20 bill as a donation. His name was Penn and he offered to escort me until I could leave the highway. The way the last few hours had gone, I was grateful for any assistance on offer. I ran in front of his car for half a mile until I made it onto a pathway, but it was so narrow that Caesar couldn't fit on it.

It was a balmy 5°C, so everything was soft and slushy, making it nearly impossible to run. I was exerting all my energy in exchange for a pace of no more than 3 mph. To make matters worse, I hit a major incline. Yes, I had arrived at the foothills of the Rockies.

Nightfall took me by surprise. Once the path ended, I found myself again on the highway with no hard shoulder, but now in darkness. I tried to make myself more visible and face the traffic, but I feared the cars wouldn't have enough time or space to move out of my way. After a few close calls, I reluctantly switched back to running with the traffic, something I normally avoided doing because I wanted to see the vehicles.

I stayed with the incomparable Mike Pedersen that night. Here's what he wrote in his blog about it:

We headed east down the #1 highway until we saw Jamie and Caesar on the other side of the road. After a quick turnaround, we pulled up behind Jamie and I jumped out to give him a massive hug. We told him how excited we were to be able to help, especially on Christmas Day.

He was able to pull in some of that positive energy and use it the rest of the way. He and I hopped out and hit the road. I figured that, since I was only there for a quarter of his day's run, (less than 1/1,000th of his total run), I ought to at least push Caesar the rest of the way. Only a few minutes in, a police van pulled up in front of us and started flashing its lights. We jogged on up to their window to say hello. They were amiable and wanted to know what we were up to. They noted that they were here because of a strange call about someone running with a wheelchair down 16th Avenue. Jamie gave him his spiel – it was obviously not his first run-in with the long arm of the law. The police officers wished him the best of luck on the rest of his journey. Fortunately, Jamie is very adept at convincing people he's not insane.

Running along with Jamie was a little surreal. We have been following his expedition for so long now and it felt like he'd stepped right out of one of his YouTube videos into our lives. I admitted to Jamie that, when I first saw the headlines about a British guy running across Canada at a marathon-a-day pace, I'd pictured someone quite different: an elite athlete who'd been competing for years. I was stunned to find out that he was just a regular guy who'd decided to do something unbelievable. He's the kind of guy you want your children to think of when you tell them they can achieve anything in their lifetimes.

The rest of our run was smooth and pleasant, given the wide shoulders near the outskirts of the city and the near-perfect weather. When we got to my house, I offered him one of my prints from Mount Assiniboine Provincial Park in the iconic Rocky Mountains and explained that we thought it was important that he have a Christmas gift to take home to help him remember his time in Canada. We also wanted to make sure that he took the time to embrace the beauty of our mountains rather than focusing on his fear of crossing them. Jamie looked genuinely surprised to be given a Christmas gift.

We went to my parents' house and joked with Jamie that we'd feed him butter and tinned fish. Instead, we gave him a full Christmas dinner: turkey, mashed potatoes, sweet potatoes with glazed pecans, stuffing, gravy, Brussels sprouts in cheese sauce and, of course, cranberry sauce. As I saw Jamie attack his full plate, I couldn't help but hear his catchphrase: 'smashed'. We both went back for seconds. To finish it off we had a bowl of my mom's Christmas pudding with lemon sauce – it wouldn't be a real Christmas dinner without it.

After dinner, Jamie regaled us with stories from his travels and insights into what makes him tick. I told him that we love him not because he has succeeded, but because he has tried. That being said, I truly believe he's going to make it.

We had one more surprise for Jamie: a stocking full of dozens of cards from our neighbours pledging donations to his cause. Jamie took them out one at a time and was able to savour all of the positive wishes in the cards and add the donations to his final tally. I'm probably biased, but my favourite two cards were the ones put in by my children. Six-year-old Evan had written a short Christmas comic involving Santa being chased by a reindeer. In the envelope he had emptied out the contents of his piggy bank, which, aside from a $20 bill, was all coins.

I sank a litre of water and a litre of organic black coffee before stuffing my face with an enormous omelette. This was my prep for tackling the foothills of the Rockies. Mike ran a couple of miles with me out of town. As we were heading over some small inclines, I sarcastically said, 'So, is this as tough as it's going to get through the mountains?'

Mike chuckled. 'They'll be a little bigger, for sure.'

After we conquered the first hilltop, Mike thanked me for what I was doing in Canada, wished me well and headed back. He left me with a spectacular view of the blue, crystal-capped Rockies.

From way before I'd even come to Canada, I'd been anticipating the moment I'd be within spitting distance of the peaks. But I was no longer scared. The build-up had been much worse than the encounter. It had nothing to do with being brave and everything to do with embracing my fear. Let's face it: why do we watch scary movies? Fear is a fact of the human condition and we can thrive on it if we want to.

About 5 miles in, the hills were loftier and a headwind was whipping up. Progress was almost impossible. Gusts of up to 45 mph were pinning me back, trying to force me back to where I had just come from. It was like wrestling with a freight train. I was soon screaming with frustration. After every minute I had to stop for a 20-second break. Even giving it everything I had, I was progressing at crawling pace. The harder I pushed, the stronger the wind grew. I would have gone faster if I'd got down on my hands and knees to crawl.

Somehow, after many painfully slow hours, I reached mile 10. I could see a petrol station ahead – the first sign of civilisation all day – so I headed straight for it. I asked if I could sleep somewhere, either in or around the building, but the attendants weren't keen. At least they let me use their microwave to reheat a tub of the Pedersens' Christmas dinner. Happy days.

I wasn't proud of only having covered 11 miles, but I took comfort from having edged a little closer to what they call 'the Lump', the main part of the Rocky Mountains.

'I'm bigger than the Rockies!' At least, that's what I kept telling myself.

I ran all day, climbing, huffing and screaming. Kelly, who had come out with her kids in the storm, drove to meet me once again. This time she brought me flowers.

'What the hell do you want me to do with these?' I said, bewildered.

'Take them because a few kilometres up the road there's a camper van, candlelit dinner and a hot Canadian girl waiting to go on a date with you.'

'Are you joking?' I laughed.

'No.'

Feeling a mixture of exhaustion and nerves – I hadn't been on a date for nearly two years – I soon fell asleep in her car. When I awoke, Kelly said she was going to tail me until my date arrived.

I worked my way to the top of a mile-high hump – apparently one of the tallest summits on my route – but I didn't notice it because I'd been climbing so gradually for a while now. I found a sheltered rest spot next to a Native Canadian reserve. A couple of hours passed and there was no sign of the date. Was this girl playing hard to get?

Eventually, Karli arrived in her vast, old-school motorhome. Kelly introduced me to my date, a petite girl with a good tan and long, dark hair, who'd been following my journey through social media for months. 'Follow me,' said Kelly, going back to her car. She gave me the bouquet of flowers to take out to Karli while she laid the table and lit the candles. When I handed them to my date, she laughed nervously and then looked touched. Her cheeks went rosy.

Kelly left Karli and me to enjoy our dinner. It was time for Karli to get me back. She handed me a card. When I opened it, $200 fell out and the card played a tune from the 1990s by En Vogue: 'What a man, what a man, what a mighty good man.' She'd written a sweet message too: 'I think you are one of the most amazing, inspirational people I have ever met. I hope to one day have half the determination and drive that you do. I know it gets hard to keep going sometimes, but I believe there is no other crazy bastard that could pull this off like I know you will.'

When I closed the card, the music kicked back in: 'What a man, what a man…' We giggled like kids.

When I reached for the caravan door at 8 a.m. the following morning, I saw that a flash-freeze had struck. The temperature had dropped 25 degrees to −20°C. It had been more than a week since I'd run in this climate and I wasn't keen to do so again. Surely if the wet slush froze it would be dangerous? That was it – I'd talked myself out of running that day. I sent out some tweets to try to ascertain if anyone knew about the current road conditions and 95 per cent of respondents told me not to even dare go outside.

I lingered in the warm camper van, ashamed of myself for not making any progress that day. At least Karli was still there to keep me company. At 2 p.m., a silly thought came to me: surely the Flash should be running in the weather phenomenon named after him – the flash-freeze? Leaving the motorhome behind, Karli and I set off and, for the first few miles, the roads were firm and my trainers got good traction on them. Karli kept asking to take Caesar, but I'd always say no. Caesar was mine. I wanted him, I needed him and it was me who was going to push him. The voices in my head were on repeat, chanting, 'I'm the man, I'm the man!' I had to live up to the expectation of the card she got me. 'What a man, what a man, what a man...'

In the course of a few moments, three cars pulled in to make donations. One gentleman took out every single dollar in his wallet and said, 'I don't even know what your cause is, but whatever it is, it must mean a lot to you, so take it all.' Although $120 is a good amount of money, his lovely words made it feel like he'd just given me a million.

Karli was worried about us running in the dark so we stopped while I got out my new flashing lights and put them to the test. It just so happened that they strapped perfectly to my chest, in front of my nipples. Flash, with new added flashing boobies – it was ridiculous.

As we continued in the dark, I noticed Karli struggling. She would sneak in the odd walk every once in a while and then try to catch up with me.

'You're doing really well, Karli,' I said, trying to pep her up.

She snapped back, perhaps feeling like I was patronising her. 'No, Jamie, *you're* doing really well.'

With just a few hundred yards left to go, she told me to jog on, as she would have to walk the rest of the way. I didn't want her to finish like this and on her own, so I said, 'No worries, let's both take a little break.'

Once we got going again, she couldn't do much more than fast-walk. I slowed my pace so we could be together the whole way. I knew how she felt; I'd been there a million times before so was aware of how the pain was dragging her down.

Eventually we made it to the Stoney Nakoda Resort, which was in the middle of nowhere. A man with a huge bushy moustache and long, ragged hair, appeared to give me a high five and shouted, 'My name is Crazy Larry!' He stamped his feet. 'Jamie, I've been searching for you for so long! You don't know how much this means to me. Jamie, you're my Christmas present!' He then stomped about in the busy hotel lobby with his video camera on, in front of lots of people, shouting: 'This is *the* Jamie McDonald, he's insane. I am with him, yes, I am with him. Do you know who this guy is?'

I remebered someone telling me I'd meet a guy called Crazy Larry out West, who doesn't have a fixed abode, cycles around constantly and people treat him like some sort of pilgrim – they help him out from the goodness of their hearts. He's something of a local legend. He then asked me if he could cycle alongside me the following day.

I'm not going to lie, I was anxious about my run with him – he'd earned his nickname for a reason, after all. We were blown to bits by the 60 mph wind, but it didn't seem to dampen Larry's spirits. 'Man, I've never been in winds like this before – I feel alive!' He crackled with laughter. He reminded me of the way kids go potty in the wind. As we continued to scale the foothills, we almost came to a standstill, crawling slower than a snail.

Larry put his butt on the top frame of the bike so that his feet could touch the ground to keep him balanced. He must have nearly fallen off 50 times. He still managed to edge in front of me to try to cop the worst of the wind. It was a selfless gesture.

A wonderful surprise was in store for us: Robin Melling from the British Army Training Unit in Suffield. Of all of the army officers, Robin was the one who'd been the least happy about my run through the Rockies. But now, a month later, he was by my side, in his running gear, saying, 'I still think you are absolutely mad, but can I run with you?' It was good to have a voice of reason to counter the eccentric Larry. I could see Robin trying to measure up Larry to check he was all there, as most people do when they first meet him.

A few more miles went down, inch by inch, and I noticed that the mountains around us were getting higher. 'Jamie McDonald!' whooped Larry. 'You are officially in the Rocky Mountains, you've made it. Say hello, my friend, because the mountains are saying hello to you!' The three of us battled into a steep incline on the fringe of a valley. The wind was behaving like a turbine, channelling all of its condensed power into a narrow corridor. Robin and I took it in turns to run with Caesar, although quite a few times Robin would refuse to let me take him back. 'Don't worry. Use my energy while I'm here.'

Larry started singing, rhythmically but also maniacally. I thought he was finally about to lose what few marbles he had left. 'Ain't nothin' gonna break my stride. Nobody's gonna slow me down, oh no, I got to keep on movin'. Ain't nothin' gonna break my stride!' He rustled up dormant emotions in

Robin and me and, before we knew it, we were all singing our hearts out. 'No one's gonna slow me down, oh no!'

Robin started to use his hands as though he was swimming through the wind; Larry had broken his scepticism down too. How ludicrous we must have looked: one guy dressed as the Flash, the second in luminous biking gear and the third clad all in black like an undercover agent, all singing and dancing down one of the busiest highways in Canada.

Robin's wife, Charlotte, and their two children, Harry and Ben, joined us to run the last half mile. At the Copperstone Resort at Deadman's Flats, Crazy Larry initiated some hip-hip-hoorays with everyone joining in.

After the usual five hours' sleep, I bumped into Larry in the lobby. His grin was as wide as his eyes. 'Are you ready?' he asked, like a wrestling referee. We hit the road to Canmore, a town encircled by gorgeous snow-topped peaks.

Larry would talk and talk and when he got bored of talking, he would talk some more. Occasionally, he'd play music on his phone and sing along to it. He put on 'Isn't She Lovely?' and nodded his head like Stevie Wonder does. It wasn't quite the tune to propel me forwards, but nonetheless the singing passed the time. Often we would lose our breath and double over from laughter, which is not the thing to do when you're trying to run a marathon through the Rockies. I wondered whether Larry was in fact a sports psychologist who'd been planted on my route to help keep me going.

We went to the Communitea Cafe in Canmore for a spot of lunch. Larry gathered together all sorts of people to cheer and applaud us. I met Clara Hughes, a six-time Olympic medallist in cycling and speed skating. With all the buzz around us, we were unable to have a proper chat, but I later discovered that Clara sent out this delightful tweet:

Just had a chance to say hi to a wonderful human being in Canmore. He's run all the way from Newfoundland! I think he makes people smile wherever he goes. Canada is lucky to have him travel our land!

Being tweeted by an Olympic medallist was another great honour.

As I was devouring some delicious pad Thai, some little girls came over to say hello. 'Did you know that no girl has ever run across Canada before?' I said. Their faces all lit up. 'Let's hope we see a girl run across Canada in the near future. I think it would be awesome for Canada and the world.'

Larry and I carried on towards Banff, joined by a very special runner. Colin Harris ran across Canada a few years ago in aid of Take Me Outside, a campaign to tell children to stop staring at screens and get outside. It's a brilliant message, I think. As we ran together, Colin told me all about his journey. He'd had a support vehicle for all but two months of the trip. He'd have to park up, run and then hitchhike back to his vehicle.

'That's pure determination,' I said, with my arm around him. 'Did you have any emotionally difficult times?'

'The first day I ran with my dad driving alongside me. I covered 30 miles and he got out of the car to say that nobody would ever understand what I was going through. And then my dad began to cry. It was a seriously proud moment for both of us.'

I thought about my own dad, whom I'd be seeing very soon. Then Larry cycled in between us with his massive smile, shouting at the top of his voice, 'Can you feel the love? Can you feel it? I'm feeling the love!'

Near Banff I had to tell Larry that it was time for me to continue solo. I think he would have cycled with me all the way to Vancouver and then probably got on the flight home to England if I'd asked him to. It was a sad time because, for three consecutive days, Larry had been by my side and I'd come to love his huge moustache, big heart and chirpy personality. His charisma had helped me to conquer a major part of the Rocky Mountains. As tough as it was to say goodbye, this journey was about letting people go, and allowing new people in. But there's only one Crazy Larry and I'll never forget him.

———————

New Year's Eve would become a night I'd never forget, either.

I'd been running for so long that I thought, *Sod it, let's go out for a few beers to celebrate the new year*. I went to a bar and people soon recognised me. My Flash outfit probably helped. We drank until the stroke of midnight and a few of the guys asked me back to a hotel in Banff to carry on the party. I was worried about being hungover for the next day's run but I was having such a good time and I was so close to the finish that I thought, *What can go wrong?*

The hotel's corridors all looked the same. Parties were happening on every floor and I spotted two girls talking outside a room. I wished them a happy new year. The door to the room flew open and a guy in his early twenties launched himself at me, grabbed hold of my collar and dragged me inside. He pushed me into the toilet and started punching me. Two of his mates appeared and laid into me too. I tried to scramble out, but they were too strong and tall. I'm 5'9" and weighed about 10 stone, and was being thrown around like a toy. The girls were screaming at the men to get off me. 'What do you want?' I shouted. Thumps kept raining down on me, as I tried to wriggle away from them. I thought they wouldn't stop until I was dead.

One of the girls managed to haul the bigger guy off me and I was able to escape into the corridor. I sprinted down several flights of stairs and out of the hotel, towards the house I was staying in, half a mile away. My head and shoulders were bruised, and my hip grazed and bloody. None of the punches had landed on my face. I reached for my manbag, but it wasn't there. With it had gone my video camera and around $300 in cash. The money was less important than the days of footage I hadn't yet backed up or posted in order to encourage people on social media to give.

I had no idea what I'd done to deserve this, and still don't to this day. I can only guess at a few possible motives: perhaps the guys thought I was carrying a huge sum of money on me or they had taken offence at me tipsily talking to the girls. Or maybe they were just nutters.

I called the police, but they said they couldn't deal with it immediately, as they had other priorities. I wrote a tweet and a Facebook post:

Putting a call out. My bag was taken on New Year's Eve in Banff, everything I own including my hard drive, camera, and my wallet and all my possessions. Please RT, share & help find it, the bag could be worth a million dollars in fundraising. Please help.

At 6 a.m. I got a call from a man with a British accent. 'What happened?'

I was still half asleep and didn't think to ask who it was. 'I got beat up and my bag is missing. I really need it back.'

'OK, I'm a reporter from the BBC and we'll be sharing this information. Hope you get it back. Goodbye, Jamie.' I didn't even know where they had got my number from. As soon as the BBC reported the news, the world followed. My phone didn't stop ringing.

Unfortunately, before I could tell my mum what had happened, someone sent her a text message, saying, 'We're really sorry to hear about your son Jamie.' She obviously thought the worst and broke down. I called her and Dad to tell them I'd only been robbed and was still alive. I didn't mention the beating I'd taken.

I went to the hotel and asked about the bag. Luckily, it had been handed in, with everything in there but the $300 of my own money. The citizens of Banff were wonderful – they put me up in the poshest hotel in town and really looked after me.

Sadly – and strangely – a small number of people claimed I'd made the whole thing up. The internet is full of conspiracy theory nutters, as we all know. Trolls targeted my social media accounts, firing some vicious stuff my way. Some said I was just doing it for attention, while others thought I was dragging the town's good name down. Banff is a popular holiday resort and that was the last thing I wanted to do.

One local paper, which should have known better, quoted police officers who said I had no injuries, but those quotes were entirely made up. Had the guys who'd robbed me been caught, the cynics might have believed my story.

The same day, both the Canadian police and the media got involved. My plight went viral to an estimated 50 million people. I spent 24 hours straight doing Skype calls with every media outlet you could imagine. One positive to come out of this trauma was a further £30,000 raised for the charities.

Although phone calls and messages were still coming in thick and fast, I had to get on with the journey. Given that a big storm had just hit, I couldn't start until very late. Before I'd got out of town, Leigh Clark and his two children stopped me. 'I'm really sorry to hear what happened. I feel kind of ashamed as a Canadian to think this happened.' One of his kids handed me a $20 bill.

'Thank you, Leigh, that's really nice of you. No need to be ashamed, though. My whole journey has shown me how amazing Canada is, despite the struggle of the run. It's just a pity that, of the thousands of positive interactions I've had, it's one bad incident that blows up in the media. The world as we know it through the media isn't often how the world truly is. Good news doesn't get as much attention. I just hope people got my message that my perception of Canada and the world hasn't changed in the slightest.'

As I departed Banff, people were shouting good luck wishes and donating large sums of money. This told me everything I needed to know about what most people in Banff made of me. Once the distraction of the crowd had gone and I was on the highway, my bruised hip began to cause me discomfort. One of the punches I'd taken on New Year's Eve had made me land on the hard tiled floor. I wasn't going to let the discomfort stop me – it just added to all the other injuries I already had. I kept embracing the pain, which seemed to be helping, almost fuelling me. The pain was becoming my friend in some twisted way – it was the one constant in my life.

I was pleased to see that the snowploughs were out, clearing the hard shoulder. Previously, in my Flash outfit I would earn regular toots from passing cars, but now people were hanging their heads out of the vehicles, shouting, 'You can do it!' and 'Keep going!'

A few miles in, Martha Birkett, who was part of the Mamma Bear clan, pulled over to wish me well for the remainder of my journey. Martha's another hero. She rode a horse from coast to coast in this beautiful country, raising hundreds of thousands of dollars for children too.

Although my hip was sore, after a couple of days off, my legs were fresh and I was running at full strength. The knots of pressure were easing with every mile. It was marvellous to be back on the road.

The sun fell behind the mountains, reminding me that I needed to carry on through the night if I was going to make it to a berth at Mountain Castle Chalets. It was either that or digging a snow cave. I attached the red flashing boobies to my chest and emitted enough light to guide a plane to landing. Numerous cars stopped to check I was all right. My legs were handling the gradual incline well. I kept telling myself, 'I'm running through the mountains, not up them.'

As the snow piled up on the hard shoulder, I dreaded the extra hassle this would add when overcoming the inclines. I reached into Caesar for the snow grips that the military gave me for the bottom of my shoes. Due to the lack of light – I had only my head torch – I couldn't attach them.

The last mile to Castle Mountain was off the highway and hadn't been ploughed. 'Come on, Caesar,' I huffed. My arm muscles inflated and became painful as I pushed my trusty chariot through the thick snow. The reward was a night in a heated and well-appointed cabin. I did all my strength and conditioning exercises, yoga and self-massage therapy with a stick before retiring to bed. I wanted to focus on my usual routine that had got me that far. I didn't want anything else to go wrong.

Still groggy at dawn, I staggered over to open the front door. Caesar was buried in the snow. On top of the mound were two Budweisers and a note: 'Good morning! We hope your run goes smoothly and you stay safe for your last jaunt. Please have a couple of beers as a gesture of Canadian hospitality. Sincerely, your neighbours in cabin 12. Cheers!'

A little way into my run, I battled with some horrific inclines, the 3,000-foot altitude adding to the struggle. But after ascending one, the views were extraordinary: networks of silvery iced-over streams criss-crossing the mountains. The water looked so pure I felt like sticking my head in it, but that would have likely given me a heart seizure. It was soon growing darker by the second and the cars could no longer see me. I opted not to put on my flashing lights because it would mean exposing my bare hands, which were already near frozen, to even more cold.

I then heard a stout British accent. 'Jamie, I found you!' Car headlights lingered on the alpine trail to my right. I removed my gloves, grabbed everything I needed and sprinted into the car, where I came face to face with Sally, someone I remembered meeting before. We gave each other a hug and she handed me a bag of treats from the UK, including a classic: pickled onion flavour Monster Munch. I took one bite and knew instantly it would take days for my taste buds to work again.

I was soon running again and as I was turning off the highway, a man named Ralph asked if I was 'that guy'.

'I think I am,' I said.

He asked if I fancied coming back to his WWOOF (Worldwide Opportunities on Organic Farms) farm for dinner. I was so hungry I'd have been a fool to refuse. As we made our way there, Ralph lit a cigarette and told me that what I was doing was pure art. Pure art? I'd never looked at it that way. I wondered what was in that cigarette.

After a litre of coffee in the morning, I sped downhill for 2 and a half miles before the road suddenly became so sheer that I couldn't see the top of the incline. I wheezed to the top and hoped to find an escort vehicle waiting – at least that's what someone had promised on Facebook. There was nothing. I had no signal for my phone, so I couldn't call anyone to ask where it was. Knowing that in an hour or so it'd be dark, cold and dangerous, I dashed back downhill, waving my hands madly on all of the blind corners. The biggest threats were the lorries barrelling around them; I evaded them by tearing into the sections of the road with no traffic. To settle my nerves, I kept singing mine and Larry's favourite song, 'Ain't nothing gonna break my stride...'

The following morning, I ran past a sign that said, 'WELCOME TO BEAUTIFUL BRITISH COLUMBIA'. Eight provinces down, one to go.

BRITISH COLUMBIA

After an interview on CBC News, I met the local mayor Christina Benty at the Eagle's Eye, the highest restaurant in North America. I took a gondola up a whopping 8,033 feet, past a sign that freaked me out: CAUTION: AVALANCHE CONTROL. The magnificence of the surrounding mountains was more than compensation for the fear, though.

Christina really understood my caveman eating habits. As soon as we were served, she handed half of her meal over to me. I used my hands to polish off everyone else's leftovers, as Christina stared at me in shock. By the end of the lunch, I'd demolished five plates' worth of pork, *poutine*, vegetables, cheese… – the list could go on. 'I could watch you eat all day,' said Christina.

After the epic lunch, I went to the College of the Rockies to address students learning about 'adventure tourism'. A girl came up to me in tears and said, 'My family and I have been submerged in everything you've spoken about. You have no idea how many lives you've touched, Jamie. You have to keep going.'

I was able to fit in one more foot treatment at the Golden Physiotherapy and Sports Clinic with Stephen Dykes. After he made his assessment, he informed me that the arch of my foot had been under so much stress – and for so long – that the inflammation and scar tissue build-up had calcified. I now had a hefty bone spur sticking out from the top of my foot. I'd been spooked for some time by the risk of long-term injury, but there was no question of quitting now, not since I'd seen the fundraising totals so far: Canada: $111,174/£61,946 and UK: £32,321/$58,026. The total was $169,200/£94,267.

As a tennis teacher, it would have taken me six years to raise this kind of money. By running like a madman across Canada we'd generated this figure in just ten months.

I was approaching the 4,360-foot Rogers Pass, in the centre of the Glacier National Park. I started on it, afraid I'd go through elevation hell, but then, happily, I could barely tell if I was in fact climbing at all. I was having a jolly in the Rockies. Who would have predicted that?

A train sloped along the jagged alpine horizon that was peppered with Christmas-type trees. I reached for my camera to take a once-in-a-lifetime shot. I then looked at the photo on the screen and noticed that one of the train carriages had CANADA stamped on it. It was one of those near-perfect pictures that you couldn't have staged any better if you'd tried.

I could smell fragrant trees and flowers as I ran, as well as the stench of cannabis when certain cars went by.

In the clotting darkness, I dashed over some railway tracks and landed in a quiet, isolated forest with some desolate buildings. It was eerie. Had I found the right place to sleep? I envisioned an axe murderer coming at me, accompanied by some bloodthirsty wolves. As my paranoia swelled, a guy with a massive Hagrid-style beard materialised from the dark trees. For a split second I thought this was the nightmare coming true.

'Hey,' said the beard. 'You must be Jamie.'

'Who are you?' I asked, still suspicious.

'I'm John and I've got somewhere you can sleep if you want to take me up on it?'

John walked me over to his house beside a frozen lake. He introduced me to his wife Judy and asked me if I wanted a drink.

'If you're having one, I'll have one.'

'Heck yeah!' One thing I've learned from my adventures is that if you're a guest in someone's home – and you want to connect with them – you should do as they do. Plus I was another day closer to the ocean and I'd probably earned a beer.

After John and Judy's, the Rogers Pass ascent was well and truly underway; I was about to climb the furthest I'd climbed in one go for the entire journey. I had to race before a snowstorm hit, and that was coming in fast. My lungs were working erratically and I had no control over my oxygen intake for the first few miles. Every quarter of a mile, maybe less, I had to stop to catch my breath, before running on.

At mile 5, I was ravenous. I could have scoffed an entire bear. It was unusual for me to want to eat during a run, as my preference had become building up an appetite while on the move and then stuff my face at the end of the day. However, I knew I'd burnt every last calorie in the space of those 5 miles. Checking Caesar for supplies, I found a tin of chilli tuna, canned sardines and a bag of nuts. I spooned the slightly frozen fish into my mouth. It was hardly *haute cuisine*, but it filled the gap. I added in the crunchy texture of nuts, which I'd learned was a good distraction from the nastiness of it all. I was energised and ready to continue on the steep ascent of Rogers Pass, and I even managed to find a rhythm with my breathing.

Caesar was upsetting me again, which was unfair because he couldn't defend himself. I began to rant in high pitch. 'Why? Why are you such a pain? Damn you, Caesar!' As my arms burned with the exertion of him, I ranted some more. 'I hate you!' Then another, saner, voice took over. 'It's not his fault he's overweight, it's really not his fault.'

The incline levelled out. The flatter terrain brought hope that the rest of this run wouldn't be as brutal as it had been so far but that hope was dashed when I came upon some soft slush on the roadside. Caesar's wheels wouldn't grip; he was sliding all over the place like someone trying to ice-skate for the first time. 'It's your fault you're overweight, Caesar!'

Caesar, who'd been my friend through thick and thin, was now my enemy.

I reached an expensive ski resort where the receptionist, Becky, explained that the rooms were fully booked, but there was a couch for me to sleep on. As soon as I sat in front of their cosy fire, the chef walked over with a delicious steak dinner. I apologised to Caesar as I chowed down.

Before going to bed, I discovered that a huge storm was coming and I saw online that avalanche control work was about to begin, necessitating the closure of various roads. There'd be no way I could run for the next two days. At least I was at the sort of place I'd dreamed about before I had the idea to run across Canada. One of the main reasons I obtained a working holiday visa was so that I could work in a ski resort, mingle with other travellers and, of course, ski, which I'd never done before. And here I was at a ski resort without even having planned to go to one. Sometimes the 'naive' approach to travel yields rewards.

Having said that, I was never going to ski and risk breaking my leg at this stage so I passed the time playing oversized Jenga with the seasonal workers. There was a twist to the game, though. After pulling out a block, the rule was to hold some ice cubes in your trousers for one minute. I love a challenge and, luckily, the ice slipped straight through and out of the bottom of my trousers. I don't think anyone noticed.

On the morning of day two I decided to go outside to check the amount of snow that had landed after the storm. The further I stomped in the snow, the deeper I sank into it. You'd have had to have a death wish to try a marathon in this.

When I was walking back to the ski resort I received this message from Carolyn:

'Hey Jamie,

As you head into what might be the hardest and most dangerous part of your journey, I thought it might inspire you to be reminded what you are running for. You might recall Samuel, a little guy in an orange hat that you met in Thunder Bay (at the Terry Fox monument and selling cupcakes at the market). No worries if you don't recall, you've met a million people. Anyway, Sammy's cancer has returned and he is out of treatment options. For now, we are enjoying every day and he is living a full, joyful life as best he can. It is devastating for us, obviously, but it is also motivating to make sure you know that what you are doing is going to help change the outcome for kids like him in the future! We really love reading your posts. As a normal mom, I have to say first, "Be careful, Jamie." But as a mom of a child facing the end of his beautiful life, I say, "Keep going, Jamie!"'

Let's face it: running the Rockies in winter is one big risk. There's never a perfect time or day to do it. Today, though, the snow was holding off, so after reading the message I packed up Caesar and set off to conquer my fear of the summit. As I was leaving the lodge, the staff all huddled at reception and shouted good luck. Then they pelted me with snowballs.

A few miles in, an employee of Parks Canada showed up on the side of the road. He put an avalanche tracker around my waist and said, 'If you're buried in snow, we'll know exactly where you are. When you're buried, you only have one minute before your oxygen cuts off. This equipment has saved lives.' I thanked him for his concern and felt terrified.

He continued, 'After the storm we've had, there'll be stretches on your run today with no hard shoulder because it's piled up with snow. You'll need to watch out for those blind corners. I'm going to be with you for these stretches with my flashing lights.' What he said next wasn't so welcome. 'You'll be heading towards the tunnels on this run. They're pretty tight and some of them don't have lights. I'd like you and your stroller to get on the vehicle with me and I'll drive you through these sections. How do you feel about that?'

I tensed up. 'I've run every inch from St John's to here, and to get in a vehicle now would devastate me.'

'OK, let's compromise. Your stroller goes in the back of my truck. That way, when vehicles drive by you can jump out of the way and move to the concrete edges.' As much as I wanted Caesar to do the mileage with me, his suggestion seemed like the only realistic option.

I went fast, but not fast enough to miss the scary signs reading: AVALANCHE ZONE – DO NOT STOP. Then I began the toughest climb of the journey: a 5-mile 6 per cent incline right up to Rogers Pass. Pushing Caesar there felt like trying to push him over a skyscraper. I put my head down, gasped for oxygen and fantasised about punching the air at the top like Rocky Balboa.

At 4,200 feet, I was light-headed and belly-sick. I wondered if altitude sickness would be kicking in. I tried to distract myself by concentrating on the dreamy, candyfloss-like clouds floating by at eye level. I ran through tunnels intended to protect the roads and traffic from avalanches. For this section two Parks Canada trucks arrived, one flashing its lights at the beginning of the tunnel and the other flashing its lights at the end. We loaded Caesar on board and off I hurtled into the black hole of the tunnel. Inside I found a high ledge that could serve as a pathway to run on, making me safe from the trucks as they sped by on the road. Had I been tugging Caesar along behind me, he'd have been flattened by one of those.

After running a mile uphill, mostly in darkness, I was relieved to be back into the open air and the alpine breeze. Parks Canada had already left Caesar sitting by the roadside, waiting to be pushed to the summit, which was now only a mile away.

'Do you still wanna go over the summit?' asked Brett, the Parks Canada guy.

'Yes!' I shouted. 'I have to do this.'

He shook his head furiously. 'This is the wrong time of year, wrong month, wrong day.'

I'd been living in a state of fear about this moment for months but now I was in the thick of it – living it, breathing it – I had total control and was certain that I'd triumph. I was bigger than the Rockies, after all.

I pushed hard on the last vertical, my leg muscles bulging like bunches of grapes. I felt the blood drain out of my face and a bit of sick landing on my tongue, which I swallowed and held down. I must have had altitude sickness prompted by the sudden rise of 1,600 feet.

I was surprised to see a long queue of vehicles just below the summit. As I ran past, heads poked out of windows to shout encouragement. 'Keep going, you're nearly there!'

One guy shouted out, 'Hey, you're that runner! I have some Chinese stir-fry here, do you want some?'

'I'm really, *really* OK, thank you.' If there was one thing in the world I didn't want at that point it was Chinese stir-fry. I gave an immense war cry to see me up to the summit: 'Aaaaaah!'

There it was: the sign. ROGERS PASS ALT. 1330 M. Unfortunately, there wasn't much of a view from the top – the snow banks on the summit were twice my height and several times my width.

It was time to enjoy the downhill run to where I'd be staying for the night, 2 miles away. My legs felt heavier than lead, but they were happy to now be working on the side of gravity. I stopped off to thank Brett, but when I held out my hand, he didn't reciprocate. 'You don't have to thank me,' he said gruffly. 'I'm just doing my job.'

We arranged a time for the following day so he could continue to assist me through the National Park. Just before getting back into his car, Brett offered his hand. Why hadn't he shaken it the first time? Maybe this was his way of saying, *I shouldn't be out here helping you at this time of year* or simply *You're an absolute idiot.*

I still had to cover a mile on the trail to the alpine hut where I'd be staying. Having slogged up to Rogers Pass, I really wasn't in the mood for this last leg to be too challenging. The snow was getting deeper, so I left Caesar in the empty parking lot and took everything I needed for the night: my phone, laptop, manbag and sleeping bag. Every step I took plunged me knee-deep into the powdery snow. It was like trying to traverse a desert, albeit an extremely cold one. Strangely, I was sweating as though this were a desert. 'Should I sweat on or stop and dig a snow cave?' I asked myself out loud. My anger grew: the very fact this was such a difficult task only strengthened my resolve to fight and win. Moreover, I didn't fancy sleeping in snow that night. That just seemed daft when there was warm shelter available, if only I could get to it.

I panted away, step after step, carrying my laptop under my arm and everything else around my shoulders. After the toughest run of my life – which felt like a double marathon – here I was, stuck in knee-deep snow, still going. My entire body was burning, tip to toe. I felt like one big ball of lactic acid.

In 45 minutes I had covered just 1,000 yards. I was missing something. At first I couldn't work out what exactly, I just had that feeling. Then I worked it out: there was a gap under my arm and I realised my laptop was gone. This was graver than losing my passport or my phone. I dropped everything and started retracing my steps, my heart going bombastic. At almost the start of the trail, I spotted a tiny black spot by my foot. I leaned down to touch it, and I was able to pull it out of the snow. 'Come on!' I yelled. It was my laptop. What were the odds?

One and a half hours later, I had made it to the hut – and just before nightfall.

Exploring the space with my head torch on, I noticed a wood stove. As I was leaning down to light it, I heard some pots and pans clanging in the kitchen. It sounded like someone was making dinner. How could that be? I shone some light at the source of the noise but I could see nothing. 'Hello, is anyone there?' Silence.

Later on, three Quebecers arrived at the hut after a long ski. They were my new bunk mates. We sat down and shared stories of our adventures, as well as 10 kg of high-quality meat that the chefs at the resort had given me. Before heading to bed, the Quebecers told me that there was an extra guest in the hut, but they didn't know who or what it was. 'We think it's a killer raccoon or something,' they guessed.

'Brilliant, thanks for letting me know. I'll be sleeping well tonight.' At least that might have explained the clanging noises from earlier.

At 3 a.m. I was awoken by the sound of plastic bags being rummaged. I ran downstairs, realising that I'd been dim enough to leave the bags of meat out. I couldn't see the critter, but I noticed that one of the bags was missing. Then I heard more rustling noises in an adjoining room. I was too scared to go in there so I took the remaining three bags of food upstairs and laid them by my side before going back to sleep.

Just as I was nodding off, I heard howling and scratching noises just metres away from my bedside. The Quebecers were awake and panicking too. We grabbed our lights and pointed them at the corner of the room. We saw a vicious giant squirrel with demonic eyes. 'It's a marten, it's a marten!' cried the Quebecers.

I didn't care what it was; all that mattered to me was: did it kill humans? 'That's great that you know it's a marten, but do they attack? He looks pretty angry about me taking the rest of my food back.'

'I don't think so,' said a Quebecer.

'You don't *think* so,' I screeched.

The little bastard shouldn't have been angry, given that he'd just stolen my prime meat. I'd been looking forward to that for breakfast. If I hadn't been so scared, I would have strangled the bugger and had him instead.

The marten howled and scratched a bit more before scuttling out of the room.

'There goes my night's sleep,' I said to the Quebecers. I went downstairs, lit the fire and turned on my laptop. Knowing I'd covered almost 4,650 miles on my trip so far, I thought it might be fun to look up where I'd have got to had I simply run the same number of miles from Gloucester. It turned out to be the equivalent of running to Kenya or Mongolia! After an hour went by in front of the homely fire, I drifted back off to sleep at 5 a.m.

The following morning, after hardly any rest at all, I said my goodbyes to the skiers and traipsed back towards the number one highway, retracing the exact same steps that had helped to pack down the snow the day before. I hung around the approach waiting for Brett. When he came, I tried to lighten yesterday's tense mood by saying, 'Good morning' in the most chipper voice I could manage. I didn't get one back.

I opened up my stride and allowed Caesar to pull me downhill. Three snow-sports dudes – Tyler, Brent and Rob – from Trappers, a company that builds snowboards, appeared on the fringe of the highway with food, drink and a brand-new tent. I thanked them dearly but explained that Caesar couldn't get any chubbier.

Running on, the warmth was increasing every half an hour as I continued to descend west. Knowing that I'd left the *really* low temperatures – such as –40°C – behind in the Prairies was doing wonders for my mood. We came upon more tunnels. 'Do you want to do the same as yesterday?' asked Brett.

'Yes, please,' I said. Maybe he was entertaining the possibility that I might have changed my mind. Now and then on this trip, I came across people who hadn't quite got what I was trying to achieve. I was philosophical about that because I remembered the negative reactions of those close to me, like my mum, when I'd first told them about my intention to run across Canada. As time went by, she got it for sure. I felt Brett would never get it, but that was fine by me.

These latest tunnels were claustrophobically narrow and there was no room for Caesar. Often I had to squeeze my back up to the wall to ensure that I missed the tops of the big trucks as they groaned by.

The snow began to melt and created streams of water running sharply down the hills at the same pace I was going. Every step was soaking wet. Once again, my feet metamorphosed into ice blocks. One corner with no hard shoulder – due to the 7-foot-tall snow banks towering around it – nearly ended my whole adventure. The banks rendered it impossible for oncoming vehicles to see me. Two trucks driving side by side ate up the entire road and headed straight for me. I was aware of them, but they weren't aware of me.

I frantically jumped up and waved my hands over the bank, which was more than a foot taller than me. Surely they had to spot my Flash colours? It took all my upper body power to launch Caesar into the rigid snow. I dived head first after him. The trucks barrelled past and missed me by inches.

I got up and brushed myself down. Near the Selkirk Tangiers helicopter hangar, the snowboard dudes returned to surprise me with a portable barbecue. With a warm place to stay and the grill all fired up, I was happy that another mountain was history.

Waking up in the hangar, I was invited to do some heli-skiing at the top of the Rockies. My blood rushed to my legs as the helicopter ascended quickly. While the vantage point from up there was magical, it was hard to comprehend height through such a small side window and the glass panels under my feet – I was only catching the tips of the mountains. We hovered over the rock face of one of the loftiest summits. Reaching the tip, I could finally understand the magnitude of the Rocky Mountains. It was like looking over the entire world. I couldn't come to terms with the fact I had just run through this landscape. How did I do it? I squealed with excitement.

As I set off running from the hangar, I kept picturing the finish in the Pacific Ocean. What was I going to do? Put my hand in the water? Dive in?

Getting to Revelstoke, just south of the enormous Revelstoke Dam, I was pleased to mark another day down. I went to the Last Drop Pub to sink a couple of beers and demolish a rack of ribs – all on the house. After this particular run, I was to do another puck drop at a hockey game and receive a blessing from Native Canadian Chief Ernie Phillips.

At the halfway point, I'd successfully blanked out all the pain. It was starting to be all about the mental – rather than the physical – game. I think my acceptance that all this strife would be over soon helped me to maintain the right psychological attitude.

Finally, I made it to Kootenay International Junior Hockey League, where I had the privilege of meeting Chief Ernie Phillips. He has met Queen Elizabeth, amongst other dignitaries, and has travelled the world giving blessings for all kinds of occasions. He had deep-set, wrinkle-framed eyes like a wizard. We walked onto the rink together and he incanted in his Native language and burned sweet grass. It was all in aid of keeping me safe until the end of my odyssey. The crowd looked on in awe.

After the game, I met a guy called Ed, who wanted some advice on how to do his own run across Canada for charity.

His variation on the theme, though, was doing the journey three times over! I told him over dinner about getting the foundations right, especially a solid social media presence. But after that, he'd be on his own. I could give Ed a whole lecture on how to run Canada, but it would be about how *I* did it. His run across Canada was *his* run across Canada. My first instinct was that he was three times madder than I was.

The next day, I set off on the infamously difficult Coquihalla trail, nicknamed 'the highway through hell'. It would take me a day and a half to reach the summit: it was time to run uphill. I was about to conquer my final Rocky Mountain.

Dashing over a minor hilltop, I could see one of those green signs that display the locations of cities and towns with the distance next to them. As I got closer and closer, the white lettering emerged until there it was: VANCOUVER 170 MILES. I went into hysterical laughter. I pictured the crowds, the Pacific Ocean, the donations rolling in and my dad waiting there for me. It was all within my grasp.

As happy as I was to see the sign, a snowstorm erased all visibility and increased the risk of vehicles losing control and squashing me. I blew hard, climbed harder and hauled Caesar with every tiny ounce of energy I had left. I stepped onto the summit at 4,081 feet and whispered, 'Who's the daddy.' Saying it once wasn't enough, so I said it again, a little louder this time. 'Who *is* the daddy!' Before I knew it, I went into another screaming fit. 'Who! Is! The! Daddy!' As vehicles tooted their horns I got more excited and I fist-pumped them in reply. Then a huge snowplough began tooting and I lost control once more. I turned to the snowplough ready to give him the biggest fist pump of my life, I screamed once again: 'Who! Is! The...' SPLAT! I instantly knew it was an error. Grit, snow and salt flew straight into my eyes and mouth. I nearly spewed after the filth hit the back of my throat. 'I'm still the Daddy,' I coughed.

On a couple of hairy occasions, Caesar almost fell off the edge of the mountain and I took a battering to save his life.

I was greeted by Rod Wharram 2 miles below, at the Deer Crest Rental Villas in Chilliwack. He directed me 400 feet up a mammoth hill. My legs were no longer working and I could only manage baby steps. Every car that went by I thought, *Is this my dad?* I was waiting for some smarmy comment.

Then I got it. 'Call that running?' But it wasn't my dad's voice; it was Rich Leigh's. I didn't know he was coming too! Then my dad said, 'I've seen snails run faster.' This was the furthest he had ever flown and it was so dreamlike to see him. My dad got out of the car, and I spun round and fell into his arms. As we hugged, tears streamed down both of our faces and I felt this warm bubble inside my tummy explode. I hadn't realised how emotional it would be to make my dad proud.

Days passed, flying downhill from the Rocky Mountains to the outskirts of Vancouver. The final day, I woke up in the hotel to see my Flash costume hanging before me. I'd worn nothing else for eight months straight. Dad came into the room. 'J, are you ready for today? It's finally here.'

My guts were going round in circles. We went down for breakfast, which felt like the last supper. Jody Gooding also flew in from the UK to join us and that really touched my heart too. My dad came in, dressed as Captain America, and put two slices of orange in his eye sockets. 'I'll say it again, J. Are you ready?' We all chuckled and I replied, 'Yes, I'm bloody ready.'

Outside the hotel, waiting for us, were 20 runners, 20 police motorbikes and tons of people I'd met along the way who had flown from all over Canada to be there, including many of the Mamma Bears.

'What have you done, you naughty boy?' my dad quipped. One of the policemen strutted over all leathered up prim and proper with a large round helmet and some cool shades. 'Jamie, we're your escorts for the day and hope to get you through Vancouver to the beach,' he said with a stern Canadian accent. Yeah, I had escorts. I felt bigger than Rocky Balboa. Further along, an entire school came out to run with me – we were like one big army.

We stopped at one of the key destinations of my journey: the final hospital I was raising money for, British Columbia Children's Hospital. I could barely move for cameras prodding me. Two cameramen were almost wrestling each other to get closer. 'Hey dude, get out of the way!'

After my interviews, someone foolishly handed my dad a microphone. 'I'm really proud of my son,' he said, 'like any father would be. I also know that Jamie wouldn't have done it without the support of the amazing people of Canada. Thank you.'

We were then heading to the Terry Fox memorial statue outside at Place Stadium, Pacific Boulevard. As we crossed an enormous bridge, I realised that our police escort were closing down streets as we ran. All this VIP treatment for a skinny bloke from Gloucester?

More runners – hundreds of them – accumulated around me. We were like a magnet: people on the streets were dropping what they were doing and joining our carnival of running. I felt like the Pied Piper of Vancouver! A mother followed us for 3 miles with her two daughters before she shouted, 'Sorry, Jamie, we're too beat to see you to the end, but enjoy the finish.'

'Here,' my dad said to one of the girls, 'get on my back. I'll piggyback you to the end'. I ran over to the other girl and told her to jump on Caesar. The mother clamped her hands to her mouth in shock.

Two men in suits approached and started running alongside me. 'Hey, Jamie, we met your dad on the plane over here. He got on the pilot's tannoy to let all the passengers know what you were doing and tell them how proud he was as a dad. The whole plane cheered. We had to run today, just had to, man.'

We made it to Terry's monument where a crowd of 50 people clapped me in. I stopped, closed my eyes and took a little bow in front of him. It was essential that I paid my respects to his memory.

'Come on!' I yelled. We were off again. As I ran, it was as if my feet weren't touching the ground. At English Bay Beach I slipped my trainers off and my feet puffed through the sand.

Overcome by emotions, I put my left hand in the ocean and turned to the hundreds of people. 'This hand is for the sick children we have all been raising money for.' A huge cheer. Then I dipped my other hand in. 'This one is to show that anyone can be a superhero.'

I dived into the sea. It was insanely cold and I'm fairly sure my heart stopped for a few seconds. When my head popped out of the water, all I could hear were roars and cheers.

I'd done it. I reached the Pacific, 200 marathons later, raising more than £250,000 ($500,000) for children's hospitals.

PART 5

THE FINISH, BUT NOT THE END

I couldn't have claimed to have gone 'the whole way across' Canada if I hadn't run on Vancouver Island. I caught the ferry across to it with Dad. We wanted to finish off our very last marathon together with two Mamma Bears, Jolene and Sherry, driving with us.

This was the easiest marathon I'd done so far. I felt like I was floating. A guy kept handing us beers every few miles, which made things go more smoothly.

As you can imagine, that mad, wonderful, inspiring and terrifying run across Canada had all sorts of impacts. After crashing into the Pacific Ocean, the first thing I wanted to do was visit the Terry Fox School, just outside Vancouver, in order to pay further tribute to the great man. I talked to the students about how his fine example had cast a long, stirring shadow over my own epic journey. I declared Terry Fox a national and international hero who is way out of my league.

A healthy bloke like me running across this vast country is one thing, but a bloke with cancer and only one leg doing it was something else. I was privileged to meet his brother Fred that day, who told me that Terry would have been proud of what I'd achieved. Not for the first time on this adventure I broke down in tears. Of all the praise I've received in my life, what Fred said will always mean the most to me.

As soon as I touched down in the UK, I went to Gloucester Children's Hospital to see the difference the fundraising had made. They'd built a fabulous new playroom and schoolroom. I know from my own experience that entertaining *and* educating kids is vital to their recovery.

Walking around the hospital, my Flash suit amused everyone but a ten-year-old girl who was struggling with cancer. When I tried to give her my 'superhero' bracelet – I explained that it had helped me through tough times – she looked right through me and said, 'I don't like superheroes.' Everyone went critical with laughter – you have to love the honesty and innocence of children. At least I now know that next time I'd be safer offering her a Peppa Pig or Barbie doll.

For me, the hardest part about the whole experience was seeing the kids fighting their illness and the families going through their own battles, trying to support them. But I knew that my fundraising had given those children a much better chance of winning.

Jogging into King's Square in Gloucester city centre, near Gloucester Cathedral, I was greeted by over a thousand people, many dressed up as superheroes. Rich Leigh had arranged this fabulous homecoming for me. The well-wishers had followed my journey on both social media and in the news. In a way, they'd been with me the whole time and their kind messages of support had helped me through the dark patches.

One guy shook my hand and said, 'My name is John Cunningham. I'm a huge fan of Terry Fox and I just can't believe a Gloucester boy finished off what he couldn't. I am your biggest fan.' I'd seen so many comments on Facebook from John and it was lovely to finally meet him in the flesh.

His friend Gary next to him said, 'He's not joking, Jamie, he really is your biggest fan. He'd stalk you if he could.'

'I love to be stalked!' I laughed.

Gloucester's town crier, Alan Myatt, rang his bell and boomed in his famous voice, 'Oya oya oya, superhero Jamie McDonald coming to receive the key to the city.' Alan then assembled us all into a marching line and we linked arms to walk to the cathedral. Wearing all his gold chains, our mayor, Chris Chatterton, presented me with the Medallion of the City of Gloucester and there was a huge roar when I raised it above my head, like Andy Murray lifting the Wimbledon trophy. As a tennis-obsessed kid, my dream was to win Wimbledon but, right at that moment, lifting the Gloucester Medallion was even better. It has been without doubt the proudest moment of my life.

The crowd then quietened down. I opened my speech with a quip that referenced the mayor's chains. 'I never thought in a million years that I'd be awarded such an accolade by Mr T.'

'I ain't no fool,' shouted Mayor Chris over everyone as they laughed.

That night was some party! Hundreds of people were at Dr Foster's pub, listening to some fantastic bands, drinking far too much beer and eating the most extraordinary spread of food. Dawn, the owner of the pub, had even baked me my very own Flash cake. I'd never felt prouder to say I'm from Gloucester.

Weeks later, I didn't see the post-adventure blues coming. For the last two years I hadn't stopped thinking about the goal ahead, whether it was pedalling my heart out for a world record or running my socks off to cross the second largest country in the world. Well, I'd just achieved my biggest goal – my life's dream if you like – by completing 200 marathons, raising over £250,000 and sharing my story with 100 million people. Why was it that so soon after my happy homecoming I felt sadder than I'd ever felt before?

I moped about at home, my parents, our foster kids and our friends witnessing my despair. Every time my mum spoke to me, I'd mumble something back ten seconds later as if I wasn't listening. I often wasn't.

Life on the road had been simple, ordered and disciplined. Everything I did had a point to it. In Canada I'd donned one superhero suit every day – the decision of what to wear was made for me. Now with ten sets of clothes, in all different colours and designs, I couldn't choose between them and it was weirdly agonising. Every coffee I drank in Canada had the purpose of propelling me forward. Back home, drinking coffee just seemed pointless. I didn't even like the taste any more.

Accompanying – or maybe contributing to – the black mood was this huge pressure to keep doing challenges and raising funds for good causes. This was a pressure I placed on myself as much as others placed on me.

Then I had a fortuitous phone call from Des and Gina Gillingham, asking me if I'd like to go for a coffee and a chat with them. Des and Gina were inquisitive and wanted to know all about my adventures. 'I'd like to tell you about our friend Andrew,' said Des. 'He was a cheeky fella, a really down-to-earth, lovely bloke. Sadly, he died 18 months ago. He wanted to leave all his money to charity, and to someone in the West Country who had achieved an amazing feat. You were top of the list, Jamie.' Des presented me with a cheque for £15,000.

It was just churlish to remain depressed after an astonishing act of generosity like that.

Another moment that lifted me was the Pride of Britain Awards 2014. It was only right that I took my mum with me. Before the ceremony I met all the incredible nominees and heard their stories – this was the most inspiring aspect of the whole thing.

On the night, celebs were everywhere. I got a cheeky photo with the legendary Phillip Schofield and, to my mum's delight, one with Fiz from *Coronation Street*. I considered getting a pic with Simon Cowell and Cheryl Cole, but I chickened out and didn't want to bother them.

Carol Vorderman read out the nominees for our category. 'And the winner for Fundraiser of the Year is...'

I held my breath.

'...Tony Phoenix-Morrison.' I'd be lying if I said that I wasn't gutted. But after a few minutes, I was overjoyed for Tony. He runs with a fridge on his back – yes a fridge! – raising money for cancer research. He's got a huge heart, probably bigger than a fridge!

My mum turned to me and said, 'I hope you're OK, J. Me and Dad spoke about this, and we agreed that now doesn't feel like the right time for you to win something as big as this. You've got so many more years ahead of you.'

Just when I thought the fun was over, in the morning we all got to visit Number 10 Downing Street to meet David Cameron. I tend to stay out of the political world and know that many of you will have your own feelings about him – good or bad – but I have to say it was an honour to meet the Prime Minister of our country. As he approached, I was a little nervous so I thought I'd break the ice with a joke. 'David, I've been necking your Ribena the last hour like it's going out of fashion.' It got a laugh and so, slightly less nervous, I then shared my story with him. He seemed impressed.

The other difficulty with being back home was money, or lack of it. On my various adventures I'd spent all the cash I'd saved up for the house I never bought. A charity called to ask me if I would speak at their fundraiser.

'Sorry,' I said, 'I don't even have the bus fare to get to you.'

I asked my trusty dad for advice on how I should earn a living. He looked at me gravely and said, 'Son, it looks to me like you've found what you love. It's your pathway, no one else's. You gotta keep doing what you're doing.' I skipped off feeling really motivated and thinking he was so right. However, minutes later I realised that I still had no money.

Then I got an email from Nigel Purveur, asking me to meet him. Nigel is a director of Capita, an enormous business with over 70,000 employees. Over coffee he asked me to come in and motivate his staff. 'We'd pay you, of course.'

'Yes,' I accepted nervously. As the day of the talk approached, I grew even more nervous. On the Canada adventure I realised I had a natural flair for public speaking, but what did I know about the business world? And if I was being paid, what came out of my mouth ought to provide some value. But I didn't think I had anything valuable to say to these people.

I wasn't sure what to wear to the talk. I considered a suit and tie, but that just wouldn't have been me. As the day got nearer, I said to myself over and over again, 'Just be yourself, you plonker! You can't be anything else.' So I turned up in a pair of shorts and flip-flops.

'Right,' I began, 'I don't know a single thing about business.' I looked down at my flip-flops, and everyone chuckled. 'I'm just going to share my story, so feel free to take whatever you want from it.' When I was done, I received a message on Facebook from someone who'd been in the audience:

Jamie, I've seen corporate speakers over the last 25 years but I've never had anyone make me feel the way you made me feel. You're a real and refreshing change from what you would normally expect in the corporate affair. Thank you.

It made my tummy go all fuzzy. Nigel then asked me to go to Scotland, Ireland and other parts of the UK to speak to his other employees. This time I said yes with a lot more confidence.

I now do motivational speaking for a job. I speak at charity events, schools, corporate dos and after dinners all over the world. It's an adventure in itself, and I get to tell stories about beating the odds and how we as human beings are capable of so much more than we realise. Oh, and we usually laugh. A lot.

I was honoured when the BBC made a short documentary that beautifully captured the full experience of my Canada run. Kathy, the director, told me that making the film was tough for copyright reasons: I was wearing the Flash suit for almost the whole time. I didn't give this a moment's thought at the time – I just wore the outfit because kids related to it and loved it. I decided to run a competition, in which schools across Canada and the UK could take part, to create a new superhero.

Connor Reddy, a ten-year-old who has dyspraxia, was the winner. He absolutely nailed the picture opposite. So, my new alter ego on all my next adventures will be... Adventureman! Hopefully, this will be a superhero whose superpowers kids really feel they can emulate.

As I stared to ponder what came next, I began thinking: *When you're dead, you're dead.* I've often risked my life on my adventures and some day I won't be around. That's when my cousin Kev and I co-founded Superhero Foundation.

Soon after our charity was born, it got its first call from Kate Bottger, the mother of a little local girl called Charlotte who was suffering from spastic cerebral palsy. She needed a tricky operation that would reduce her pain – which was constant – and give her the chance to walk. The catch was that the op would cost over $100,000 and had to be performed in the US. Kate and Charlotte's dad, James, had already raised more than $60,000, but public interest in the cause had fizzled out.

Kev and I went to visit the family and I asked which one of the parents wanted to be the superhero. James and Kate pointed at each other. I then asked who would be up for a challenge and this time James stepped forward. Kev and I had worked out that if he walked up and down Robinswood Hill in Gloucester 75 times, that would equate to the same height as the summit of Mount Everest. When we told James that, he glared at us in horror. Then he looked at Charlotte and said, 'Bugger it, I'll do it!'

We spent the next month training him up. With help from our friends, we got him doing yoga, as well as strength and conditioning exercises. James smashed the first 12 hours of climbing and descending the hill, but began to deteriorate quickly as he got to his twentieth consecutive hour. His knee was giving him a lot of pain and he said that he couldn't take another step. I told James about Terry Fox and what he had overcome to try to achieve his goal. I explained about Terry's cancer, and how he had lost his leg and then ran across Canada. James got back to his feet instantly.

He hobbled back up the hill but 20 hours later he was vomiting and could hardly stand. After an hour and a half's sleep, we fed him and read some of the Facebook messages of support, such as: 'Every step you take is another step forward for your daughter. You are giving her a future.' BBC Radio Gloucestershire were there and shoved a microphone in his face. He cried live on air.

We pinned pieces of paper on the Attwoolls marquee to represent how many ascents he had left to complete. As James came down and touched the tent, he would rip off one of the sheets. It was something for him to focus on, but as the pain and the leg cramps grew, he had to start walking down backwards. James is normally a quiet, humble guy, but with just four laps to go he grabbed the paper and screamed 'Come on!' Then shoved it in his mouth and ate it. It reminded me of Andy Murray's primeval cry when he won Wimbledon.

We all joined him for the last lap at 10 p.m. When he reached the top, we allowed James and Kate to hug and have a moment on their own to realise what they had achieved. James also had a moment with his best friend, whom he hadn't seen for nine years, but had heard about the challenge and driven down to join him. They had rekindled their friendship – another great example of the challenge bringing people together.

James had, in a sense, conquered his Everest. We cracked open a bottle of champagne and he went down the hill to meet Charlotte, who was waiting in her wheelchair with a 'number one' sign for her daddy. He gave her a massive hug as the fireworks went up. It seemed very Hollywood, but this was real life. And he had raised more than $60,000 in real money for his daughter's operation.

His adventure reminded me of what ordinary people can achieve when they put their mind and body to it. The hill climb was a template for future fundraising ideas to empower other real-life superheroes to change and save lives.

James is just a normal bloke. I'm just a normal bloke. But we dedicated ourselves to achieving something with the right motivation and we saw it through to the end, no matter what obstacles were put in our way. We were inspired and, in turn, we inspired others with our deeds. Inspiration can save the world. It is more powerful than any medicine or medical equipment.

There's no reason why anybody else – anybody at all – can't do what James and I did. Anyone can be a superhero.

ACKNOWLEDGEMENTS

MY BOOK JOURNEY

Having mild dyslexia and having no idea how to write a book, I began to collect my Facebook blogs from my Canada run and to pour out the rest of my life from the heart, from the isolation of my friend David Redvers' beautiful annex. He even told his kids 'don't disturb Jamie', which made me feel a bit like a grumpy granddad, so I ended up playing a lot of football with his kids behind David's back. Once I'd written more than 180,000 words (I quickly found out that that was the equivalent of two books), I got in touch with the editor of our local newspaper, Jenny Eastwood. 'What the hell do I do?' I asked. As she is a busy bee she led me to another editor and friend, Nick Webster. Nick had a good go at reading it, correcting a lot of my misspelt words and said, 'Jamie, it's brilliant. This has to hit the shelves, now go find a publisher.' That confidence made me believe that maybe I could. So the next day I strutted into the Penguin Random House building in London to find myself minutes later being escorted out by the receptionist, who was saying 'This is not how you get a book published, waltzing in here like that. What were you thinking?'

Back to the drawing board: I asked adventurer and author Al Humphries, who led me to Leon McCarron, also a lovely guy, and an adventurer and author who put me in touch with the amazing Debbie Chapman. When I emailed Debbie she responded, 'I tweeted you a year ago to ask if you were going to write a book!' Then that led me to a great editor, Tom Sykes, who was able to cut my book from 180,000 words to 80,000 (apparently standard book size) – something I could never have done, as every person in the book meant so much to me. The 'naked' editor, Daniela Nava, worked her eagle-eyed magic on my grammar and spelling. My friend and legal guru James the Cat helped me with the contract – I literally had no idea what I was looking at and couldn't have done it without him! I feel incredibly lucky to have landed my first publishing deal with Summersdale and the journey so far has been nothing but brilliant! Oh, and tough: I'm not one to sit still.

SUPERHERO FOUNDATION

Thanks to all the friends who have selflessly helped over the years, and who currently help with Superhero Foundation. For someone who beats their body to a pulp by running too many miles, Ed Archer, my movement specialist, keeps me in working order. Thanks to Jody Gooding for his creative brain and for filling me with the confidence to 'step up as a role model'. Nigel Purveur, who uses his business-like brain (very unlike mine) to help see my blind spots. Wendy Fabian for always caring and sharing her charity expertise so we can continue fundraising as best we can. A special thank you to Rich Leigh, who continues to use his talent for PR for the greater good. Rich helps us reach a wider audience and increases donations so we can make an even bigger difference.

OTHER THANK YOUS

Thank you to my cousin Kev Brady for the friendship throughout my adventures. To Jamie Richards who helped me with all my nutrition and for telling me the right stories, at the right time – just when I needed them. Also, to Rob McEwan and Nick Williams from Argyle PR who helped increase the donations in Canada. Also, my good friend Mario Peters, who had the vision and funds to help get Superhero Foundation off the ground. 'As an agent for good, it's the best money I've ever spent,' he said – Mario has this enormous gift for making you feel like you were born for all the right reasons. To Keiran Montagu, who saw potential in me as a teenager with a tennis racket. I didn't make it as a tennis pro as he thought, but he helped develop me as a person, which has led me to what I'm doing now. And finally, to the love of my life: Anna McNuff. As I'm writing this, she's currently cycling as many summits as possible in South America – a different kind of 'getting high in the Andes', you could say. Anyhow, I've found my match. Anna is that person that I'll be having sproggs with, so yes, couldn't do it without her.

FAMILY THANK YOUS

It would be illegal to not mention my mum Ann, dad Donald McDonald (real name) and my brother, Lee. My brother was very naughty as a kid, and he always dragged me along into his mischief, probably giving me the confidence to somehow embrace and enjoy fear.

THE DIFFICULT THANK YOUS

If you helped with any of my adventures, especially in Canada, I want to include your name within this book and shout it from the rooftops – a million times over! When I sat and wrote the book, it was 180,000 words long and included every single person that helped me along the way. Every single person. The tricky part is that for it to be published, it would need to be cut closer to 80,000 words. Yes, this hurt, and with my pure emotional attachment to every single person that helped me, it was something I would have found impossible to do alone. Please know that even if you're not in this book, you are in my heart. Forever. Anyhow, I feel like Canada is my second home, and I'm planning on a Canadian book tour, so hopefully I'll get the chance to see you again and give you a proper 'thank you', and a hug, of course.

And lastly, thank you to you. For buying this book. One hundred per cent of the royalties from every book sold will go to our charity, Superhero Foundation, helping sick children and their families across the world.

SUPERHERO FOUNDATION

Aiming to empower real-life Superheroes to change, and save, lives around the world. We help ordinary people through their fundraising challenges to support families in need – raising funds for inaccessible medical treatments, and children's hospitals worldwide, with the aim to relieve mental or physical illness. Our mission is to build a superhero-hub, where people can be part of a community and learn to be happy by making a difference.

ANYONE CAN BE A SUPERHERO

Simply make a donation now, or take on your own fundraising challenge. We believe that everyone has the potential to become a superhero – sometimes all that's needed is a little helping hand – so please get in touch, and make a difference.

www.superherofoundation.org

ANN CONROY TRUST

Jamie is also a proud patron of the Ann Conroy Trust, which is the only charity that helps people in the UK with syringomyelia, the illness he had as a child, and people with Chiari malformation. The charity needs more awareness, support and donations. If you'd like to know more, please visit: www.annconroytrust.org.

ABOUT THE AUTHOR

Jamie has delivered motivational, inspiring and entertaining talks for schools, corporates, not-for-profits and after-dinner events all around the world.

'Jamie has an inspiring story to tell, using his stories to motivate others with his incredible adventures'
   Sir Steve Redgrave, rower, five-time Olympic Gold medallist

'Are you an adventurer, or a comedian? Phenomenal'
               Sir Geoff Hurst, former England footballer

'Fast-moving, inspiring and funny. You left us wanting more' NHS

'Jamie has a hugely entertaining story and [it] is one of great personal endeavour; his tenacity in achieving his goals and in overcoming barriers is inspirational'   Capita

'Fundraising is easy with a superhero mentality. We'd love you back'   NSPCC

'We know from Terry Fox, my brother, [that you need] to have determination, commitment, dedication and living mind over matter, and you've shown all of these characteristics and especially shown these students today that anything is possible. Incredible presentation, thank you'   Fred Fox, at Terry Fox's School

'Seeing Jamie speak was like watching an episode of Only Fools and Horses. Complete comedy and every once in a while you get socked with a heartwarming moment'   Liverpool Victoria

To book Jamie, or find out more visit:
www.jamiemcdonald.org/speaker

You can also follow Jamie's adventures on Facebook, YouTube, Twitter and Instagram, or at www.jamiemcdonald.org.

Have you enjoyed this book?
If so, why not write a review on your favourite website?

If you're interested in finding out more about our books, find us on Facebook at **Summersdale Publishers** and follow us on Twitter at **@Summersdale**.

Thanks very much for buying this Summersdale book.

www.summersdale.com